TURNING YOUR
PAIN
INTO
GAIN

It is my prayer that you will learn how to turn your stumbling blocks into stepping stones; that victims of child abuse and spousal abuse can reclaim lost ground. With all my love in Christ,

Dr. Michael D. Evans

#1 *NEW YORK TIMES* BESTSELLING AUTHOR
MIKE EVANS

TIMEWORTHY
BOOKS

P.O. BOX 30000, PHOENIX, AZ 85046

This book is dedicated to
the multiplied thousands of hurting people
tortured by the pain of abuse;
trapped in destructive relationships;
plagued by powerlessness, low self-esteem,
anger and false guilt; tormented with insecurity,
rejection, and many other fears;
those who are longing desperately for healing,
wholeness, and a new way of life.

PART I: EXPOSING THE ROOTS AND FRUITS OF ABUSE

—CHILD ABUSE—

1/ HOPE FOR HURTING PEOPLE....................................9

2/ PSYCHOLOGICAL ABUSE 21

3/ NEGLECT 35

4/ SEXUAL ABUSE...43

5/ PHYSICAL ABUSE 69

—SPOUSAL ABUSE—

6/ BATTERED WOMEN 85

7/ DANGER SIGNALS!...101

8/ RESCUER, PERSECUTOR, OR VICTIM..........................115

9/ BATTERERS AND THEIR VICTIMS 135

PART II: RECLAIMING LOST GROUND

10/ DISCOVERING THE POWER OF FORGIVENESS 159

11/ MAKING OFFENSES WORK FOR YOU 177

12/ OVERCOMING REJECTION 193

13/ REBUILDING SHATTERED SELF-ESTEEM.......................221

14/ FINDING A GOD YOU CAN BELIEVE IN.......................239

15/ EXPOSING FAMILY CURSES.................................259

16/ BREAKING FAMILY CURSES.................................277

17/ CONQUERING THE TIGER WITHIN 291

18/ OVERCOMING DESTRUCTIVE HABITS & BEHAVIORS 307

19/ WELCOME TO A WINNER'S WORLD!...........................323

ENDNOTES..333

ABOUT THE AUTHOR 335

PART

EXPOSING THE
ROOTS & FRUITS
OF ABUSE

1

IF YOU'VE EVER tended a garden or flower bed, you know how hard it is to get rid of unwanted weeds. It's not enough to simply yank off their leafy tops or chop them off at ground level: the roots supporting and feeding the pesky plants must also be exposed and destroyed.

Just so, it's not enough to attack the flourishing out-growth of symptoms, pain and problems produced by abuse. The underlying root system must be exposed. The poisonous fruit that abuse has produced in our lives and relationships must be recognized and resolved. Only then can the unproductive, untilled soil in our souls be reclaimed.

❧ 1 ❧

HOPE FOR HURTING PEOPLE

"PLEASE, DADDY, let me out! I didn't steal the knife. I found it in the snow. Honest, I did. Please unlock the door, Daddy! Please!"

Muffled screams erupted from my skinny, terrified seven-year-old frame as I pounded and clawed at the rough door of a dirt-walled, rat-infested canning cellar beneath the house. Pencil-sized welts crisscrossed my back, buttocks, and legs. Pain and panic had caused me to wet my pants, now grimy with dirt. Sticky cobwebs streaked my tousled black hair.

After what seemed like hours, the heavy door burst open, but my father had not come to rescue me. Shouting curses and armed with an extension cord and a coat hanger, he jerked me out of the cellar, beat me for screaming, and then tossed me back into the blackness.

Sobbing, I scrambled to the crack of light at the bottom of the door and drew my shivering, throbbing form into a ball. I hoped somehow to distance myself from the squeaking rats and bone-chilling cold.

I had become accustomed to my father's violent anger. As a toddler, I had instinctively learned to sleep *under* my bed, not *in* it, to avoid my drunken father's middle-of-the-night beatings. At four, having never been loved, hugged, nor even once called "Son," I actually ran away from home. I wandered the streets until well-meaning policemen found this dark-eyed Jewish boy and took me back home.

Although my entire family was abused, I always had been singled out as my father's favorite target. And the sadistic arsenal of curse words, angry fists, coat hangers, extension cords, belt buckles and heavy boots always found their mark.

In 1958, I was eleven and still mystified as to why my father despised me. At the same time, I wondered if I could really be garbage, the never-amount-to-anything piece of trash my father said I was.

Upstairs in my room, I cringed as I heard the front door slam. The Friday night ritual began as my drunken dad screamed my mother's name: "Jean! Jean! You get yourself in here!" I crept to the top of the stairs and peered over the railing as my father shoved my mother into a chair. I could see the terror on her face as he began battering her face with his fists.

"How could you do such a thing to me?" my father ranted. "That stupid moron is not my son. It's your fault that bastard is living in my house!" he yelled. Each word was punctuated by bone-jarring blows. "He is a moron. He is a coward. He is NOT my son!"

I longed to dash down the stairs and through the front door into the dark night. Instead, I tried to intervene and he turned his anger on me. By the time he was done using his fists on my scrawny frame, I had been dumped unconscious on the floor of my bedroom. Sometime later I awoke, my body curled into a fetal position with my face and pajamas covered in dried vomit. Every bone and joint ached. I tried to push myself up from the floor of that dark room but fell back, the room spinning. I closed my eyes, clenched my fists in total agony, and, shaking uncontrollably, cried out to no one in particular, "W-w-why was I born? W-w-why?!"

I saw no purpose for my life. My father hated me, and my mother suffered because of me. All I knew was my father's warped version of Christianity: Booze on Friday, beatings on Saturday, and church on Sunday. My dad's favorite Bible verse must have been Proverbs 23:14: "You shall beat him with a rod, and deliver his soul from hell." He paraphrased that as "Spare the rod, spoil the child." There were no spoiled children in his home—only abused ones. He had never given me one word of affirmation. Not once had I heard "I love you" from his lips that so tenderly and lovingly caressed a glass of amber whiskey. Jack Daniels was his "friend"; I was "moron."

That night in my room, I had a life-changing encounter with Jesus Christ. As quickly as I had whispered those words, the room was flooded with a light so bright it blinded me. I thought Dad had come back to finish the job—to beat me to death, and this time I could not escape. My first thought was to crawl under the bed to protect myself. I covered my face with my hands and closed my eyes as tightly as I could. After what seemed like an eon, I realized there was no other sound in the room. Now there was only a brilliant light. I slowly spread my fingers and eased my eyes open as imperceptibly as possible.

Instead of seeing my dad's anger-deformed face, I saw two hands reaching toward me. In the center of each wrist was an ugly scar. I had seen those scars in Sunday school literature. They were supposed to represent the nail scars of Jesus. Someone was playing a trick on me, but who? Did I dare look beyond the wrists to the face? Was I having a nervous breakdown? Was I going crazy?

Rather than the cold, stark fear that had filled the room earlier, I now actually felt warmth. I felt a Presence that brought both power and peace. I was being immersed in an invisible liquid love that poured over me and lodged deep within my soul. I slowly raised my head, and as my eyes followed the arms upward, I saw standing there in my bedroom the Lord Jesus Christ. He was either clothed in light or in the most brilliant white imaginable—whiter than fresh snow; whiter than the clouds that float in the sky; whiter than anything I had ever seen. Draped from His shoulder to His waist was a deep purple cloth—more purple than the heavens at sunset.

As I lifted my head to take in His face, I was instantly drawn to His loving eyes. They were happy eyes filled with every color of the rainbow. It was like looking into an illuminated bowl of the world's most highly prized jewels. I felt as if I could see through them and beyond to heaven and the promise of eternal peace. They were like magnets drawing me into their depths. Keeping His arms outstretched, He looked at me with an all-encompassing expression of love. He smiled and then said three things I had never heard before. They were like a healing salve to my wounded soul and spirit.

He said, "Son." It was the first time anyone had ever called me "Son." It was said so gently, with such love and respect for me—for me!—that I felt my heart melt. The word *son* echoed in my spirit again and again.

"I love you." Someone really did love me. What joy! I felt as if I'd just escaped a death sentence and was free. That statement alone was enough to sustain me for the rest of my life. But He continued, "I have a great plan for your life." The power and presence of Jesus were like a holy fire igniting my soul. I had a purpose! God had something for me to do. Then there was silence. I am sure only a few seconds had passed, but it felt like an eternity.

I closed my eyes, and tears slid slowly down my face. I was consumed with an inexplicable happiness. Eventually I realized that the light had departed but the overwhelming warmth remained. He was gone from my room but not from my spirit, not from my heart. I never wanted to lose that feeling of love and peace and warmth.

I knew better than to share my special secret with anyone, especially my mother. "The Pope, Billy Graham, Adolf Hitler have all claimed to be Christians, and they're all the same," I had heard her snort angrily. "Why would you want Christianity? It has killed six million Jewish people. Jesus is the gentile God, and He's dead. Don't try to dig Him up!"

Still I managed to get a Bible and began reading it faithfully. In the coming years I was somehow kept from the destructive vices and snares around me.

Yet, I could not throw off the terrible shyness that had plagued my early childhood. The jeers of my gentile classmates and their sarcastic remarks about the welts and bruises I was unable to hide in gym class were becoming more than I could endure. My habit of skipping school accelerated and just before high school, I dropped out altogether.

By 1963, I was an awkward, lanky sixteen-year-old, nervously laughing with my friend as we walked through the front door of my house. This was the first time I had ever had the courage to invite anyone home with me; my heart was beating in my throat. As I attempted to quietly steer my friend past my father and uncle and upstairs to my room, my father sneered loudly, "Well! It's my moron of a son!"

I was angry and embarrassed beyond words. I cast a glance at my father and kept climbing the stairs, hoping he had achieved his aim of humiliating me and would say no more. That was not to be. With great agility for a man of his stature, he was on his feet and across the room in a flash. Cursing viciously, he took the stairs two at a time. "I saw that dirty look, you bastard," he roared. "No moron is gonna look at me like that and get away with it!" Terrified, my friend bolted for the front door.

A blow to my head spun me around. Huge, vise-like hands grabbed me by the throat. I was lifted six inches off the floor as the very life was choked out of me. My struggles were no match for my father's brute strength. As blackness overtook me, the screams and curses seemed farther away. The room whirled faster and faster and then went completely black as my father tossed by limp body to the floor and stalked away.

In 1964, I realized I would have to leave before my father killed me. I had studied a world map, searching for the farthest place I could find away from home. Consequently, after joining the army, I was stationed at Wong Tong Ne, a compound on a mountaintop in Seoul, Korea. I served as a medic in the 44th surgical hospital. Two years later this exact site would become known as Prayer Mountain. It had been purchased by Dr. David Yongii Cho, a minister who would ultimately pastor the largest church in the world.

Early one morning as I strolled mountain trails not even thinking about God, the Holy Spirit fell upon me. I wept as I was gently reminded of the words Jesus had spoken to me those many years ago when I was eleven. Every morning thereafter, I returned to that hallowed spot to commune with God.

When in 1966 I had to leave my beloved mountain in Korea, I returned to Philadelphia to work as a recruiter. In my sparsely furnished room at the Philadelphia YMCA, I shut myself in with God for a week, praying and reading straight through the New Testament. Hoping Jesus might visit me again, I pointed to a battered rocking chair in the corner and said, "Lord, this is your chair. If you want to sit there and be comfortable while talking to me, that is fine."

A few days later I was baptized in the Holy Spirit. Filled with boldness, I spent every available minute in the streets, passing out gospel tracts and sharing Jesus.

About two weeks later, while eating breakfast in a run-down restaurant, once again I was enveloped by the presence of God and began to weep. "Lord," I cried, "I don't even know what an evangelist does, but I know You're calling me to be one. I'm just garbage, but if you can use garbage, I'll give my life to You."

After being discharged from the Army, I felt compelled to attend a Bible college in the South to prepare for ministry. During the next two years, I spent many nights in the dormitory prayer room. Fasting and interceding before the Lord, I sought divine direction and pled for healing from the never-ending pain of rejection that had, all my life, gnawed at my insides like a starving rat.

It was in Bible College that I met and married Carolyn, but fearing her rejection, I never told her of my past abuse or of not attending high school.

In 1978, after so many years of repressing my feelings, I found myself in a cardiology ward. There, I underwent a heart catheterization at the tender age of thirty-one. I had undergone a complete breakdown—emotionally and physically. I was still afraid to tell anyone of my fears lest I be rejected. I had yet to realize that I was in search of a father figure.

For the previous twelve years, I had worked as hard as humanly possible in the ministry. Although I told myself it was because of my passion for souls, deep in my heart I knew it was also the driven little boy inside crying out for acceptance. Feeling inferior to other preachers who had bigger ministries, wore better clothes and were better educated, I shrank from close relationships, always avoiding opening up and being real. Longing for the approval I had never had and believing that worth and significance had to be earned by performance, production and perfection, I strove for achievement.

Every time a pastor said, "We can't schedule a meeting with you right now," if was as if my father had rejected me yet again. Finally, the time came that I was holding back-to-back revivals and crusades. My ministry was housed in its own 66,000-square-foot headquarters complex in New York. As a young evangelist, I spoke at Giants Stadium to 60,000 people, at Arrowhead Stadium to 45,000, and was written up in *Time* magazine. Driving myself eighteen hours a day, seven days a week, I felt sinful if I rested, and even apologized for being tired.

But now, as scalding tears trickled down my cheeks and machines monitored every heartbeat, I knew I must confide in someone. I reached for the phone and called one of the few men I had been able to trust, the beloved Christian author and journalist, Jamie Buckingham.

"Jamie," I sobbed, "this is Mike Evans. I'm hospitalized in a cardiology ward and I'm afraid."

"Mike," Jamie answered, "it's okay to be afraid."

I desperately needed to hear those words because I believed that if people found out I was afraid, they would think me weak and I would face more rejection.

When I ended the call, I lifted my hands to God and pled for the grace I would need to be honest with my wife and others. Warm tears dripped down my face, and an indescribable peace descended.

It took most of the night, but sob by sob, hurt by hurt, I told Carolyn everything. Then I confessed my failures and fears to God, asking His forgiveness.

"Will you let Me set you free from the destructive soul ties between you and your father," I sensed the Lord asking. "Will you go to him and ask his forgiveness?"

"Yes, Lord; yes, I will."

"Now, you are ready to minister," Jesus answered.

Early the next morning, I disconnected myself from the machines, dressed, and explaining to the astonished nurses that I was well, walked out of the hospital.

I found my father in a bar trying to pick up a young woman. He and I drove to a quiet place so we could talk. Obeying the Lord's leading, I did not speak of my father's wrongs against me. Neither did I speak of my own successes, as I had in the past, vainly struggling to gain my father's approval. Instead, I wept and confessed my failures.

The presence of God settled upon us, and my father's hard exterior crumbled.

"Mike," he admitted tearfully, "my father abused me like I abused you. He had me working in the fields when I was five or six, and I couldn't go to school to learn to read and write." He had to choke back sobs before he could continue. "Son, I should have been put in prison for the way I treated you."

Suddenly, I found my heart overflowing with love and compassion for the man I thought I could never forgive.

The healing process continued as God steadily worked in my life to demolish the big lie. The constant, stabbing pain of rejection has diminished to a mere twinge now and then. My old, negative self-talk has been replaced with what God's Word says about me as His child. I increasingly comprehended that it is Mike Evans—not what my pride and compulsive workaholic nature can produce—that God values.

Today, my life is filled with joy unspeakable. Carolyn and I have celebrated over four decades of ministry and marriage, as we have worked side-by-side to fulfill what God has called us to do. We now have four children and ten grandchildren.

Wonderful doors of opportunity continue to open wide so I can minister to heads of nations. The Lord has allowed me to preach face-to-face to hundreds of thousands of people. I have been asked to appear on television and radio shows such as Good Morning America, Nightline, Crossfire, CNN World News, and numerous Fox Network shows in defense of the Jewish people. To date, I have published nearly fifty books and produced eighteen television specials based on the books.

Best of all, as I dare to share the story of the atrocities I once endured, the story of a frightened, rejected little boy's terrible suffering is being used to bring healing and hope to hurting people— people struggling for perfection, performance and praise; people with plastic smiles on their faces and gaping holes in their souls; people of all ages and from all strata of society who so desperately need to hear that a smiling Savior with nail-scarred hands loves, accepts and values them and has a wonderful plan for their lives.

TAKE A LOOK IN THE MIRROR

Are you the victim of a painful past? Have you come to grips with that pain and resolved it, or are you still a prisoner of the past? This checklist may help answer those questions for you.

_____ 1.   Are you a workaholic?

_____ 2.   Are you a perfectionist? Do you believe any error on your part detracts from your worth as a person?

_____ 3.   Do you feel you must perform in order to prove your worth?

_____ 4. Do you seek approval and acceptance by striving to produce and achieve?

_____ 5. Are you afraid of taking leadership?

_____ 6. Are you torn between fear of failure and fear of success?

_____ 7. Do you avoid being placed in a position requiring you to be evaluated or criticized?

_____ 8. Is your self-concept so fragile that even this most harmless negative statement made by someone you love or admire damages you emotionally?

_____ 9. Are you so afraid of rejection you won't allow people to get close to you?

_____ 10. Do you reject or belittle any compliment you receive?

_____ 11. Do you always seem to feel inferior to everyone?

_____ 12. Are you so filled with self-hatred that you despise who you are, what you are and everything you do?

_____ 13. Has your chronically low self-esteem resulted in an exaggerated sense of self-importance—a false grandiosity where you pretend to be something you're not?

_____ 14. Do you have a strange tendency to sabotage your own successes?

_____ 15. Are you constantly assuming the blame and/or apologizing for things that aren't your fault?

_____ 16. Do you always place yourself in positions or relationships that are painful?

_____ 17. Are you afraid of losing control?

_____ 18. Are you afraid of the dark or of going to bed?

_____ 19. Do you have difficulty trusting people?

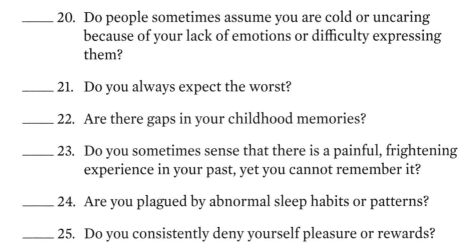

_____ 20. Do people sometimes assume you are cold or uncaring because of your lack of emotions or difficulty expressing them?

_____ 21. Do you always expect the worst?

_____ 22. Are there gaps in your childhood memories?

_____ 23. Do you sometimes sense that there is a painful, frightening experience in your past, yet you cannot remember it?

_____ 24. Are you plagued by abnormal sleep habits or patterns?

_____ 25. Do you consistently deny yourself pleasure or rewards?

The questions you have just answered describe some of the traits springing from long-buried seeds of abuse. Each case is individual, of course, since the long-term effects of abuse vary, based on the severity and frequency of the abuse, the amount of trauma each victim may have experienced, and the internal strength of the victim.

If you found yourself answering yes time after time—either because you were seeing a reflection of your own self or someone you know—you will find hidden keys and practical explanations for those feelings in this book. At times its probing may make you cry or become angry. You may find long-buried fears or memories surfacing.

Remembering can be unpleasant; it can hurt. When that happens, remember this: Recognizing, rebuilding and redirecting damaged emotions, attitudes, thought processes and behavior patterns can be painful, but in the end, it will lead to wholeness.

2

PHYSICAL ABUSE

*"The degree to which people are convinced that they are loved
unconditionally; that they are valuable, gifted and special; and
that they are not alone to face life's struggles is the same degree to
which they will be able to love, serve and build others up. The degree
to which individuals are not convinced of these things is the same
degree to which they will function out of emptiness and shame."*

—JEFF VAN VONDEREN[1]

THE FOLLOWING incident really happened: It was 1989, and I was ministering in Atlanta, Georgia. I had just completed my sermon and had invited people who desperately needed a special touch from God to come forward. As people surged into the aisles, my heart was drawn like a magnet to a young couple and their little girl who looked to be about seven years old. The child had the eyes of a tormented old woman. I knew the bitter tears the mother and father were shedding could only be coming from shattered, hopeless hearts.

Those parents' terrible pain spilled over onto me as I listened to their tale of horror. The father spoke in hushed tones, giving few details, sparing his fragile daughter more suffering. He shuddered: "Our little girl was kidnapped, held captive and abused for over a year. We've had her back home now almost six months, but she's still in such a state of shock she cannot talk, and she won't let a man touch her."

Unable to hold back the tears, I knelt so my face was even with hers while I related the pain and abuse I, too, had suffered as a child. At first, looking into her eyes was like staring into a dark, abandoned house. As I continued to share, a tiny light of hope flickered then flamed, illuminating her little face.

Suddenly her lips quivered and hot tears began to roll down her cheeks. "Thank you!" she hiccupped. "Thank you!" Then, she buried her face in her mother's shoulder and began to cry, "Mama, Mama!" No one had to tell us her journey of healing had begun..

Every time I recall that precious little face, a strange mixture of joy and pain washes over me--joy because God's healing power is at work in that little child's life, and pain for the thousands of other children, teenagers and adults who endure insults, assaults and atrocities more terrible than your worst nightmare. Am I exaggerating? I wish I were.

CHILD ABUSE: WHAT IS IT?

As defined in the Child Abuse Prevention and Treatment Act (PL 100-294), child abuse is:

> ...the physical or mental injury, sexual abuse, or exploitation, negligent treatment or maltreatment of a child under the age of eighteen, or except in the case of sexual abuse, the age specified by the child protection law of the State by a person...who is responsible for the child's welfare under circumstances which indicate that the child's health or welfare is harmed or threatened thereby...

In 1990, the United States Advisory Board on Child Abuse and Neglect published a major report warning that the United States is now in a state of emergency in regard to child abuse. The Board stated: "Each year hundreds of thousands of children are being starved and abandoned, burned and severely beaten, raped and sodomized, berated or belittled."[2] In 1992, for example, nearly 1.9 million reports were received and referred for investigation on approximately 2.9 million children who were the alleged subjects of child abuse and neglect.[3] As you will see later, those numbers have changed dramatically.

Starvation; abandonment; beatings; rape; sodomy; belittlement; what horrible images those words evoke. But child abuse in its four ugly forms—*psychological, abuse, neglect, physical abuse* and *sexual abuse*—includes all these despicable acts and more.

PSYCHOLOGICAL ABUSE

In *Cry Out*, an autobiography of a child who was severely abused by adoptive parents, Peter Quinn paints a somber word-picture of psychological abuse:

> When Peter's parents spoke to him, they always pointed out how bad, stupid, or ugly he was. Never was he hugged, held on their lap, or kissed goodnight. To them, he was like an enemy living under the same roof or a limb grafted onto their body which they rejected by cutting the flow of any life-sustaining nourishment in the hopes that the unwanted limb would die, rot or fall off.[4]

Psychological abuse, sometimes referred to as emotional abuse, is an habitual pattern of behaviors, such as belittling, humiliating, shaming and ridiculing a child through verbal abuse, or engaging in bizarre acts of torment such as locking the child in a closet.

From my earliest memories as a toddler to the day I left home to join the Army at the age of seventeen, emotional abuse was a way of life. My father's philosophy of child rearing was, "children should be seen and not heard." But I learned very early that it was best not to let him even *see* me lest I incur his wrath. If my father walked in the front door, I scooted out the back. If he wandered into the living room, I slipped into the kitchen.

My father didn't call me "Mike" or "Son." His names for me were "Trash, garbage, liar, thief, coward, stupid moron, good-for-nothing @#$%^." Judging by the frequency with which he used it, my father's favorite term for me was simply "moron."

He seemed to delight in accusing me of lying or stealing. When I denied doing or saying whatever my father happened to denounce at any given moment, he beat me until I "confessed." I can't recall the number of times I was locked in that dark, damp canning cellar and made to feel that I belonged with the rats and spiders.

While I could go into more detail and give you a myriad of personal examples, I think you are getting a clear snapshot of emotional abuse. We are not talking about a rare, one-time experience where a weary, worried, wound up parent blurts out unkind words that he/she immediately regrets. No parent is perfect; we all make mistakes. That's not what we are referring to here. Emotional abuse is a habitual pattern of behavior, a never-ending assault using words and tormenting fear as weapons.

In our competitive society, we must remember that psychological abuse can also involve a parent placing excessive, perfectionistic demands upon a child—academically, socially, athletically, or artistically. Unable to accept the child's limitations or differences, the parent may attempt to press the child into the prescribed mold by withdrawing affection and approval, withholding physical or verbal contact, and using verbal put-downs and fear.

One woman who had experienced such a relationship with her father wrote a letter describing what it was like to be the child of an angry parent who both loves and hurts:

> I loved and adored you so much, but I'd tremble with fear when you were angry with me. I did everything to try to please you, but no accomplishment ever seemed enough for you. You compared me to all my friends. This one was prettier, that one was smarter. Then if I achieved something, you belittled it. If I didn't achieve what you wanted me to, you called me a failure. You constantly humiliated and degraded me in front of others. I never knew what you wanted from me.[5]

Bruises and lacerations on the spirit of a child can hurt just as much as welts and cuts on the physical body. And often the pain and scars last a lot longer.

The saying, "Sticks and stones may break my bones, but words will never harm me," is not correct. Combined research on the effects of verbal abuse on a child's later development reveals that verbal abuse alone is more harmful than physical abuse alone but, in combination, verbal and physical abuse have the greatest chance of producing children who have interpersonal problems, are delinquent and aggressive.[6]

In addition, verbal aggression undermines the parent/child bond and promotes the "labeling effect." Here, a child takes on the characteristics of the insulting, demeaning label used by the parent, such as "stupid, whore, troublemaker, lazy" and acts out that role.

I was called "garbage" so often by my father I actually began to believe I was just a piece of valueless human trash that deserved to be discarded. I talked to and treated myself like trash. I took for granted that everyone else must have thought I was trash as well. That's why I was not surprised to learn that the more verbal aggression to which a child is subjected, the greater the probability of the child becoming delinquent, physically aggressive, or having interpersonal problems.[7]

SCOPE OF THE PROBLEM

Just how bad is the problem of psychological abuse? A recent report by The American Humane Association, citing some of the most recent and reliable figures available, estimated that: Every day in America, approximately 2,463 children are determined to be victims of abuse or neglect.[8]

DETECTING PSYCHOLOGICAL ABUSE

People sometimes ask, "If a child is being emotionally abused, what signs or symptoms might be present that could alert an outsider to the problem?" A child who persistently shows several of the following physical or behavioral characteristics may be experiencing psychological abuse:

> » Physical indicators: Eating disorders, sleep
> disturbances (nightmares), failure to thrive,
> developmental delays, speech disorders (stut-
> tering), bed-wetting by a school-age child,
> asthma, ulcers.

» Behavioral indicators: unsuitable sexual behavior, other inappropriate behavior, i.e., bullying, biting, overeating, suicide attempts, poor peer relationships, aggression, withdrawal, anger, academic underachievement, fearful, and a disregard for personal safety.

If you experienced psychological abuse as a child, you may recall exhibiting several of the physical and behavioral indicators listed.

INSIGHTS INTO THE ABUSIVE PERSONALITY

What about those individuals who deliberately inflict pain through psychological abuse? What should we know about them since it is obvious that such abuse occurs not only in the parent/child relationship, but can happen in other relationships as well?

In their practical book, *No Longer a Victim*, Burton Stokes and Lynn Lucas share many helpful insights that have been gleaned through years of ministry to abusers and their victims:

Verbal abusers usually know how to accomplish their abuse in public, and do it so subtly that only their victims know what is happening. Should these victims react, knowing well the message behind the remarks, those observing the exchange usually assume the victims to be the person(s) with the problem...

Most who abuse psychologically are also masters at subtly controlling the environment of their victims until only those of whom the abusers approve have free access to the victims. Abusers also tend to control the outside activities of the victims...Abusers are fearful of their victims forming trusting relationships with authority figures lest the authority figure expose the abuser, and their victims break free!

We must understand that psychological abuse occurs not only in marriages, but between parents and their children, employers and employees, roommates and even friends. Victims will always form at least one abusive relationship. Victims cannot live without abusers, nor can abusers thrive without victims.[9]

A few words of explanation may be necessary here. Many victims of psychological abuse, as well as victims of other types of abuse, develop psychological needs for abuse, know how to provoke abuse, and are drawn to abusers when forming relationships. Simply put: Victims attract victimizers. Because these victims have come to believe they are inferior and deserving of punishment, they unconsciously gravitate to certain abusive personalities, just as abusers are drawn to individuals upon whom they can act out their aggression.

THE ABUSER'S FAVORITE WEAPONS

The two primary weapons of abusers—intimidation and ridicule—combine to cause victims to keep trying to perform and produce in a vain attempt to gain validation from their abusers. Sometimes the abusers use a third weapon and belittle their victims, attacking their sex or the core of their identity. As Stokes and Lucas explain:

This attack wounds so deeply that the victims question their very foundations, concepts and values. If this wound is inflicted often enough, victims begin to experience such confusion that they feel unable to reach the simplest conclusions. They begin to question their most basic rights, concluding that these standards are also wrong. The abusers now have gained such a level of control that, with a little planning, they can even determine the kind of treatment their victims will expect to receive from others. For example, an abuser might say to his victim, "If you do that, so-and-so will see how dumb you are." His victim is by now so weakened that she accepts such statements as fact. In order not to appear "dumb" the victim retreats within herself and says nothing. It is even possible for the situation to deteriorate so much that the victims begin to look to their abusers for validation of their value systems, their choice of friends and their outside activities.[10]

Some abusers will attack an area in which the victims already believe themselves to be handicapped or inferior. The most severe damage seems to occur when abusers attack areas of fear or insecurity within their victims and make them a public laughingstock. This may actually produce some of the same personality problems as being raped.

Abusers enjoy public scenes that illustrate their point. As illogical as it may seem, victims become so programmed to sensitivity concerning these issues, they often give the abuser an opening to attack. This serves to eliminate some of the helplessness victims feel since they still have enough control over their lives to determine when the abuse will occur.

THE VICTIMS

Victims of psychological abuse often are more damaged than victims of either sexual or physical abuse. However, as Stokes and Lucas point out, victims of psychological abuse have no moment to pinpoint as the specific time of abuse, whereas the physically or sexually abused can attribute their encounter and the resulting problems to the violence or lust of certain persons at specific times.[11] In addition, neither sexual nor physical exploitation can occur as often as psychological abuse.

Stokes and Lucas pinpoint several characteristics and problem areas frequently found of victims of psychological abuse.[12] I will list several and summarize them for you. As you read, be alert with characteristics or problem areas that may be present in your own life.

Inability to Form Healthy Relationships

Victims of psychological abuse instinctively perceive their self-worth to be under attack. Consequently, such manipulation causes deep wounds to the identity and self-esteem of its victims that they are hindered in forming healthy relationships.

Need to Feel Valuable and Appreciated

Victims of psychological abuse often have a desperate need to feel valuable, but cannot specify any behavior that would achieve this important end. They are easily threatened and feel insecure because of their perception of how others view them and the way they execute their jobs and responsibilities. They seldom feel indispensable or appreciated, and often feel taken for granted.

Need for Perfection

Victims usually believe, perhaps unconsciously, that the world has set a higher standard for them, allowing absolutely no room for mistakes or less-than-perfect performance. They perceive everyone to be drawing from them, demanding answers, support and direction.

Yet this leads to panic and depression since the victims do not believe they have any of these resources available, even for themselves.

Need for Approval and Affirmation

Psychological abuse leaves its victims in continual need of affirmation and reassurance, even when performing the simplest tasks. This may make the victims appear conceited, wanting everyone to appreciate their performance. However, since victims think they always fail and never do anything right, and because they have no realistic idea of their own value, accomplishments, appearance, competence or effect on others, they truly do need ego reinforcement.

Fear of Performing Before Others

Psychologically abused individuals have virtually no confidence in their own talents or abilities. Therefore, being asked to perform produces intense anxiety, terror, or even panic attacks. They expect to be critically evaluated and exposed as a failure or a fraud. Although victims may pray and beg God for an opportunity to do something, when the opportunity comes, they try to get out of the very thing they are asked to do.

Tendency to Compare God with Abusers

Victims tend to fear that God has much the same personality as their abusers. They fear that love and respect will be withdrawn any time their performance is not up to the standard others set for them.

Need for Abuser's Affirmation

As Stokes and Lucas explain, victims of psychological exploitation, like victims of other types of abuse, seem to need the affirmation of the abuser. As a result, victims are not at peace until they have achieved some measure of approval from the source of manipulation.

All my life I longed for a few words of praise or approval from my father. That's why as a little boy, I foolishly took the chance and showed him the pretty jackknife I found in the snow. That's why, as a young minister, I made it a point to call home and crow about my successes. No matter how much glowing praise I received from my wife, fellow ministers, or people I respected in the business world, I would gladly have exchanged it all for a tiny crumb of verbal affirmation from my father.

The Need for an Abuser

Even when the initial abusers are no longer in the picture, many victims merely look for a surrogate. Seeing themselves as valuable only when someone else says they are, they form relationships to validate their accomplishments. But the authority figures they choose will likely also be abusive, and the cycle continues. The need for abuse and punishment becomes so powerful that if no others are available, some victims find ways to undermine their own goals.

Yesterday Does Not Have to Determine Today

Whether a child is the victim of emotional abuse, emotional neglect, or both, the consequences can be damaging and far-reaching. But they do not have to be final.

I, and many others—victims like me—know from experience that restoration and wholeness is possible. We have discovered that the pain, shame, and bondage of the past can be left behind for a walk into the freedom and hope of a new life. So, let me encourage you to take heart. If I can, if others can, *you* can too!

UNCOVERING THE ROOTS OF YOUR FEELINGS

Childhood abuse can lead to emotional difficulties in adult life. The following checklist may help you identify some of the sources of your pain.

YES   NO

____   ____   1. Did you *really* feel loved as a child?

____   ____   2. Did you ever consider running away because you were hurting so bad emotionally or felt that no one really cared about you?

____   ____   3. As a child, did you ever wish you had never been born or that you had been born into a different family?

____   ____   4. Did your parents express interest in and attend special events in your life, i.e., games, plays, awards ceremonies?

____   ____   5. Were you continually subjected to any type of communication that was critical, humiliating, destructive to your emotional security, self-image, self-worth and development as a person?

____   ____   6. Did either of your parents subject you to unrealistically high standards and goals, producing feelings of failure, inadequacy, self-hatred or shame?

____   ____   7. If you disappointed your parents, did either of them withhold love and affection as a means of punishing you?

____   ____   8. When your mother or father got upset, do you remember being told or made to feel that it was your fault?

____   ____   9. Were you ever subjected to artificially imposed environmental controls that made you the psychological or physical prisoner of another?

Did one or more of these questions evoke painful emotions? Take a moment now to put those feelings into words.

3

CHILD NEGLECT

*According to data from the National Child Abuse
and Neglect Data System (NCANDS), [50 states and
the District of Columbia]States reported a total
of 1,545 fatalities. Based on these data, a nationally
estimated 1,570 children died from abuse and neglect
in 2011. This translates to a rate of 2.10 children
per 100,000 children in the general population
and an average of four children dying every
day from abuse or neglect.*[13]

IN NOVEMBER 1991, residents of White Settlement, Texas, a small town just west of Fort Worth, were stunned when police responded to a 911 hang-up call from a woman who said her son was making gurgling sounds and having difficulty breathing. They found thirteen-year-old Stephen Hill unconscious and chained to a cabinet in his parents' home. Deprived of sufficient food for months, Stephen weighed only fifty-five pounds—about half the weight of a normal boy his age and height. Hospitalized immediately, Stephen was reported to be in very critical condition with minimal brain activity. He died two weeks later.

The boy's engineer father and college-educated mother told police their son was hyperactive and, as a form of punishment, they were not feeding him. The couple's twelve-year-old son was placed in the custody of State Child Protective Services. Police feared the abuse may have gone undetected for years.[14]

CHILD NEGLECT: WHAT IS IT?

Stephen's story is an extreme case of child neglect, a second category of child abuse. It is defined as the habitual failure of a parent or caretaker to provide a child under eighteen with basic needs such as food, clothing, shelter, medical care, educational opportunity, protection and supervision.

Neglect is an act of omission rather than a physical act of commission. Parents or caretakers who neglect are either unable or unwilling to provide appropriate and adequate care. Many often blame external powers for their problems. Some may view the child as a "mistake" or as having "ruined" their lives. Others see the child as a source of trouble with which they are unable to cope; therefore, they give up and ignore the child. Some neglectful parents are mentally deficient; most lack knowledge or sufficient parenting skills and tend to be discouraged, depressed and frustrated in their role as parents. Alcohol and drug abuse may also be a factor. Studies indicate that in neglect cases, age, not gender, is the important variable, and the numbers of child victims rapidly decrease with age.[15] Some emotionally neglectful parents may be unable to accept their children as immature or fallible human beings and may expect or demand too much of the child.

Researchers have noted an observable difference between abusive mothers and neglectful mothers. The abusive parent tends to be tenser, more interfering and not actively involved with their children. The neglectful parent is apt to show little or no affection, have little interaction with their children and seem uninvolved or withdrawn.

As a child, I had sufficient food and clothing, but I experienced emotional neglect. I can recall what it is to feel starved for appropriate support, attention and affection. I remember sitting on the front steps of the shabby government-subsidized apartment where we lived when I was four years old. I was crying because I had been left home alone. I recall how frightening it was, but even worse than the fear was the terrible loneliness that came from feeling I was unwanted and unloved.

EVERYDAY EXAMPLES OF CHILDREN AT RISK

Three-year-old Michael is a victim of child neglect. His pregnant nineteen-year-old mother is foggily attempting to figure out what she is going to feed him after having blown two welfare checks on drugs.

Two-year-old Chrissy is a victim of child neglect. Workers at the day care center where her young single mother has been unceremoniously dumping her each morning for the past two weeks are appalled at the child's condition. Even on the coldest days, Chrissy arrives in one of her three or four torn cotton sunsuits. The child smells so badly, some of the workers have to force themselves to touch her. Each morning Chrissy's teacher winces at the sight of the underweight, unsmiling little girl hobbling into the center still wearing the diaper she had worn the day before.

Seven-year-old Derrick and his three-year-old sister, Jenny, are victims of child neglect. Much of the time their drug-addicted mother leaves them all alone in their filthy, roach-infested apartment while she picks up men in local bars. Most meals, which Derrick prepares for his little sister and himself, consist of peanut butter or bologna on stale bread.

SCOPE OF THE PROBLEM

When thinking of child maltreatment, most think of abuse, not neglect. However, in taking the various kinds of abuse into consideration, surveys reveal that neglect is the more frequent problem.

> Research indicates that very young children (ages 4 and younger) are the most frequent victims of child fatalities. NCANDS data for 2011 demonstrated that children younger than 1 year accounted for 42.4 percent of fatalities; children younger than 4 years accounted for four-fifths (81.6 percent) of fatalities. These children are the most vulnerable for many reasons, including their dependency, small size, and inability to defend themselves. Frequently, the perpetrator is a young adult in his or her mid- 20s, without a high school diploma, living at or below the poverty level, depressed, and who may have difficulty coping with stressful situations. Fathers or mothers' boyfriends are most often the perpetrators in abuse deaths; mothers are more often at fault in neglect fatalities.[16]

Only as we try to imagine multiplied thousands of children like Stephen Hill, Michael, Chrissy, Derrick and Jenny, do we begin to grasp the incalculable suffering caused by child neglect.

DETECTING CHILD NEGLECT

A child who persistently shows several of the following physical or behavioral characteristics may be experiencing neglect:

Physical indicators include height and weight significantly below age level; malnutrition—paleness, low weight relative to height, lack of body tone, fatigue, inability to participate in physical activities, lack of normal strength and endurance; torn or dirty clothing or inappropriate clothing for the weather conditions; untreated illnesses or injuries, lack of routine medical attention for correctible conditions, i.e., poor eyesight, dental care, immunizations; poor hygiene—including lice, body odor, scaly skin or unkempt appearance; inadequate supervision for extended periods of time or when engaged in possibly dangerous activities; lack of safe, warm, sanitary shelter; abandonment.

Behavioral indicators include irritability, begging for or stealing food; taking lunch money or food from other children; chronic hunger and/or hoarding available food; falling asleep in class, lethargy; tardiness or poor school attendance which may signal overwork, exploitation, or the child being kept at home until outward evidence of abuse fades. It is also manifested by a dull, apathetic appearance; repressed personality, inattentiveness and withdrawal; extremely aggressive, disruptive and demanding in an attempt to gain attention and love; assuming adult responsibilities for the needs of a parent or siblings; running away from home; vandalism; drinking; prostitution; drug use.

The behavioral indicators for abuse and neglect vary widely and may also include a drop in school performance, attempted suicide, hypochondria, phobias, and anti-social behavior.

LONG-TERM EFFECTS OF NEGLECT

Some of the effects of childhood neglect were clearly visible in the life of "Gwen," a homeless runaway whose mother and drug-addicted father split up when she was four. At first, Gwen and the other children were shifted from relative to relative. When the family finally moved into its own shabby apartment, Gwen was the one charged with doing the cleaning and cooking after she got home from elementary school.

"I was the family peacemaker and caretaker," says Gwen. "I was the one who stayed home to cook and clean while the other kids were playing and having fun."

When, at age fourteen, Gwen got stoned on drugs, rebelling against her "good kid" role, her mother threw her out of the house. Gwen spent the next five drug-and-alcohol numbed years cooking and cleaning for any man who would give her a place to stay. "I was always old," recalls Gwen, "but I never grew up."

Child neglect is a very real problem that will be around until informed, alert people care enough to open up their hearts, roll up their sleeves and reach out to hurting children who cannot help themselves. *Hurting children grow very, very old before their time.*

UNCOVERING THE ROOTS OF YOUR FEELINGS

We have already seen how childhood abuse can lead to emotional difficulties in adult life. The following checklist may help identify some additional sources of your pain.

YES   NO

____   ____   1. Did you learn at an early age that you couldn't depend on anyone but yourself?

____   ____   2. During your childhood, was your mother there when you needed her?

____   ____   3. Were you expected to perform heavy household responsibilities at an early age?

____   ____   4. While you were still a child were you frequently placed in charge of your younger sisters/brothers?

____   ____   5. Were you frequently left home alone?

____   ____   6. Were you sometimes deprived of one or more of the basic necessities of life such as food, warm clothing, and/or medical attention?

If one or more of the above questions triggered painful memories and emotions, take a moment to describe and surrender those memories and emotions to God. Ask Him to transform your past hurts into victories for today and tomorrow.

4

SEXUAL ABUSE

For it was not an enemy that reproached me; then I could have borne it: neither was it he that hated me that did magnify himself against me; then I would have hid myself from him: But it was thou, a man mine equal, my guide, and mine acquaintance. We took sweet counsel together, and walked unto the house of God in company.

PSALM 55:12-14, KJV

THE YEAR WAS 1902. A little girl, Corrie ten Boom, and her watchmaker father were on a train traveling from Amsterdam back to their home in Haarlem, West Netherlands. The two had been on a trip to get the exact time from the clock atop the Naval Observatory tower. Within forty years or so, Corrie, her father, several family members and friends would be imprisoned for hiding Jews and helping them avoid the horrors of Hitler's concentration camps. She would know what it was like to be beaten, starved, and forced to stand naked before leering Nazi guards.

But for now, little Corrie was blessed to be growing up in a child-safe, womb-like environment shielding her from many of the sorrows and responsibilities of the adult world. In her wonderful book, *The Hiding Place*, Corrie recreated a special scene for her readers:

> Often I would use the trip home to bring up things
> that were troubling me, since anything I asked at

home was promptly answered by the aunts. Once—I must have been ten or eleven—I asked Father about a poem we had read at school the winter before. One line had described a "young man whose face was not shadowed by sex sin." I had been far too shy to ask the teacher what it meant, and Mama had blushed scarlet when I consulted her. In those days just after the turn of the century, sex was never discussed, even at home.

So the line had stuck in my head. "Sex," I was pretty sure, meant whether you were a boy or girl, and "sin" made Tante Jans very angry, but what the two together meant I could not imagine. And so, seated next to Father in the train compartment, I suddenly asked, "Father, what is sex sin?"

He turned to look at me, as he always did when answering a question, but to my surprise he said nothing. At last he stood up, lifted his traveling case from the rack over our heads, and set it on the floor. "Will you carry it off the train, Corrie?" he said. I stood up and tugged at it. It was crammed with the watches and spare parts he had purchased that morning.

"It's too heavy," I said.

"Yes," he said. "And it would be a pretty poor father who would ask his little girl to carry such a load. It's the same way, Corrie, with knowledge. Some knowledge is too heavy for children. When you are older and stronger you can bear it. For now you must trust me to carry it for you."

And I was satisfied. More than satisfied—wonderfully at peace. There were answers to this and all my hard questions—for now I was content to leave them in my father's keeping.[17]

No, I am not suggesting that we return to an era where sex is a dirty, unmentionable word. God created Sex and gave it as one of His good and perfect gifts to mankind. It has, in turn, been perverted and misused.

Neither am I suggesting that sex education is wrong or unwise. Tragically, you and I live in a Sodom-and-Gomorrah society that has made it necessary for parents to arm their children with the information they need to defend themselves against the evils of our day.

Whenever I read Corrie ten Boom's story, I cannot hold back the tears. Tears for a beautiful, simple way of life most families will never know. Tears for little children forced to carry knowledge far too heavy for their delicate spirits.

CHILD SEXUAL ABUSE

Sexual abuse, the ultimate misuse of a more mature individual's power over a child and of a child's trust. Child sexual abuse is the exploitation of a child or adolescent for the sexual gratification of another person. It includes behaviors such as intercourse, sodomy, oral-genital stimulation, exhibitionism, voyeurism, fondling, involving a child in prostitution or the production of pornography. It is hard for me even to write some of the above words, yet think of the tens of thousands of once-innocent children who have had such horrors forced upon them. For many years it was believed to be largely a trauma for girls. However, many boys are also victims of this third major type of cruelty.

Incest is sexual abuse that occurs within families. The abuser may be a parent, step-parent, grandparent, sibling, cousin, or other family member. Research indicates that up to 50 percent of incest offenders also molest children outside their families.

In his book, *Healing of Memories*, David Seamands refers to a statement made in 1983 by Karl Menninger, a respected psychiatrist that in the United States, incest was becoming as common as shoplifting.

Frankly, Dr. Menninger's observation did not surprise me. For years, disturbed, depressed young people have been coming to me following a meeting and tearfully confiding that they had been victimized by family members. Being sexually abused by a stranger is horrible enough; but, just imagine the avalanche of emotions triggered by being molested by a loved, trusted member of the family.

Several years ago, four young girls came to my office seeking help after having heard my own personal testimony. Three of the four had been victims of incest: One girl had been molested by her father; another by an uncle, the third by her brother. The fourth had been gang-raped. All of the girls wanted to be free and gladly received my prayers for their deliverance.

On another occasion, a man and wife came to my office for counselling and prayer for their thirteen-year marriage. Unable to shoulder the unbearable weight of her guilt any longer, the woman broke down and confessed that none of their three children had been fathered by her husband. For years, while her husband was at work, she had picked up men at different bars. This woman, who had attended church all her life and who sang in the choir, had been repeatedly sexually abused by a trusted relative as a child. Like so many victims, she had become convinced that she was wicked, evil, and had acted out those feelings. As I ministered to that heart-broken woman, eight different masculine voices spoke through her. Some people might say they were demons, while others might call those voices "multiple personalities." I dealt with them as I see Jesus dealing with similar situations in New Testament accounts.

The husband was stunned by his wife's shocking revelation. But as I prayed and counselled with the woman, her husband began to comprehend the unspeakable pain and guilt his wife had carried so much of her life. It was then that the long, difficult healing process in their marriage began.

Other people naively assume that faithful, respectable church families, such as the one I just mentioned, are untouched by the problem of child sexual abuse, but that is not the case. A disturbing number of people in the church, young and old alike, are sobbing out stories of sexual abuse.

A Bible college freshman confided:

> The first time it happened, I was about eleven. My family and I were on a camping trip. As soon as I could get my mother alone the next morning, I told her what had happened. She patted me on the shoulder, looked away and said, "Don't worry about it, honey. Daddy just thought you were me." After that, I never even bothered to tell her. I knew she wouldn't stand up for me.

Denial is often used as a defense mechanism in incestuous families. Mothers must use enormous degrees of denial to overlook such sexual abuse in their husbands. Family members who participate in such secret sexual abuse can deny it is happening, referring to it as "sex education," "helping Daddy," and other euphemisms. But as we can sense in the following poem written by a young victim of incest, the trauma inflicted by denial is immeasurable:

DANGER

Danger threatened!
I knew I had to get away,
But there was no place I could go.
A girl of six
Can hardly leave the yard alone.
I stayed.
Instead, I ran into my mind.
I dodged between the messages
Of Mother's eyes
And Grandma's sighs—
Messages which said:
Don't tell the truth;
We cannot bear to hear.
Cowering in the dark recesses
Of an attic in my head,
I crept behind the broken furniture
Of my unacceptable rage and fear.
Dust of decades
My forbidden secret,
Settled over me as I choked in guilt.
Abandoned and abused,
I sealed the doors
So that no one would know.[18]

Said a pretty Bible college sophomore:

Although my mother is a Christian and always took
us kids to church, my father rarely went with us. The

first time my father tried to molest me and I went to my mother for help, she got very angry and accused me of lying and trying to make trouble between them. After that, I put up with my father's nighttime visits to my bedroom for years because I thought I had to, but when I went away to college, I made up my mind that I wasn't going to let him bother me anymore.

The first time I went back home for the weekend, I bought myself a little hook and latch like the kind that goes on a screen door, and I put it on my bedroom door. When mother asked why, I just told her I wanted privacy like I had in the dorm at college, but I could tell by Daddy's eyes that he knew exactly why I had done it.

That night he came to my room. He tugged at the door, trying to get inside. But when the hook rattled loudly, he stopped and went away.

Mary Ann, A Bible college sophomore, still battles bitterness toward her mother and father:

They got so caught up in attending religious seminars on weekends they forgot that my older brother and I needed parents. Two or three weekends a month, Mom and Dad would drive to another city or state for the latest seminar on whatever spiritual topic happened to be the "hottest" at the moment, leaving my teenage brother and me at home alone. He started messing around with me, threatening me with all kinds of stuff if I told our parents.

After a while, my brother began inviting his friends over to "play" with his little sister. By that time, so much had gone on I felt trapped. I despised my brother and his raunchy friends, and I hated myself. I started gorging on food, getting fatter and fatter, partially to punish myself, but also hoping that if I looked fat and repulsive, they would leave me alone.

I wound up 100 pounds overweight. As soon as I graduated from high school, I chose a Bible college as far away from home as I could get. But I feel so empty and lonely, and I can't stop gorging myself. My parents still have no idea what I've gone through.

Many sex offenders appear to be responsible and respectable citizens. They may be married and appear to function well in many areas of life. Researchers tell us that 80 to 90 percent of sex offenders are known to the child. They are neighbors, baby-sitters, family members and friends. But kinship or friendship should never cause parents to become careless when it comes to protecting a child.

One young man, who was faithfully reared in the church by his devout Christian parents, places much of the blame for his homosexual lifestyle on his mother and father:

When I was about twelve years old, my parents invited an older teenage cousin of ours to spend a week at our house. Even though they knew he was gay, my parents thought nothing of having him share my bedroom.

For several nights I resisted his advances. But then, overcome by curiosity and my own newly awakened sexual urges, I yielded. Since that time, I've experienced tremendous shame, guilt, and sexual confusion over the things he and I did together. But worse than that, I've done the same things my cousin did to me to several young boys. I'm filled with anger and bitterness, and I have doubts now about God and a lot of the things my parents and the church taught me.

SCOPE OF THE PROBLEM

Children of all ages are sexually abused; over one-third of the victims are five years old or younger. Verbal threats and coercion are frequently used to force children to participate. Although child sexual abuse may be a one-time occurrence, it more typically is an abusive relationship that lasts an average of one to four years.

The National Children's Alliance reported that in 2012 "197,902 children reported sexual abuse."[19] Many researchers consider that number to be an absolute minimum since it does not include stranger abduction for sexual purposes or cases which did not come to the attention of the authorities. Nor does it include the victims of child prostitution and pornographic exploitation, both known to involve multimillion dollar businesses.

CORRECTING FAULTY ATTITUDES
TOWARD CIHLD SEXUAL ABUSE

Parents and other adults who are not aware of the true nature of the problem of child sexual abuse cannot give children the useful, accurate information they need to help avoid abuse.

For example, many adults still believe some common myths:

> » Children are molested primarily by strangers;

» Girls are the exclusive targets of sexual abuse;

» Sexual abusers are violent, aggressive or mentally ill;

» Sexual abuse is immediately apparent; and

» Children will naturally outgrow the effects of sexual abuse or incest.

You can see the problem: If parents warn a child only about strangers, then the child is poorly prepared. If a parent does not realize that boys are also victims of sexual abuse, a male child giving obvious signs of alarm and distress may be ignored.

One of the most horrifying aspects of childhood sexual abuse is the casual, almost flippant attitudes some adults hold toward it. In discussing with a worried uncle the safety of his three-year-old niece who had been repeatedly molested by the man her mother had recently married, a social worker casually commented, "Well, you know, some little girls get where they like that sort of thing."

Certainly the qualified social worker should know better than to make such a statement. But as social work professor Jane F. Gilgun reminds us, sexual abuse "involves a misuse of power, where an older, stronger and more sophisticated person takes advantage of a younger, smaller and less sophisticated person in order to satisfy the wishes and feelings of the more powerful person without regard for the less powerful person."[20]

What we think sexual abuse is and how seriously we take it affects how we react toward it. Our attitudes help determine the steps we do or do not take in protecting the child, reporting the incident and attempting to prevent further abuse.

DETECTING SEXUAL ABUSE

Because many children and adolescents cannot or will not report their sexual abuse, someone else must be informed about specific physical and behavioral indicators and care enough to report them.

A child who persistently shows several of the following *behavioral and physical characteristics* may be experiencing sexual abuse.

Be alert for behaviors such as: Sexual play with dolls, excessive or public masturbation, inserting objects into the vagina or anus, seductive behavior, sexually attacking playmates, requesting sexual stimulation, acting out sexually.

Other indicators such as the following may also signal sexual abuse: Sexual knowledge or behavior beyond the child's developmental level; drug or alcohol abuse; decline in school performance; sudden avoidance of familiar adults or places; complaining frequently of headaches, backaches, or stomachaches. Markers may also include: running away, lying, stealing, sadness and/or depression, suicidal thoughts or tendencies, compulsive behavior, overeating or anorexia, anxiety, aggression, loss of bladder or bowel control. Victims have also shown symptoms of post-traumatic stress disorder which is manifested by insomnia, impaired memory, nightmares, and poor self-esteem.

Certain *physical indicators* may also alert an adult to sexual abuse of a child: Complaints of genital pain or irritation, sexually transmitted diseases, unexplained sore throats, yeast, or urinary infections, and of course, pregnancy in young adolescents.

PROBLEM AREAS IN VICTIMS OF SEXUAL ABUSE

Many sexually abused children appear to show no symptoms. However, some studies conclude that these victims may exhibit symptoms later, that they are the most psychologically resilient or that these victims suffered the least damaging abuse.

Studies also indicate that the following factors may lead to increased symptoms: A close related abuser, high frequency of contact, penetration, long-time abuse, use of force or threats, lack of material support at the time of the abuse.

Other elements such as psychological abuse, parental neglect, or family disorganization can make the long-term effects of childhood sexual victimization even more traumatic or devastating. On the other hand, strong maternal support seems to be the most important factor in reducing symptoms over time.

Research leaves no doubt that childhood sexual victimization results in serious, long-term consequences for individuals. Studies, when divided by the ages of the victims, reveal that certain symptoms manifest themselves at different points in the abused child's life.

For *preschoolers,* the most common symptoms include nightmares, anxiety, sexual behavior and general post-traumatic stress disorder.

Symptoms in *school-age children* include aggression, fear, nightmares, hyperactivity, school problems, general mental illness and regressive behavior.

In adolescents, the most common behaviors include withdrawal, suicidal or self-injurious behaviors, depression, illegal acts, substance abuse, and running away. Some researchers propose that sexual behavior in preschoolers may be suppressed during the elementary school-age period only to resurface in adolescence as promiscuity, sexual aggression or prostitution.

Childhood abuse can affect an *adult's* sexual feelings and behaviors. Some victims report compulsive erotic activity or else total abstinence. When measured for "sexual self-esteem," both men and women victims as children reported lower levels of sexual satisfaction and adjustment than did other people in the research sample.[21]

Also found in research literature are repeated suggestions that female targets of sexual abuse as children become victims later in life. Several investigations have found unusually high incidents of victimization among women who suffer rape and/or spousal abuse. The increasing number of reports that point to some connection between childhood and adulthood subjects should not be dismissed.[22]

Actually, a number of factors could be at work in regard to the connection between childhood and later victimization:

> » There is evidence that childhood sexual victimization may force children out of their families at an earlier age as they seek to escape the abuse or blame associated with it. Some women marry early, probably to men who have little more to recommend them than the fact they were willing. Being young and unable to return to their families, these women are in extremely dependent positions and vulnerable to physical, verbal, emotional and sexual abuse. Those who do not marry immediately, but who do run away from home, may also find themselves living a dire existence that makes them more vulnerable to additional abuse.

> » Childhood sexual abuse may have a corrosive effect on self-esteem. Women who feel bad about themselves may be conspicuous targets for men who exploit women. They may also

lack assertiveness to short-circuit encounters that could put them at risk.[23]

Some clinical reports note connections between child molestation and later homosexuality. In a student study conducted by David Finkelhor, boys victimized by older men were over four times more likely to engage in homosexual activity than were non-victims. Close to half the male respondents who had had a childhood sexual experience with an older man were then involved in homosexual activity.[24]

Authors Burton Stokes and Lynn Lucas in their book, *No Longer a Victim*, discuss ten problem areas often experienced by victims of sexual abuse:[25]

1. Fear

Victims of physical and sexual abuse experience some of the same fears; however the way these fears are expressed and the behaviors they produce are somewhat different. The most common and universally expressed fears of sexual abuse targets—consciously or unconsciously—are: (a) fear of being successful; (b) fear of failure; (c) fear of God or any authority figure; (d) fear of taking leadership; (e) fear of losing control; (f) fear of the dark and going to bed; (g) fear of violence or pain; and (h) fear of those who resemble their abusers.

2. Mistrust of people

Victims expect most people to inflict emotional or physical pain, and some believe that people only associate with them for what they can provide or produce. However, victims seem to keep at least one abusive personality type around.

3. Lack of feelings and emotions

This symptom appears more often in those who were physically or psychologically abused; it usually occurs in those who were sexually abused and used their imaginations as defense mechanisms to escape the assault.

4. Language patterns

Victims seem always to apologize for everything. Their communication is centered around a pattern of continuous acquiescence—giving in and stepping back, until they can no longer tolerate their pattern of retreat. They need to be peacemakers and know how to avoid confrontation. They often have difficulty accepting gifts and will explain away anything they own that has the appearance of being above the poverty level because they feel totally unworthy of any luxury.

5. Expectations

The life theory of sexual abuse victims seem to be that if something good happens it will be followed by something bad, so why allow the good. In their spiritual lives, it is as though they stand before God with their hands closed, refusing His blessings.

6. Amnesia

Loss of memory breaks down into four categories,

depending on the severity of the problem and the coping mechanism used:

a. *Total*—The victims have very little memory of childhood, which leads to fear and frustration.

b. *Selective*—Victims remember only the good events that happened, form a false adulation of family members while growing up, and always make themselves the villains in any problem.

c. *Partial*—Victims have a mixture of both good and non-threatening bad memories of the past. Although they may remember one or two instances of abuse, their memories may be protecting them from the perpetrators, the initial acts, and frequency of attacks.

d. *Fantasy*—Victims have created memories with just enough truth to pass inspection and give them an identity, but that create conversations and positive relationships that never existed with family members. This intensifies guilt feelings about admitting that anything less than total love has transpired in their families and places victims in positions of continually striving to earn love and approval in their families.

However, in all four categories there are periods when the victim knows that some event in the past was a painful experience. This may manifest as a dream in which the figures are slightly shapeless, unidentifiable and disjointed; a vague fear that someone is hiding under the bed; or a fleeting impression that a form is standing in the doorway—and panic results.

7. How they view themselves

Victims feel inferior to everyone else; they work overtime at being accepted, liked and valued; they try to earn love and respect, yet are not able to accept it. They express these feelings by acting as if everything is satisfactory, or as if they are in complete control. One defense mechanism employed to avoid judgment or exposure is their need to know something about everything; another may be a tendency to suffer from inertia. Prone to self-destructive behavior, sexually abuse victims usually hate who they are, what they are and what they do.

8. Relationships

Victims must have an abuser around somewhere. If they cannot find or force someone into that role, they will abuse themselves by overwork, denial of pleasure, set unreachable goals, or place themselves in positions of receiving pain.

9. Sexual attitudes

These may break down into one of the following expressions:

a. They avoid all sex because they believe sex is dirty.

b. They find the marriage relationship almost impossible because they feel that sex is a service and not a means of intimate communication.

c. Uncomfortable with and afraid of warmth and intimacy, they will find it difficult to give and receive affection.

d. They may have a low sex drive even if married. For male victims, venting their repressed feelings of rage and indignation, the sex act will become more like rape than love. A female victim may tend to be passive and completely uninvolved because as a child, the method of coping was withdrawal.

e. Male victims may tend toward perversion.

f. Male victims may tend more toward masturbation, while the female may have a problem with touching her own body.

g. The victims—male or female—may become so sexually active as to run the risk of promiscuity.

10. Damage to parenting ability

Abused parents may subconsciously instill in their children a sense of mistrust or fear of close family members. Some will fight incestuous urges toward their own or molest other children.

Their ministry to abuse victims led Stokes and Lucas to conclude:

Sexual abuse leaves no area of its victims' lives intact. The influence of the abusers is stamped deep into the nature and personalities of their victims.[26]

Stokes and Lucas also add these insights:

Victims of sexual abuse believe they can never be freed from the shame and guilt and that they must always feel dirty inside, evil and unworthy...They find it difficult to accept as fact that the motivation for [the abuser's] acts was not love, but was indeed lust, hatred, or contempt.

Every victim seems to feel deep sorrow, even grief...as if something had died...At some point during the violation, their sense of self-respect and even their identity as an individual died... When a victim comes to realize that abuse has occurred, it is not uncommon for the response to be uncontrolled crying. Such crying may occur at a later stage of recovery.[27]

Others have also compiled a checklist of behaviors associated in adults sexually abused in childhood. Some of these include: an inability to trust, low self-esteem, rigid control of one's thoughts, risk-taking behavior, sexual difficulties of all kinds, self-destructiveness and suicidal tendencies, and compulsive behaviors such as drug abuse or eating disorders. Such checklists also include other aftereffects of childhood sexual abuse, such as feeling distant and disconnected from one's own body, nightmares and fears of being alone in the dark, gynecological and gastrointestinal problems, blocking out parts of one's past, avoiding mirrors, multiple personalities, stealing, desire to change one's name. However, these symptoms are found in many people and do not necessarily indicate abuse.

VICTIMS WHO CARRY BLAME

Why do many child and adult victims of abuse often believe they are to blame for the exploitation? Some victims were punished when someone found out. Some were accused of lying. Some were told by their abusers that it was their fault. Some blame themselves because they took gifts and special privileges.

Also, as Dr. Dan Allender points out, "The experience of pleasure in the midst of powerlessness and betrayal sets off a profoundly convoluted spiral of damage."[28] Some victims recall feeling a sense of power, attractiveness and dominance resulting from the abuser's attention, while despising both the abuse and the perpetrator. Others remember a sense of mingled pleasure and intense self-loathing. The confusing, contradictory feelings related to abuse may establish patterns of relating to others that can affect a victim's current relationships.

However, the victim who felt some degree of sensual pleasure during molestation should be reminded that bodies were designed to respond to touch, and no abuser has the right to take advantage of that. These victims were not betrayed by their bodies; they were betrayed by the persons who abused them. Children have neither the skills, power, maturity nor responsibility to protect themselves. It is *always* the adult's responsibility not to be sexual with children.

Childhood victims of sexual abuse should also understand that when they were assaulted as children, their capacity to set boundaries and to say no was severly impaired. Because of that damage, even if the abuse continued into teen years or beyond, they were still responding from the perspective of a powerless child whose boundaries had been violated, a child who was trained to submit dutifully to the pleas or pressures of another.

A NEW BEGINNING

The victim of sexual abuse who determines to seek and attain healing and wholeness is not doomed to play out the melody of life in a sad, haunting minor key. Life can begin again, this time on a triumphant note.

If you are a victim of child sexual abuse longing to be healed, read these words of hope from Stokes and Lucas and believe them with all your heart:

> The eventual change within the personality will be so great that when the healing process is complete, those closest to the former victims feel as if they have met a different person.[29]

A different person! That's how I'd describe 45-year-old Rebekah—thirty pounds thinner, eyes sparkling with laughter and love of life. But things weren't always that way.

Rebekah grew up in a dysfunctional home amid an atmosphere of bickering and rivalry. As a single adult, Rebekah fought a continual battle with obesity and depression. As far back as she could recall, her depression always deepened during the Christmas holidays.

In her late thirties, Rebekah had begun having eerie, recurring dreams in which she saw the faces of an uncle and of the minister who had been her father's best friend. She was also disturbed by strange thoughts and impressions of a sexual nature.

Fearing that she was headed for suicide or a nervous breakdown,

Rebekah sought out a Christian counselor. Over a period of months as they prayerfully probed into her past, the strange flashbacks and dreams began to come into focus. Finally, like ghostly corpses, two horrible scenes that had been submerged in her subconscious for years rose to the top: Rebekah distinctly remembered being molested by her father's minister friend and also by an uncle she had loved and trusted. Both instances of abuse had occurred around Christmas.

Today, Rebekah is well on her way to wholeness and well-being. Every Christmas now finds her more free and joyful than the last.

In counselling, Rebekah discovered that putting her thoughts and feelings into written form served as a tremendous release and healing force. She wrote the following poem about her past:

RESTORATION

A little girl—"shy" they would say.
If only they knew: They made me that way.
Did anyone care? Did anyone see
The sadness and fear and shame in me?
Was it fun for them to toss me around?
Those angry words...in my mind they still sound.
Father to Mother. Brother to brother.
Was it *me* they all hated, or just one another?
So many years have slowly passed by,
Yet remembering all this still makes me cry.
The pain, still there, I'd thought time would heal.
Be quiet, little girl! Who told you to feel?
A frightened young girl on his basement stairs.
Stolen from home, but nobody cares.

Stripped and ashamed—that smile on his face.
I stand there abandoned, alone in that place.
Another year, a young lady, all grown
With questions and memories and pain all my own.
Could I be safe in this room where I am?
Wait! The door opens, oh no, not this man!
Unable to move, I endured the abuse.
He destroyed what was left. Oh, God, what's the use?
He left me sick and all covered with shame.
Ugly. Repulsive. A thing with no name.
I tried hard to forget. I worked and I schemed,
But it kept reappearing in thoughts and in dreams.
Maybe someday I'd forget the words that he said.
Or better yet, find a way to be dead.
Though years have passed, the pain is still real,
But I'm discovering now that it's okay to feel.
Not alone anymore—friends working together.
I'm doing my part, and I'm getting better.
What was done to me should never have been.
All of it happened when someone else sinned.
God despises abuse. He was angry, too.
His plan never included all I went through.
Now His Spirit's at work, searching the deep.
Exposing dark secrets I thought I could keep.
Before Him old hurts and all bondages fall.
I bring them to Him, and He heals them all.
I'm learning to laugh, to love and believe.
I trust now in One who cannot deceive.
He knows my name. I'm precious, adored!
Because of His grace, I'm being restored.

—A SURVIVOR

A different person. A new beginning. That's exactly what God wants for you. As Rebekah discovered, the damage from sexual abuse can be healed once for all. Victims can become happy, whole survivors!

WHAT HAS POWERLESSNESS DONE IN ME?*

Sexual abuse produces a sense of powerlessness, a feeling of helplessness. Deep helplessness usually leads to a lifestyle marred by the loss of our sense of pain, for the only way to survive despair was by deadening the parts of our soul that still felt rage, pain and desire. That loss of a sense of pain makes us lose our sense of self—our sense of who we are, which in turn impairs our judgment and wisdom about relationships.

Do your relationships reflect any of these traits?

_____ I have a pattern of being the victim in relationships.

_____ I have to be in control.

_____ I prefer to be around people less clever than I am.

_____ I usually feel controlled by the other person.

_____ I tend to hold the core of myself aloof from others.

_____ It's as though there's a chasm or wall separating me from those around me.

_____ I feel unable to make myself understood.

_____ Because I know I'm no good at relationships, I avoid them.

Do these signal the way you tend to think deep down?

_____ I'm not good enough to be involved with a truly loving man/woman. A really wonderful man/woman would never want me.

_____ It's more important to be to be in control of a relationship than to have it be deep and intimate.

_____ If I had a terrific man/woman and lost him/her, it would be far worse than never having had that relationship.

As Dr. Allender explains, one root of poor judgment is shame: "I'm not worthy to be in a relationship with a truly loving man/woman." The other root is contempt for self or others. The person capable of deep relationships is more dangerous; abandonment by him/her will hurt far more than abandonment by an uncommitted person. The good individual is also far harder to control, and we hate feeling powerless to control someone. For both reasons, we often opt for those who are incapable of sustaining a deep relationship.

With that understanding, look back over your answers in the above exercise. Overall, how would you say experiencing powerlessness has affected your inner self—your attitudes, feelings, and commitments?

*This exercise was adapted from the book, _The Wounded Heart: Hope for Victims of Childhood Sexual Abuse_, by Dr. Dan Allender.[30]

5

PHYSICAL ABUSE

"I have suffered too much in this world not to hope for another."
—JOHN JACK ROUSSEAU

TWO-YEAR-OLD STEPHANIE is at risk. Her mother, who works as a waitress, makes an income below the poverty level, so it's tough for her as a single parent to make ends meet. The money factor and loneliness are part of the reason Stephanie's mom has allowed a boyfriend, a convicted sex offender with violent mood swings, to move into her apartment.

The helpless little girl is living with a ticking time bomb that could explode into at least two devastating types of abuse. Her mother, the one person who could rescue her, has chosen to ignore the danger.

Tragically, family members, neighbors or caseworkers often become aware of children like Stephanie who are at high risk for physical abuse after it is too late to intervene.

WHAT IS PHYSICAL ABUSE?

Physical abuse, this fourth category of child abuse, is defined as any non-accidental injury to a child under the age of eighteen by a parent or care taker. Non-accidental injuries may include beatings, shaking, burns, human bites, strangulation, or immersion in scalding water.

Like other categories of abuse we have mentioned, physical abuse is rarely a single attack; instead, it is a pattern of behavior that repeats over time. Such maltreatment occurs:

> a. When a parent or other person willfully or maliciously injures or causes a child to be injured, tortured or maimed;

> b. When unreasonable force is used upon a child; or

> c. It may result from over-discipline or from punishment that is too severe. Physical abuse means bruises, cuts, welts, scars, pain—even death.

SCOPE OF THE PROBLEM

Just how serious is the problem of physical abuse? In 2011, 6.2 million children were referred to Child Protective Services (CPS) of which 18 percent were victims of physical abuse. The most likely age group to be victimized is children under the age of two years. It is estimated that in the US 1,570 children die yearly because of maltreatment. That is an average of thirty children weekly. Of those who are killed, 81.6 percent are under the age of four years and almost half of those children were less than one year old.[31]

According to domestic violence statistics from the University of California at Los Angeles:

> a. Child abuse is reported every **10** seconds.

> b. Five to six children die each day as a result of child abuse or neglect.[32]

DETECTING PHYSICAL ABUSE

Indicators of physical abuse include the following:

» Wearing long sleeves or high necklines on hot days in order to hide bruises, burns, or other marks of abuse.

» Bruises or welts in various stages of healing on the face, lips, or mouth, i.e. black eyes; large areas of bruising on the torso, back, buttocks, or thighs (may be in unusual patterns reflecting the instrument used to inflict the injuries.)

» Lacerations and abrasions to the mouth, lips, gums, eyes, or to the external genitalia.

» Burns (cigarette or cigar); doughnut-shaped burns on the buttocks indicative of immersion in hot liquid; rope burns on the arms, neck, legs or torso; patterned burns that show the shape of the item—an iron, for example—used to inflict them.

» Human bite marks.

» Fractures of the skull, jaw, or nose; spiral fractures of long bones (arm and leg); fractures in various stages of healing; multiple fractures; any fractures in a child under the age of two.

» Loss of hair; bald patches.

» Retinal hemorrhage.

>> Abdominal injuries.

>> Missing teeth.

Anyone in close contact with children should be alert to untreated injuries—especially in very young children; multiple injuries, a history of repeated injury, or new injuries layered on top of old ones. But do we have to rely solely upon a child's physical appearance? His or her behavior may also indicate physical abuse.

Behavioral indicators of physical abuse include:

>> Wariness of physical contact with adults, especially parents.

>> A young child who, when being treated by doctors and/or nurses and is afraid or in pain, does not look to the parent for help, but simply cries hopelessly.

>> Suggesting that other children should be punished in a harsh manner.

>> Crying excessively and/or sitting and staring.

>> Requesting or feeling deserving of punishment.

>> Fear of going home and/or requesting to stay in school or daycare.

>> Showing apprehension when other children cry or when an adult approaches a crying child.

>> Demonstrating extremes in behavior, such as extreme aggression or withdrawal.

>> Reporting injury by parents or giving unbelievable explanations for injuries.

FACTORS CONTRIBUTING TO ABUSE

Research reveals a lengthy list of factors contributing to abuse. For example, certain characteristics of the children may contribute to abuse. Researchers tell us that a family may be at risk for abuse if the child:

>> Is "different"—smaller than average, sicklier, disabled, or considered to be unattractive.

>> Is more demanding, or otherwise has more problems than other children in the family.

>> Resembles or reminds the parent of someone that parent dislikes.

>> Is unwanted, viewed as a mistake or burden, or as having ruined a relationship for the parent.

Although certain characteristics in a child might trigger maltreatment, it is the abuser, not the innocent child who bears responsibility for the abusive behavior.

Risk factors for abuse include unemployment and financial stress, dysfunctional families, a history of abuse as a child. Although the following list is by no means complete, check to see if any of the risk factors might apply to you:

>> Families in which the husband is not working have a significantly higher rate than other families.

>> Parents who have constant conflict between themselves are more likely to abuse their children.

» Parents who verbally abuse their children are more likely to physically abuse them.

» Husbands and wives who verbally attack each other are more likely to abuse their children.

» In families in which the husband strikes his wife, the rate of child abuse is much higher.

» Fathers and/or mothers who have seen one parent hit the other have a higher rate of child abuse than those who have not.

» The greater the inequality of power between husband and wife, the greater the risk of violence in a family.

» Child mistreatment is more common in neighborhoods that have been depleted of job opportunities, economic resources, and social and educational role models.

Parents who had troubled childhoods and learned not to trust or rely on others for emotional support are often socially isolated. This signals danger, for socially isolated families are much more prone to abuse than families with connections and support. Feeling alone and trapped, parents may react with violent abuse or depression resulting in neglect in stressful situations. On the other hand, statistics reveal that parents who attend church groups or other support meetings during the previous month have much lower rates of abuse.

Every parent needs a support system of neighbors and friends, community and church activities to help maintain a healthy emotional balance. All of us need someone we can reach out to when the pressures and frustrations of life—and especially childrearing—begin to mount. If you are a parent and do not have one or more people to whom to talk when you need a listening ear and an understanding heart, you owe it to yourself to begin developing a support system now. Remember: An ounce of prevention is worth a pound of cure.

PROBLEM AREAS

What happens inside an individual who has experienced physical abuse from someone the person should have been able to trust? Often, the victim's abilities to trust, obey and relate to God and to others out of love instead of fear will be severely hampered. In addition to mistrusting people and their motives, the victim also mistrusts God and His motives, not understanding that God's thoughts and plans for us are always perfect and good.

In *No Longer a Victim*, Stokes and Lucas discuss some of the major problem areas in the personalities of physical abuse victims.[33]

1. Fear

The victim of physical abuse may be controlled by many fears:

a. Fear of being successful, but not understanding that they—not God or fate—are sabotaging their own efforts just as success is within reach.

b. Fear of failure since failure reinforces the negative thoughts and feelings they have about themselves.

c. Fear of public recognition and honor, since others might not deem them worthy of acceptance or admiration.

d. Fear of taking leadership and of making necessary decisions.

e. Fear of God or any authority figure. Having always been told they brought their punishment on themselves, these victims believe they deserve judgment and punishment.

f. Fear of losing control of their emotions or their environment, thus opening themselves up to further hurt.

g. Fear of crowds and speaking before groups since their weaknesses might be exposed, evaluated or criticized by all present.

h. Fear of criticism—since the victim's self-concept is so shaky, any negative statement by someone he loves or values can do irreparable damage to his emotional makeup.

i. Fear of the dark or of going to bed.

j. Fear of violence or pain. Except when they feel the need for punishment, victims will do anything to avoid violence or pain.

2. Mistrust of People

Feeling that there is something within themselves valuable enough to merit approval, victims of abuse may not expect valuable interaction with anyone.

3. Lack of Feelings and Emotions

Victims may seem to be arrogant, aloof, patient, or not easily alarmed, excited or confused. Because these victims dare not judge others lest their own weaknesses become more noticeable, they will work with people and in situations others find almost impossible. Filled with latent rage, anger, resentment and hatred, and fearing loss of control, they work hard at repression.

4. Expectations

Programmed to expect the worst and not understanding that they have placed limits on themselves, such victims may not expect to receive any reward or benefit from their labors.

5. Amnesia

Unless their abuse has left scars on their bodies or almost resulted in death, these victims experience less severe problems with amnesia than sexual victims. However, if there is a tendency toward amnesia, one of the following patterns may be observed: a problem with retention that could be mistaken for a lower I.Q. or a learning disability, or a problem with short-term memory that gives the appearance of not listening or paying attention.

6. View of Self

These victims often feel inferior to everyone, are filled with self-hatred, are afraid to share their lives and inner feelings with anyone and tend to self-destruct.

7. Need for an Abuser

They will usually have an abuser in their environment. If they cannot find one, or make someone in their environment into one, they will suffer abuse somehow, even if it is by depriving themselves of a want or need.

8. Need to Maintain a Protected Position

Victims often seek to maintain a protected position regardless of their stance and will usually appear frightened, shy or easily intimidated.

9. Prone to Abuse Spouse or Children

10. Propensity to Abuse Frustrating Individuals

Prior to receiving ministry, these victims should not work in daycare centers or nursing homes since they may have a tendency to abuse individuals in their environment who cause them frustration.

11. Difficulty in Giving Emotionally

Finding it difficult to give on an emotional level to those who are important to them, victims may overcompensate by giving too much to those who mean much less.

12. Love/Hate Relationship with Abusers

Although a victim may not allow others to attack

the abuser in any way, the victim may frequently fight the urge to harm their abuser.

13. Working to Gain the Abuser's Approval

Believing that the abuser's approval would make them valid and worthwhile, the victim may work to gain the approval of an abuser even after that person is dead.

There's no denying it: Physical abuse can wound and scar much more than just the bodies of its victims.

"When an abused childhood leaves us with too few healthy memories to paste together for a hopeful future," says Elia Wise, "we need help." When Elia found that help in a gifted therapist, she wrote "For Children Who Were Broken" as her way of saying thank you.[34]

FOR CHILDREN WHO WERE BROKEN

For children who were broken,
It is very hard to mend...
Our pain was rarely spoken
And we hid the truth from friends.
Our parents said they loved us,
But they didn't act that way.
They broke our hearts
And stole our worth,
With the things that they would say.
We wanted them to love us.
We didn't know what we did
To make them yell at us and hit us,
And wish we weren't their kids.

They'd beat us up and scream at us
And blame us for their lives.
Then they'd hold us close inside their arms
And tell us confusing lies
Of how they really loved us—
Even though we were BAD,
And how it was OUR fault they hit us,
OUR fault that they were mad...
We who grew up broken
And somewhat out of time,
Struggling to mend our childhood,
When our peers are in their prime.
When others find love and contentment,
We still often have to strive
To remember we are worthy,
And heroes just to be alive...
There's a lot of digging down to do
to find the child within,
to love away the ugly pain
and feel innocence again.
There is forgiveness worthy of angel's
wings for remembering those at all,
who abused our sacred childhood
and programmed us to fall.
To seek to understand them,
and how their pain became our own,
is to risk the ground we stand on
to climb the mountain home.
The journey is not so lonely
as in the past it has been ...
More of us are strong enough
to let the growth begin.

LET THE HEALING BEGIN

If you were abused as a child through neglect, suffered physical, sexual or psychological abuse, what better time to pray this simple prayer?

"Dear God, I have been broken. I am frightened, ashamed and confused. But the frozen pain inside my soul is beginning to melt. I am ready now. Let the healing begin!"

PREVENTING CHILD ABUSE

Do you know what to do if a child tells you about child abuse?

What should you do if a child or adolescent tells you, directly or indirectly, about abuse in his/her family? Since talking about such abuse could get a child into trouble or even a life-threatening situation, it is important that you handle the disclosure as wisely and sensitively as possible.

To test your knowledge about helping victims of abuse, answering the following true or false statements:

T F 1. Provide a private time and place to talk.

T F 2. Promise not to tell.

T F 3. Do not express shock or criticize the child's family.

T F 4. Offer reassurance that the child has done the right thing by telling you.

T F 5. Use the child's vocabulary to discuss body parts.

T F 6. Assure the child the abuse is not his/her fault, that the child is not to blame.

T F 7. Tell the child you are required by law to report the abuse.

T F   8. Determine the child's immediate need for safety.

T F   9. Let the child know what will happen when you
          report the abuse.

T F   10. Report the abuse to the proper authorities rather
          than taking the problem into your own hands.

(Only answer #2 is false.)

REPORTING SUSPECTED ABUSE

A report should be made when an individual has reasonable cause to believe that a child or adolescent has been abused or neglected, or is in danger of being abused. If additional incidents of abuse occur after the initial report has been made, the individual should make another report.

When reporting, the following information will be requested:

>   » Name, age and sex of the child and other
    family members

>   » Address, phone numbers and/or directions to
    the child's home

>   » Parents' place of employment

>   » Description of suspected abuse

>   » Current condition of the child

The person making the report does not need to prove the abuse before it can be reported. A report of suspected abuse is only a request for an investigation. Actual investigation and validation of child abuse reports are the responsibilities of Child Protective Services (CPS) workers.

Once a case has been reported to CPS, the situation is evaluated to determine if it is real, or if it should be dismissed. In this way, a child at risk can be identified and social service workers can intervene to protect the child from further abuse.

The evidence has been validated: Children of all age, race and economic background endure abuse in our society. You may be part of the answer to some abused child's desperate need. Keep your eyes and heart open, won't you?

6

BATTERED WOMEN

*"The battered woman lives in fear. She never knows when
her husband will punch her in the face for wearing the
wrong makeup, slap her for fixing a casserole instead of
chicken for dinner, beat her for having a different view about
politics, or threaten her because he had a bad day."*

—RITA-LOU CLARKE[35]

PREACHERS, LIKE COUNSELLORS and physicians, are supposed to be shock proof. Still, I wasn't quite prepared for what two women told me when they quietly came forward for prayer at a meeting in Houston, Texas.

At the end of my sermon, I had offered to minister to people who needed to be delivered from emotional pain and bitterness. After I'd prayed with several other individuals, two women asked if I would minister to them. Imagine my surprise when both women told me they had murdered their husbands. They said their cases had been tried and that the legal proceedings were behind them. The women were, however, still struggling with tremendous emotional pain and bitterness.

One woman told me that her husband, a doctor, had beaten her brutally and repeatedly for years. One day as he attacked her yet again, she snapped. Grabbing a loaded revolver, she simply kept firing until all the bullets were spent.

The other woman's story was very similar. She related how she, too, had undergone hellish torment for years. Times without number, she had been cursed, beaten, verbally degraded and forced to satisfy her husband's perverted sexual desires. The last time he threatened her and then came at her in a rage, all the pent-up anger exploded inside her. Struggling to hold back her tears, the woman told me how she killed her husband, cut his body into pieces, drove to California and dumped it into the ocean.

God, in his mercy, sent those two women to me that night. Yes, I was stunned and dismayed by their stories. Killing their husbands was the wrong way out of their dilemmas, but my heart went out to them as they stood sobbing. They were torn to shreds by their guilt, yet still fighting rage and bitterness toward the two men who had brutalized them. Behind their tear-stained faces, I saw my own mother's face— bruised and cut, eyes swollen shut, blood trickling down her neck... and those two women and I cried together.

Then I prayed with them asking God to forgive them and wipe away their guilt. As they walked away, I saw peace and hope on their faces.

HOME SWEET HOME?

A home should be a peaceful place—a place for renewal; a place of refuge where we can lock our doors and keep danger out. But for many women, home is the place of greatest risk: The bolt on the front door doesn't lock the danger out; it locks it inside.

Did you know that in this country, a woman's chances of being assaulted at home by her partner are greater than that of a police officer being assaulted on the job?[36] It's a fact, and it's also a fact that husbands can be the recipients of violence by wives. But several factors have led me to focus on battered women rather than battered men.

For one thing, the greater average size and strength of men, and their aggressiveness, means that the same aggressive act—a punch, for example—is likely to be very different in the amount of pain or injury inflicted. Even more important, a great deal of violence by women against their husbands is retaliation or self-defense.

In addition, most men can nonviolently protect themselves from physical harm, or if they want to leave the premises they can do so without fear of being forcibly restrained. If men choose to strike back, most can do greater physical harm than that which is done to them. Men also have a higher rate of using the most dangerous and injurious forms of violence—such as physical beatings or using guns or knives.

Social psychologist Angela Browne explains:

> Even when both partners are injured in an altercation, the woman's injuries are nearly three times as severe as the man's. Injury patterns also differ: Multiple injuries, abrasions, and contusions are reported frequently by female victims of a partner's violence, but are not seen in their mates.[37]

None of these factors is meant to condone violence by women. Even minor violence by wives greatly increases the risk of subsequent severe assault by the husband. Furthermore, if women do not stop the use of violence themselves, they cannot expect to be free of assault.[38]

Who is ultimately responsible for the specific act of violence when battering occurs? One basic fact needs to be understood from the outset: *Under no circumstances is a man justified in hitting his wife.* As Rita-Lou Clarke, author of *Pastoral Care of Battered Women*, explains:

> Although the woman may contribute to poor

communication in the marriage or may remain in the relationship after her husband has beaten her, therefore implicitly giving permission for him to hit her again, she does not cause him to hit her. The woman may appear to provoke, she may be unpleasant or act badly...but she is still not responsible for this act of violence...In no circumstance is a man justified in hitting his wife. This does not mean that a wife should not make changes in her behavior. It only means that she is not responsible for his act of hitting. For the marriage to be repaired, the hitting must stop. Then both the husband and wife can work together to build a better marriage.[39]

SCOPE OF THE PROBLEM

Keep in mind that by the term "battered women" we are referring to those women living in battering relationships, not merely to women living in unfulfilling or unhappy marriages. We are talking about the woman who is repeatedly subjected to any forceful physical or psychological behavior by a man in order to coerce her to do something he wants her to do without concern for her rights or safety.

The National Coalition Against Domestic Violence defines battering as a pattern or behavior with the effects of establishing power and control over another person through fear and intimidation. Battering occurs when batterers believe they are entitled to control their partners, when violence is permissible; when violence will produce the desired effect or prevent a worse one; and when the benefits outweigh the consequences.

The term "battering" can include economic, emotional, sexual and/or physical abuse as well as using children, humiliation, intimidation, threats, male privilege, isolation, and a variety of behaviors to maintain, fear, control, and power.

According to the U.S. Department of Justice, Bureau of Justice Statistics, the number of American women assaulted by men each year totals 2,100,000.[40] Just how often do these battering incidents occur? Information collected through clients at women's shelters reveals that the average physically battered woman sought help for abuse 28 to 29 times. Conversely, other client/shelter surveys reported women having been abused over sixty-five times per year. However national surveys by Murray Straus that did not concentrate on women's shelter clients, revealed that battered women were assaulted an average of six times per year.[41] Six times each year or sixty-five—that's too many.

For many women, physical abuse represents a very real threat of death. Intimate partner crimes include rape and sexual assault, robbery, aggravated assault, simple assault and homicide. The term "intimate partners" is defined as current or former spouses, current or former boy/girlfriends. Based on the National Crime Victimization Survey, for 1995 to 2008, and the Federal Bureau of Investigation's (FBI) Uniform Crime Reporting Program's Supplementary Homicide Reports for 1995 to 2008, statistics indicate that 551,590 women were victims of intimate partner crimes as opposed to 101,060 men who were victimized.[42] In addition, research also reveals that miscarriage rates, suicide attempts and drug and alcohol addiction reflect the horrible plight of the battered woman, as well.

PSYCHOLOGICAL VERSUS PHYSICAL BATTERING

Psychological battering is related to and often accompanies physical battering. Psychologically, the weapons are words, when the abuser uses the tongue, and not the fists, to project power over a mate in a way meant to demean and cause emotional harm.[43]

In psychological abuse, a variety of tools are at the disposal of the abuser. Not surprisingly, methods used by batterers to paralyze a woman in an abusive relationship often parallels methods listed in Amnesty International's definition of psychological torture: Verbal degradation, denial of powers, monopolizing perceptions, occasional indulgences, isolation, and threats.

By now it should be clear that I am not using the term "abuse" to describe an occasional bad mood or the expression of angry feelings that can exist in any relationship. Abuse is the systematic persecution, the deliberate inch-by-inch demolishing of one person by another.

Let me give you an example, as one of my friends, a college counsellor, related to me. The couple's names and minor details have been changed in order to protect their identity and preserve confidentiality.

Larry and Esther, a couple in their early forties, came to Bible college to study for the ministry. Larry, a smiling, neatly-dressed and well-groomed man, made a nice first impression. He looked every inch the devoted family man and hardworking student preparing to be a pastor.

His wife was a different story. Sometimes Esther made my counsellor friend think of a fragile, trembling doe caught in the headlights of an approaching car moments before impact. Nervous, quiet and withdrawn, she practically tiptoed into a room. Her entire manner and appearance seemed to whisper frantically, "Please don't notice me." Esther's long brown hair was drawn into a droopy ponytail at the nape of her neck. Her plain, but attractive, face was hidden by unbecoming, straight-cut bangs brushing the rims of out-of-date, cat-eye glasses. Shapeless, colorless clothing and clunky shoes obscured her slender form.

But first impressions aren't always correct impressions. At the end of that first semester, it was Esther's name not Larry's that appeared on the Dean's List. And as professors and classmates became better acquainted with the couple, it was gracious, intelligent Esther, not Larry, who became the focus of their admiration and respect.

Little by little, close observers noticed more and more oddities and imbalances in the couple's relationship. After Esther's name appeared on the Dean's List, Larry wrote an angry letter to the Dean demanding that his wife's name never be published again. At Larry's insistence, Esther held down the steady, on-campus job that was their major source of income. Meanwhile, Larry's temper and poorly developed people skills lost him one part-time job after another.

Larry always drove Esther to work, browsed around town when he could have been studying or working, then picked her up promptly at closing time. He became noticeably annoyed if he saw Esther holding conversations unrelated to her work. It was Larry, never Esther, who did the shopping, including grocery buying, for the family. Since Larry drove Esther everywhere and took the same classes as she did, he managed to be with her or to control her whereabouts most of the time.

After a few months on campus, a very nervous Esther began taking a few minutes off work once or twice a week so she could slip into the counsellor's office. Little by little the story emerged. It had been more than two years since Larry had allowed Esther to drive the car or go anywhere by herself. It was Larry who cut Esther's bangs and chose her unbecoming hairstyle. Although Larry bought new glasses for himself every two or three years, Esther hadn't had a new pair since their children were young. Many of the secondhand clothes and shoes Esther wore had been given to her, with Larry's permission of course, by a woman who lived down the street from the couple.

Since they had enrolled in Bible college, Larry had become more controlling and threatening than ever. Because Esther always earned better grades on tests and term papers than he did, Larry refused to allow her to study the textbooks shared by the couple until an hour or so before tests were administered. When his wife still managed to make A's, Larry became infuriated.

Esther told the counsellor that letters or phone calls from her family made him angry. Deep inside, she knew that one of the reasons they had moved was to isolate her from her relatives and concerned friends. Esther was also worried that their third child, about to graduate from high school, would leave home as had their other children due to their father's endless tirades, insults and unreasonable demands.

Larry's unbridled anger and strange obsessions

and compulsions had eroded their family life, but Esther was also becoming fearful for her personal safety. Larry had begun playing with their long-bladed kitchen knives and making subtle threats while Esther cooked or cleaned up after meals. Although earlier in their marriage his abuse had always been verbal, lately he had shoved her against the wall several times while threatening or insulting her. One evening he forced Esther to get in the car and ride with him to an isolated spot several miles from town. Stopping the car and pointing to a deep, brush-filled ravine, he stared menacingly at her and taunted, "I could kill you and throw your body down there. No one would ever find you!" When Larry saw Esther's obvious fright, he laughed. On another occasion, he drove into the country, forced Esther from the car and made her walk home.

Continually mocked and ridiculed, carefully monitored and controlled, afraid of being totally alienated from her children and fearful for her very life, Esther was walking a fraying tightrope that could snap at any time.

That, my friend, is abuse. If the results are fear and control, helplessness and/or pain, what difference does it make if the abuser's weapon is his fist or his words?

BEWARE OF UNDERESTIMATING

A survey of Protestant clergy in Canada and the United States confirmed some of the problems that battered women can encounter when they seek help from the church. One-third of the clergymen surveyed felt that the abuse would have to be severe in order to justify a Christian wife leaving her husband. Twenty-one percent felt that no amount of abuse justified a separation. Twenty-six percent of the pastors agreed that a wife should submit to her husband and trust that God would honor her action by either giving her the strength to endure the abuse or by stopping it altogether.[44]

As victims of abuse know all too well, many batterers eventually vent their violence through more than just ugly words, forceful shoves, and painful punches. Only then, when it may be too late, do many well-meaning outsiders—even professional people—become aware of the living hell in which frightened women have been forced to exist. The following true story is one such account:

A car door slammed and a familiar, frantic knock came at the door. The minister sighed as he went to answer it. Just as he'd suspected, there stood his sister, disheveled and weeping.

"What's happened this time?" he asked.

"Bob's gone totally berserk. Throwing dishes, breaking pictures, hitting and kicking me. He knocked me down and pulled my hair..." Reading the frustration and impatience on her brother's face, her voice trailed off. Crying had always made him nervous. Blinking away the tears and dabbing at the trickle of blood oozing from her puffy lower lip, she waited for his response, hoping he wouldn't notice her bare feet. There hadn't been time to grab a coat and put on shoes. She'd barely managed to ease the car keys off the table and slip out the kitchen door before her husband noticed she wasn't washing her face at the sink as he had ordered.

"What did you do to set him off this time?"

"Nothing. Nothing important. He got mad because I was late getting supper started. I'd been lying down because I haven't been feeling well, and..."

"How many times have I told you that you've got to stop provoking him? You know he has a short fuse. No man likes a dirty, sloppy house or having to eat a meal an hour late."

"I know...You've told me that before, and I've been doing better. Honest I have. But's it more than that. He's getting worse. I can't please him no matter how hard I try. He says he hates me and that he's going to kill me, and I believe him."

"That's ridiculous. He wouldn't think of killing you. He's just angry, and he's making stupid, silly threats trying to get you to shape up."

"But what am I going to do? I..."

"You're going to go back home, get that messy house cleaned up and start being the kind of wife he needs you to be. That's what you're going to do."

"But he said he would kill me! I saw it in his eyes. If you could have seen his face...He meant it. I know he did."

"Now that's enough. We've had conversations like this a dozen times. Look, Sis, I'm sorry he hurts you. I'm sorry he talks to you the way he does and scares you with his stupid threats, but this sort of problem takes time. You've just got to shape up, do your part and be patient. Understand?"

She nodded, staring at the floor.

"Now run on home. Tell him you're sorry and that you promise to do better. Okay?"

"Okay."

About an hour later, the minister sighed as he heard a car door slam and aloud knock at the door.

A police officer waiting on the other side asked, "Reverend Smith?"

"Yes"

"Your sister lives at 1522 Brookwood?"

"Yes...?"

"I'm sorry to have to tell you this, Reverend, but your sister was killed a short time ago. The neighbors said when she pulled into the driveway, her husband was waiting for her with a shotgun. He blew her head off, sir."

No, I did not make up that story. It really happened, and that pastor, who refuses to forgive himself, left the ministry.

A GROWING AWARENESS

I shrink from using sensationalism, gossip, and gory details to attract an audience. But I'm glad that talk show hosts, politicians and preachers are beginning to discuss this horrifying subject. I'm thankful that the age-old pattern of wife battering is finally becoming a widely recognized social problem in American life and that we are being made aware of the facts and issues surrounding abuse.

Because of our new awareness, women who thought they were

the only ones being beaten, and believed their spouses' lies that they deserved it or asked for it are discovering that multitudes of other women have encountered similar experiences.

As the general population is becoming more sensitized to the facts surrounding this problem, desperate women are being offered listening ears, rather than being told to "stop upsetting him and try to be a better wife." They are also being offered practical alternatives, such as safe lodging for themselves and their children in women's shelters, along with counselling and job training, if needed.

RECOGNIZING AN OLD PROBLEM

We now understand that wife battering is a problem in all religious groups and socio-economic classes, not just among the poor, the psychotic, or the criminal. The middle class and the wealthy may have more resources to draw upon, but no group is immune to the chaos and pain produced by battering.

Wife battering did not become widely recognized as a social problem in American life until the 1970s when, as a result of the women's movement and the establishment of battered women's shelters, frightened women and their bewildered children were offered long-overdue help and hope.

For generations, archaic laws and head-in-the-sand attitudes helped perpetuate the problem. For instance, English common-law doctrine allowed the husband "the right to whip his wife, provided he used a switch no larger than his thumb." This was known as the "rule of thumb" law. In the United States until the late 1800s, it was legal for a man to physically assault his wife.[45] Until 1971, a man could not be punished for "beating [his wife] with a stick, pulling her hair, choking her, spitting in her face, [or] kicking her about the floor."[46]

PREVENTING FUTURE ABUSE

For many today, the subject of battered women is still clouded by groundless claims and confusing myths: "A man's wife is his property." "Battered women like to be beaten, or have some masochistic need to be beaten. Otherwise, they would leave." "It is more socially acceptable for a man to beat his wife than to hit someone at work." "A family should be kept together at all costs." "A man's home is his castle. What happens between a man and wife in their home is their business, and police should not be expected to intervene or interfere." "Women who are beaten have done something to deserve it."

Thankfully, society is beginning to recognize and be repulsed by such groundless claims and cultural myths. But if many future offenses are to be prevented, women must become better informed. They must be increasingly on guard to detect potential batterers before becoming involved in abusive relationships. That's where we'll turn our attention in the next chapter.

RECOGNIZING DYSFUNCTIONAL HOMES

Although violence can occur in families that appear to be in no way deviant or out of the ordinary, dysfunctional homes often become spawning grounds for family violence. If one parent displays any of these unhealthy behaviors or obsessions, it is damaging to a child. If both parents are caught up in any of these practices, the results may be even more devastating.

Dysfunctional homes are those in which one or more of the following occur:

1. Abuse of alcohol or drugs.

2. Addictive behavior such as compulsive eating,

working, cleaning, gambling, spending, dieting, exercising, and so on, that effectively disrupts and prevents honest contact and intimacy in a family.

3. Battering a spouse and/or children.

4. Inappropriate sexual behavior on the part of a parent toward a child, ranging from seductiveness to incest.

5. Constant arguing and tension.

6. Extended periods of time in which parents refuse to speak to each other.

7. Parents who have conflicting attitudes or values or display behavior that competes for the child's allegiance.

8. Parents who are competitive with each other or with their children.

9. A parent who cannot relate to others in the family and thus actively avoids them, while blaming them for this avoidance.

10. Extreme rigidity about money, religion, work, use of time, displays of affection, sex, television, housework, sports, politics or other topics. (Obsession with any of these can preclude contact and intimacy, because the emphasis is not on relating, but on rules.)

11. Inability to directly confront or discuss root problems (It is the degree of secrecy—the inability to talk about problems—rather than their severity, that defines both how dysfunctional a family becomes and how severely its members are damaged.)

❖ 7 ❖

DANGER SIGNALS!

*"He had so much potential! Even though
I really don't like a lot of his behaviors and basic
characteristics, I thought he'd change."*

—A VICTIM

A COMMONLY HELD MYTH surrounding the problem of battering is that there is no way to predict a potential wife-beater. A cursory glance at certain statistics might seem to bear this out. For instance, studies of abused women have found that the majority—73 to 85 percent—do not experience physical assault until after they have married the abuser. Often the violence occurs within the first year the couple live together. Many of the first incidents are around the time of the wedding or shortly thereafter.[47] If this is the case, how can a woman determine whether or not she is entering into a relationship where she could be at risk?

Researchers who have taken the time to study case histories and to conduct interviews with batterers, their victims, and when possible, friends and families, have found early warning signs we would be wise to heed.

In her work with battered women, Angela Browne has uncovered six such danger signals.[48]

1. Intrusion

A man's desire to know the whereabouts of the woman early in a relationship, which at first seemed somewhat romantic and flattering, and made the woman feel cared for and missed, can later tighten into a leash-like existence as the woman was made to account for every hour. Unsatisfactory explanations led to violent retaliation by their partner. Women told Browne of being followed to work or to a friend's house, being telephoned constantly to make certain they were where they said they would be, and of sudden appearances to check up on them. As the man's early interest in their activities turned more and more to suspicion and distrust, arriving home a few minutes late could initiate a beating.

2. Isolation

Women usually recalled that there had been some indication of a tendency to isolate them from outside contacts during the early days of the relationship. Men had expressed jealousy of the women's friends and had not wanted the women around their families.

Once a commitment had been established, a man's need for constant knowledge of the woman's whereabouts, combined with their preference not to let her interact with people other than themselves, in most cases led to severe restrictions on the woman's activities. Eventually, many of the men succeeded in cutting their partners off from friends and family, refused to let them work outside the home, and treated activities the women wanted to pursue without them as a personal affront. As proof of their love and to keep the peace, the women were pressured to give up those things that made them unique and were an important part of who they were as individuals.

Once the women were no longer allowed to be part of a larger network, they found themselves at greater risk when the abuse began. The isolation had reduced their resources as well as their chances that others would be aware of their plight and intervene.

3. Possession

The gentle, but persistent, persuasion used by the man when he desired touch and intimacy earlier in the relationship later changed to forceful possession without regard for the woman's wishes or well-being. The woman became unable to predict when lovemaking would be affectionate, or when it would be brutal or assaultive. Physical intimacy changed from a joy to the most threatening part of the relationship.

4. Jealousy

In the earlier stages of the relationship, the man would often mask tendencies toward extremes of jealousy by emphasizing the positive dimensions of being alone. They seemed out of balance only in their constant inquiries about the woman's thoughts and activities. Yet the women interviewed reported that as time went on, the man's extreme jealousy and suspicions became a serious problem in their relationship, triggering numerous violent incidents.

5. Prone to Anger

Many of the women told Browne that even before their partners assaulted them physically, they noticed that the men seemed easily angered and that it was difficult to predict what would set them off. Without warning, their moods could change from laughter to fury. More importantly, the anger was often completely disproportionate to the circumstances that triggered it. It was this pattern that later left women victims of violent attacks over minor incidents, i.e., leaving the checkbook in the car or chatting a moment with the lady next door.

The women also noted that early outbursts of violence were frequently directed at objects or pets, rather than people. The men frequently displayed aggressive, reckless driving behavior by using the car as a weapon deliberately endangering their lives.

6. Unknown Pasts

In interviewing battered women, Brown noted another danger signal. Many of the women knew almost nothing about the pasts of their men when they first became involved with them, or even at the point at which they made major commitments.

Few of the women had mutual acquaintances who knew the man well. Most had spent relatively little time with their partner's family early in the relationship. Therefore, their impressions were based almost exclusively on their own interactions and on the sides of the man they were allowed to see. But batterers often have a history of violent interactions, if not with prior female partners, then with peers or family members. For this reason, making the effort to learn as much as possible about the man could have alerted the woman to possible future patterns. Women told of finding out later about assaults by their mates on former wives, girlfriends, relatives, or even employers.

The women interviewed by Browne confided that they were often so blinded by the men's intense interest and desire to know about their pasts that they didn't notice how little they actually knew of the men's pasts. Some women had no knowledge even of their partners' previous criminal records.

THE THREE-PHASE CYCLE OF VIOLENCE

In her extensive work with battered women clinical psychologist Dr. Lenore E. Walker discovered a definite battering cycle that women experienced over and over in relationship with their batterers. Dr. Walker breaks the cycle into three phases: the tension-building phase; the acute battering incident; and the tranquil, loving (or at least non-violent) phase that follows.[49] Some counsellors say, depending on individual circumstances, couples may take years to go through the cycle one time, while other couples may experience all three phases in less than an hour.

Phase 1: The Tension-Building Phase

During the tension-building phase, minor battering incidents occur, such as verbal tirades, temper tantrums, throwing things, slaps, pinches and psychological warfare. Believing that what she does will help prevent her batterer's anger from escalating, the woman tries to stay out of his way or works to control the situation by kind, nurturing, compliant behavior and attempting to anticipate his every whim. What really happens in this phase is that the woman allows herself to be abused in ways that, to her, are relatively minor. More than anything, she wants to prevent the batterer's violence from escalating. This desire, however, eventually backfires, because her compliant, docile behavior helps legitimize the batterer's belief that he has the right to abuse her in the first place.

To keep the man from becoming upset, the woman attempts to manipulate and control as many people (including children and relatives) and as many factors in their environment as she can. Attempting to win his favor, the woman may also cover for the batterer, making excuses to others for his bad behavior. Although she is angry inside, the woman covers and suppresses her anger through rationalization or justification of the batterer's actions. But the woman's efforts to appease are not effective in the long run. As the woman becomes more passive, the batterer becomes more possessive and aggressive. As the tension builds, it becomes harder and harder for the woman to deny and control her anger.

Violence and verbal abuse worsen as the cycle progresses. Each partner senses the impending loss of control and becomes more desperate, fueling the tension even more. But, sooner or later, exhausted from the unrelenting stress, the battered woman withdraws emotionally. Angry at her emotional unavailability, the batterer becomes more oppressive and abusive. At some point, and often unpredictably, the violence spirals out of control. Then the next phase of the cycle, the acute battering, occurs.

Phase 2: The Acute Battering Incident

Phase two, the acute battering incident, is characterized by a lack of control as well as a lack of predictability. This phase is set apart by its savagery, destructiveness, and uncontrolled nature. The violence escalates to a point of rampage, injury, brutality and sometimes death.

Anticipating what might happen, the woman may suffer from a variety of factors including sleeplessness or oversleeping, fatigue, overeating, high blood pressure, severe headaches and other physical responses to the mounting tension.

By the time the acute battering incident occurs, both parties accept the fact that the man's rage is out of control. Usually, the battered woman realizes that she cannot reason with him and that resistance will only make matters worse. The batterer starts out by wanting to teach the woman a lesson and stops when he feels she has learned it. The woman has no control over when he stops. The batterer is the one who begins and ends the incident. He is the one in power. Immobilized by fear and feelings of helplessness, the woman simply endures until it is over. She has a sense of being distant from the attack and the pain, although she may later remember each detail with great precision.

Knowing that if they try to call the police for help, the attacker will escalate the violence afterward, many battered women don't seek help during an acute battering incident. Much like disaster victims who often may experience severe depression or emotional collapse twenty-four to forty-eight hours after the catastrophe, battered women are immobilized by depression, listlessness and feelings of helplessness. They tend to remain isolated at least twenty-four hours and often wait several days before seeking medical attention, if they do so at all.

Phase 3: The Tranquil, Loving (Or Non-Violent Phase)

Once the acute battering incident ends, the final phase in the cycle of violence begins. This third phase is characterized by extremely loving, kind and contrite behavior as the batterer attempts to make up for his abusive actions. Trying to atone, he becomes loving and charming. He promises never to hit his partner again and begs for forgiveness. The batterer manages to convince everyone involved, including himself, that he really means it and can reform.

During the third phase, the battered woman may join the batterer in sustaining the blissful illusion. She convinces herself that it will never happen again, that her lover can change. She tells herself that this good man, who is gentle and sensitive and nurturing toward her now, is the real man, the man she married, the man she loves.

However, if the woman is wavering and undecided, the batterer will use every means at his disposal to keep her. Sincere promises and tearful confessions, the influence of family and friends who send her on a guilt trip by pleading that he will fall apart without her, telling her she will be depriving her children of a father if she leaves, or that she will be responsible for the consequences if she leaves. This is usually extremely effective since many battered women believe they are the sole support of the batterer's emotional stability and sanity, the one link their men have to the normal world.

Although the most common time for a batterer to get help is after the woman leaves, she often attempts to convince herself that the two of them can conquer their problems and that if she stays with her husband, he will go for help. Sensing the batterer's isolation and despair, feeling responsible for his well-being and terrified of what he might do to her if she tries to leave him, she agrees to stay.

SIMILARITIES IN THE HISTORIES OF BATTERED WOMEN

In her book, *The Battered Woman*, Dr. Lenore Walker relates how she uncovered certain similarities in the histories of women she studied:

> After completing about twenty interviews, it became clear to me that the battering histories of the women had some striking similarities. The stories became so repetitious that I found myself filling in their omissions. The women began to treat me as if I had supernatural powers. How could anyone guess what they had gone to great lengths to keep hidden?[50]

Walker then lists eleven similarities she discovered. In some areas, you will notice a familiar overlapping with the danger signs battered women shared with Angela Browne.[51]

1. Initial surprise:
A layer of gentleness masked the batterer's brutal potential. Most of the women were taken unaware by the violence and could not have predicted the men would have been so ferocious until after the initial incident occurred. Then, they could identify characteristics which led up to the actual incident.

2. **Unpredictability of acute battering incidents:** Despite the number of times a battered woman went through the cycle of violence she still could not predict exactly when an acute battering incident would occur or how serious it would become during the incident.

3. **Overwhelming jealousy:**

   Batterers were jealous of other men, women friends, family, children, grandchildren and jobs. The batterer's possessiveness of the woman and his intrusiveness into her life increased as his jealousy increased.

4. **Unusual sexuality:**

   Battered women reported unusual kinds of sexual behavior expected by their batterers in their relationships, yet they commonly spoke of the sensitivity and sexuality the men expressed toward them when not being brutal.

5. **Concealment:**

   Although battered women vividly recalled details of their experiences, they frequently denied and concealed this information to protect their batterers.

6. **Drinking:**

   Many of the battered women reported that their men had difficulty controlling alcoholic intake. Excessive drinking was a common experience.

7. **Extreme psychological abuse:**

Almost all battered women reported severe verbal harassment and criticism by the batterer. They were constantly accused of bungling behavior. The men were adept at finding weak spots and using them for their own purposes.

8. **Family threats:**

As an important coercive technique, batterers threatened to harm the families or close friends of the women.

9. **Extraordinary terror through the use of guns and knives:**

Batterers reportedly would frighten their women with terrorizing descriptions of how they would torture them. They often backed up these descriptions through the use of guns, knives and other weapons.

10. **Omnipotence:**

Battered women believed that their batterers could accomplish things others could not, both positively and negatively. While believing in the omnipotence of the batterer, the women tended to believe that the abusive partner was fragile and would fall apart at any moment.

11. **Awareness of death potential:**

Battered women interviewed by Walker stated that they were aware their batterers' threats of violence were not idle and that they were capable of killing the women and/or themselves.

MORE FACTS ABOUT BATTERING

If you are a battered woman or grew up in a home where your mother was abused, many of the facts you just read sounded hauntingly familiar. However, the average man or woman on the street or sitting in a church pew has no concept of the vicious cruelty to which many women are subjected by their batterers.

For instance, some sincere, but naïve people might ask, "How can a husband rape his own wife? After all, they're married, aren't they?" But those people are forgetting that one of the things making rape so traumatic is not simply that the violation is committed by someone the woman doesn't know, but it's with someone doing something to her that she doesn't want. Prior trust and intimate contact only make rape more traumatic.

Experts in the field are realizing that rather than being driven by a desire for romance or intimacy through sex, batterers seem to be motivated by a desire to establish control, teach a lesson, assert power and show who is boss. In addition, their unusual sexual demands often involve other men and violence.

IT IS TIME TO SPEAK UP

In the next chapter we'll learn to recognize five common coercive techniques used by batterers and take a look at revealing profiles of the battering man as well as the battered woman. Then we'll examine the damaging effects of battering upon children. Last of all, you and I will take a moment to meditate on some words of caution.

But be prepared; all of us no matter how healthy our relationships with others might be, may see a bit of ourselves in these next pages.

ARE YOU A BATTERED WOMAN?

How many, if any, of these things has your partner done to you?

_____ Humiliated you in private or public.

_____ Refused to socialize with you.

_____ Ignored your feelings.

_____ Ridiculed or insulted women as a group.

_____ Ridiculed or insulted your most valued beliefs, your race, religion, class, or heritage.

_____ Withheld affection, approval, or appreciation as punishment.

_____ Continually criticized you, called you names, shouted at you.

_____ Kept you from working, controlled your money, made all decisions.

_____ Refused to work or share money.

_____ Took car keys or money away from you.

_____ Regularly threatened to leave or told you to leave.

_____ Threatened to hurt you or your family

_____ Punished or deprived the children when angry with you.

_____ Deliberately failed to provide you with adequate food or shelter.

_____ Threatened to kidnap the children if you left.

_____ Abused, tortured, killed pets to hurt you.

_____ Harassed you about affairs your partner imagined you were having.

_____ Manipulated you with lies and contradictions.

_____ Destroyed furniture, punched holes in walls, broke appliances.

_____ Threw something at you.

_____ Pushed, grabbed, or shoved you.

_____ Slapped or spanked you.

_____ Choked you.

_____ Burned you with a cigarette, cigar, or other hot object.

_____ Hit or tried to hit you with something.

_____ Forced sex.

_____ Wielded a knife or a gun in a threatening way.

Are you, or is someone you know, a battered woman? If so, the next chapters contain information you can't afford to be without.

8

RESCUER, PERSECUTOR, OR VICTIM?

"Aggression and violence are the masks of weakness, impotence and fear. Strength is sure, sovereign and smiling."
—S. ALEXANDER,
NEWSWEEK MARCH 31, 1975

WHY DOESN'T MOTHER LEAVE and take us with her? During the seventeen years I lived at home, not only experiencing abuse myself, but having to watch my brothers, sisters, and our mother being beaten, cursed and humiliated, I asked myself that question over and over. My head knew at least part of the answer even before my heart asked the question.

I think my mother stayed with my father because she had seven children. I'm sure she must have reasoned, "If I throw our clothing into a suitcase and march out the door, will I be walking into more overwhelming problems than the ones I left behind? Where will we live? How will I support myself and seven children? What will my husband do to us when he finds us?"

Mother had been reared in an orphanage, and she didn't want a life like that for us. Her Jewish ancestors had come to the United States from Russia. Her mother had died when my mother was born, and Mother's father had lost one of his legs and couldn't handle the children, so they ended up in an orphanage.

Mother never talked about her childhood, but it must have been bad. During her teens, while still living in the orphanage, she had suffered a nervous breakdown. Then she met my father and married him even though he was a Jew-hater. After that, babies came one after another, and Mother suffered at least one more breakdown.

When Father beat us, I remember her jumping in front of her children and trying to defend us. But there was no way she could stop him. Father would just throw her off, and then turn his wrath on us again. I don't recall blaming her for those beatings. I knew she was a desperately hurting woman trapped in a no-win situation.

For many years as psychologists observed women like my mother refusing to leave or repeatedly going back to battering relationships, they wrongly concluded that there must be some flaw in their personalities. Placing the blame on the victim, they said such women were "masochistic"—that they enjoyed suffering and derived pleasure from being dominated or physically abused. The men were labeled "mentally ill" or "psychopathic," which basically meant they were being absolved of responsibility for their behavior.

I personally saw enough as a child to convince me that women do not remain in battering relationships because they like being beaten. Some stay because they are economically dependent. Some stay because they are afraid of what people might think. Many stay because there is simply no place to go. But for most of these women, their true reasons for staying may run far deeper than the issues I've mentioned.

Why does a battered woman remain in a situation where she knows it is only a matter of time until she will be beaten again?

Several important theories are helpful in making the battered woman's behavior understandable.

LEARNED HELPLESSNESS

Listening to the stories of battered women, Dr. Lenore Walker developed a psychological rationale explaining why the battered woman becomes a victim and how the process of victimization is perpetuated. The social-learning theory of "learned helplessness" developed by psychologist Martin Seligman, basically states that if an individual is caught in a position where repeated attempts to make changes in the environment fail, the individual will learn to be helpless.

In a series of experiments in the late 1960s and early 1970s, Seligman placed dogs in cages from which they could not escape and administered electric shocks to them at random. Quickly learning there was nothing they could do to predictably control the shocks the dogs eventually appeared to completely stop all voluntary attempts to escape. In addition, when researchers tried to teach the dogs to escape, they appeared to remain entirely passive, sometimes lying in their own excrement, refusing either to leave or to try to avoid the administered electric shocks.

However, a closer look revealed that these dogs had developed coping skills and were not as passive as they seemed. The dogs had learned to minimize the pain by lying in their own fecal matter (a good insulator from the electrical impulses) in part of the grid that received the least amount of electrical stimulation.

At first, even when the cage doors were left open, the dogs remained passive, making no attempt to escape. It took repeatedly dragging the dogs to the exit to teach them how to avoid the shock. The earlier in life that the dogs learned to be helpless, the longer it took them to overcome the effects. However, once they were taught that they could escape and avoid the shock, the helplessness faded, along with the self-defeating coping strategies they had used before.

When studying people, rather than animals, Seligman found that the actual facts of a situation are less important than the individual's set of beliefs or perceptions about the situation. Even if a person has control over a situation, but believes that he or she does not, the individual will be more likely to respond by merely attempting to cope rather than by trying to escape.

In the case of battered women, victims don't attempt to leave the situation, even when it may seem to outsiders that escape is possible, because the women cannot predict their own safety. They believe that nothing they or anyone else does will change their terrible circumstances.

How does Seligman's theory of learned helplessness apply to battered women? Clinical psychologist Dr. Lenore Walker theorized that repeated battering acts like electric shocks to diminish the woman's motivation to respond. Unable to predict the effect her behavior will have her response to situations changes. The woman becomes passive, preferring to live with familiar problems and fears rather than taking a chance on a response, such as escape, that could launch her into an even more frightening or dangerous unknown. Her perception is also changed. She believes that nothing will help, that no matter what she does, she has no influence. With her sense of emotional well-being affected, the woman is more prone to anxiety and depression.

Walker found that battered women seemed to be most afflicted with feelings of helplessness in their relationships with men. She observed that many women were successful and competent in their careers and other areas of life. It was only when they were relating to the batterer that they exhibited helpless behavior. Based on her research, Lenore Walker has come up with five factors in childhood she has successfully used to identify the presence of learned helplessness in an individual.[52] These five childhood factors are:

1. Witnessing or experiencing battering in the home.

2. Sexual abuse or molestation as a child or teenager.

3. Critical periods of time during which the outcome was independent of or unaffected by the child's responses or behavior, such as early parent loss; alcoholism of a parent; frequent moves; shameful or stigmatizing situations, such as poverty.

4. Stereotyped sex-role socialization supporting rigid traditionalism.

5. Health problems or chronic illness.

EXTERNALIZERS VERSUS INTERNALIZERS
Other research indicates that many battered women may also be externalizers—people who believe that things happening to them are caused by powers outside themselves, over which they have no personal control, instead of internalizers—people who tend to believe that they have great influence over the events of their lives. Externalizers seem to succumb to learned helplessness more easily than intrnalizers.

HELPLESS VICTIMS OR SAVIORS?
Are all battered women victims of learned helplessness? Others present a different angle of this complex problem, and believe that

some women need to be needed. Seeing themselves as stronger and more psychologically stable than their husbands and considering themselves responsible for their husbands' well-being, they become victims by trying to be rescuers.

These women feel they can somehow take care of the men, treat them better and soothe the hurt and pain through which they feel their men have gone. Fearing abandonment more than divorce, they make excuses for their husbands' behavior and forgive the violent outbursts.[53]

CODEPENDENCY

Codependency has become the psychological buzzword of the hour. While some counsellors may be taking the concept to extremes, others are wisely applying it to bring wholeness and balance.

Although any compassionate person feels the hurt of a person he or she deeply loves, excessive identification with a loved one's pain to the point of chronic dependency and the sacrifice of one's own self-worth, freedom and fulfillment is not healthy. Some partners are more comfortable and fulfilled attending to the loved one's problems than to their own. Some, already conditioned to giving too much of themselves and playing the role of caretaker in their original families, out of habit may continue doing so with their mates.

Counsellors have long been aware that partners of alcoholics can be addicted as well—not to alcohol, but to the alcoholics themselves and to the all-consuming caretaking that shields them from confronting their own issues. But the problem of codependency is not limited to spouses of alcoholics. An individual can become so submerged in the struggle to help, it becomes increasingly difficult to make a distinction between the partner's wants, needs, or feelings and their own.

The following true story, excerpted from *Glimpses of His Glory* by John and Elizabeth Sherrill, is a classic example:

> Her husband had been a problem drinker for eleven years. For five of them Sylvia did not buy a single new dress. Bob was too expensive. She paid damages twice to keep him out of jail (one smashed window, one wrecked car.) To keep him out of the state hospital, she took a job and sent him to private doctors.
>
> Every time he sobered up, Bob thanked Sylvia with tears of gratitude. He would promise her the world, and she would buy him a new suit of clothes. Sometimes he hocked the suit that week, sometimes not for a month or more. Then she would resume her nightly patrol of park benches. Home by cab: "He's not feeling well, driver." (Hoping it wasn't the same one as last week.) Urge him up the front steps—twelve of them. Clean up the mess. Beg. Reproach. Threaten. Her whole life was devoted to Bob's drinking.
>
> The fact that she needed help with the hard job of being an alcoholic's wife never occurred to Sylvia. But when she heard about a new group called AL-Anon, she attended, hoping this time she might find the secret to changing Bob.
>
> To Sylvia's dismay, no one even mentioned alcohol or how to make an alcoholic stop drinking. Instead of discussing other people's problems, the group members were discussing their own. After the meeting ended, an older woman, perhaps sensing Sylvia's

disappointment, explained that people had discovered that years of living with an alcoholic spouse had left scars on their own personalities—some so deep that they remained even if the drinking ceased.

Although Sylvia left the meeting feeling a little hurt—after all, she had come to discuss Bob's problems, and people had suggested she work on hers—she continued attending the sessions.

Sylvia finally came to the realization that she could do nothing to induce Bob to stop drinking and that all activities such as pouring his liquor down the sink, warning local bars not to serve him, rationing his spending money, pleading and bargaining must cease. She also began her spiritual journey out of self-pity, self-righteousness and other shortcomings toward a personal knowledge of God.

At Al-Anon Sylvia learned that the addictive personality will often lean his whole weight on any support that is offered. When that support is withdrawn he may find that he can stand alone. Sylvia also learned to stop being an enabler of her partner's self-destructive patterns. She decided to allow Bob to confront his situation without the buffer of a well-meaning intermediary, knowing it could be the shock that started him on the road to sobriety.

Sylvia had always prided herself on the fact that she kept things running. But as the weeks passed, she began to wonder if she had run things too well.

On a warm spring night about four months after that first meeting, Sylvia came home late from an Al-Anon session to find Bod asleep on the front steps. He had a door key in his hand, but hadn't managed to get it and the keyhole together. Sylvia stood for a moment, staring down at the man she'd loved and married and promised to cherish forever. Then she took out her own key, stepped over her husband and let herself in.

"I went to bed," she said later. "Slept fine, too."

The next morning as she was getting breakfast, Bob walked into the kitchen. "What time did you get in?" he demanded.

"About 11:30."

"Where was I?"

"Sleeping on the steps."

Bob blinked as though trying to understand a foreign language. "Why didn't you pick me up?"

Sylvia poured him a cup of coffee, looked him in the eye and said, "Because I didn't put you down."

For Bob, the shock of losing the support he had so long counted on was the beginning of a new life. Within six months he was in Alcoholics Anonymous and, despite some brief relapses into old patterns, Bob eventually stopped drinking altogether.

Says Sylvia, "I was so busy asking God to change Bob that I never heard what He wanted changed in me...It sounds selfish, but if we don't bring ourselves to God first—for healing, for strength, for growth—then He can't use us to help anyone else."

Sylvia's faith became real when she stepped out from behind her husband's needs and said, "God, this is Sylvia."[54]

When some battered women believe they can stop their husband's violence by acting better and others, like Sylvia, believe they can change their husbands by being their saviors, neither group is successful in eliciting change. Both groups of women are deeply dependent upon and attached to their batterers. Furthermore, some experts in the field believe it is possible for a battered woman to fall into both Walker's and Dorn's descriptions

WOMEN WHO LOVE TOO MUCH

Robin Norwood, therapist and author of the bestseller, *Women Who Love Too Much*, helps us distinguish between unwise loving and healthy loving. Norwood says women can love too much, and explains:

> Loving turns into loving too much when our partner is inappropriate, uncaring, or unavailable and yet we cannot give him up—in fact we want him, we need him even more...Our wanting to love, our yearning for love, our living itself becomes an addiction...
>
> If you have ever found yourself obsessed with a man, you may have suspected that the root of that obsession was not love, but fear...fear of being unlovable and unworthy, fear of being ignored or abandoned or destroyed.[55]

To help women determine whether or not they are women who love too much, Norwood asks the following questions:

1. Do you feel that having a man in your life could solve your problems of depression, aimlessness and loneliness?

2. When you meet a new man, do you fantasize about changing him, or helping him, or making him happy?

3. Even though he reminds you of other men who have made you unhappy, do you feel that this time it's different?

4. Does your involvement with him jeopardize your well-being, your health, or even your safety?

5. Are you terrified of the depression that will follow if you break up with him?[56]

"The more difficult it is to end a relationship that is bad for you, the more elements of the childhood struggle it contains," Norwood declares. "When you are loving too much, it is because you are trying to overcome the old fears, anger, frustration and pain from childhood."[57]

> When our childhood experiences are particularly painful, we are often unconsciously compelled to recreate similar situations throughout our lives, in a drive to gain mastery over them.
>
> For instance, if we...loved and needed a parent who did not respond to us, we often become involved with a similar person, or a series of them, in adulthood in an attempt to win the old struggle to be loved.[58]

According to Norwood, much of what the woman is attracted to is a replication of what she lived with growing up.

> The sparks, the chemistry, the drive to be with that

other person and to make it work, are not present to
the same degree in healthier, more satisfying relationships, because they do not embody all the possibilities
for settling old accounts and for prevailing over what
was once overwhelming. It is this thrilling possibility
of righting old wrongs, winning lost love, and gaining
withheld approval that, for women who love too much,
is the unconscious chemistry behind falling in love.

This is also why, when men come into our lives
who are interested in our well-being and in our happiness and fulfillment, and who present the genuine
possibility of a healthy relationship, we usually are not
interested.[59]

By the same token, a man whose life is becoming unmanageable is
attracted to a woman who, when he gets into trouble, figures out how
to help him, how to cover things over and make him and everyone
else comfortable, rather than being offended. The feeling of safety she
provides has powerful appeal to him.[60]

Norwood also believes that men who have been damaged in
childhood differ from women in that they do not develop an addiction
to relationships.

Due to an interplay of cultural and biological factors,
they [men] usually try to protect themselves and avoid
their pain through pursuits which are more external
than internal, more impersonal than personal. Their
tendency is to become obsessed with work, sports, or
hobbies, while, due to the cultural and biological forces
working on her, the woman's tendency is to become

obsessed with a relationship—perhaps with just such a damaged and distant man.[61]

And so, when the woman who loves too much meets the man who is cruel, indifferent, abusive, emotionally unavailable, addictive or otherwise unable to be loving and caring, she secretly asks, "Do you need me?" And the silent query behind the spoken words of the man who would choose her to be his partner is, "Will you take care of me and solve my problems?"[62]

But that, Norwood warns, only escalates the problem, for each of us needs to feel that we are in charge of our own lives. When someone helps us, we often resent that person's implied power and superiority.[63] And when anything goes wrong, we may choose to blame the other person.

In addition, if the woman wavers in her role as the tower of strength in the relationship, her status as the perfect woman is lowered in the man's eyes. As therapist Susan Forward, Ph.D., expresses in her book, *Men Who Hate Women,* this woman is to be an ever-flowing source of love, adoration, concern, approval and nurturing for her man. If the woman gets upset, questions him, or is ever anything less than totally giving and loving, as far as the man is concerned, she has betrayed him and no longer deserves to be treated well by him.[64] Explains Dr. Forward, "His contempt and disillusionment with her is all the permission he needs to stop expressing his love for her and to begin criticizing, accusing and blaming."[65]

A CLOSER LOOK AT BATTERED WOMEN

Some of the women interviewed by Angela Browne in her book, *Battered Women Who Kill,* came from traditional homes. They had experienced the warmth and security of a loving father who took care of them, and had no experience taking care of themselves. These women reacted to the violence of their husbands with shock and embarrassed silence, choosing not to reveal their plight to their parents or families.

A smaller group of battered women, coming from homes where violence was commonplace, appeared to enter the relationship expecting to be assaulted physically, yet believing that they could overcome the problem. Perhaps that could be one of the factors involved in the finding that abused women who have suffered abuse earlier in their lives tend to stay longer in battering relationships.

The typical battered woman is low in self-esteem, her sense of worth having been eroded by her batterer's continual criticism and disrespect. Yet is this all that is behind her quickness to assume blame and guilt? Researchers don't think so.

When an emotionally painful event occurs and the woman tells herself it is her fault, she is actually saying that she has control of it: If she changes, the pain will stop. By blaming herself, she is holding on to the hope that she will be able to figure out what she is doing wrong and correct it, thereby controlling the situation and stopping the pain.[66]

RESCUER, PERSECUTOR, OR VICTIM?

Although she is not writing exclusively about battered women as are Lenore Walker and Angela Browne, Robin Norwood defines three different roles women may play in their unhealthy relationships with their men: Rescuer, persecutor, or victim. As Norwood explains, each woman has a particular role she may especially favor.

A woman may enjoy playing the role of rescuer. Says Norwood:

It is familiar and comforting to many women who

love too much to feel that they are taking care of (managing and controlling) another person. Out of their chaotic and/or deprived history they have chosen this path as a way of staying safe and earning some degree of self-acceptance. They do it with friends, family members, and often in their careers as well.[67]

Having experienced little security in childhood, rescuers have a desperate need to control their men and their relationships.

> Living in any of the more chaotic types of dysfunctional families such as alcoholic, violent, or incestuous ones, a child will inevitably feel panic at the family's loss of control. The people on whom she depends are not there for her because they are too sick to protect her. In fact, that family is often a source of threat and harm rather than the source of security and protections he needs. Because this kind of experience is so overwhelming, so devastating, those of us who have suffered in this way seek to turn the tables, so to speak. By being strong and helpful to others we protect ourselves from the panic that comes from being at another's mercy. We need to be with people whom we can help, in order to feel safe and in control.[68]

While some women prefer playing the role of rescuer, others choose to play the role of persecutor, the woman who is intent on finding the fault, pointing it out, and setting things right.

Again and again, this woman must recreate the struggle with the dark forces that defeated her as a child, hoping to have more parity in the battle now that she is an adult. Angry from childhood and seeking to avenge herself in the present for the past, she is a fighter, a scrapper, a debater, a harridan. She needs to punish. She demands apologies, retribution.[69]

Or a woman may opt for the role of victim, the most powerless of the three. She sees no options but to be at the whim of others' behavior. To this woman, Norwood says:

> Perhaps there seemed to be no options when you were a child other than being victimized, but now the role is so familiar that there is actually strength to be gained from it. There is a tyranny in weakness, its coin is guilt, and that is the currency of exchange in the victim's relationships.[70]

But, as Norwood warns, to assume any one of these roles is self-defeating:

> To play any of these positions, whether in a conversation or in life, keeps the focus off yourself and holds you in your childhood pattern of fear, rage, and helplessness. You cannot develop your potential as a fully evolved human being, an adult who is in charge of her life, if you do not give up each of these restrictive roles, these ways of being obsessed with the others around you. *As long as you are caught up in these roles, these games, it will appear that another person is keeping you from your goal of happiness. Once you have let go of the games, you are left with total responsibility for your own behavior, your own choices, and your own life...*(emphasis mine.)[71]

What a powerful insight! Please go back and read those words again and again until you have absorbed them. They may be the very key many victims of abuse need in order to lock the door to the past and walk free into a new way of life.

ON THE OTHER HAND...

Perhaps this is a good place to interject a word of balance. We should not be too hasty to brand ourselves or others as "codependent," "savior," "helpless victim," "persecutor," and other labels. An awareness is growing that violence may be more attributable to the problems of the attacker than to something the victim has or has not done.

In contrast to other theories and studies, Professors David Sugarman and Gerald Hotaling found that abused women show no specific personality traits and are no different from non-abused women in terms of educational level, age, occupational status, race, number of children and length of the relationship.[72] A woman's poor self-esteem seemed to be a consequence, not a cause, of abuse.[73] Also, being abused as a child or seeing a parent abused did not associate a woman with being battered as a wife.[74] However, two factors (level of marital conflict and socioeconomic status) appeared significant in distinguishing abused wives from non-abused wives.[75] Women with lower socioeconomic status and those with husbands who have witnessed parental violence as children are more likely to experience severe violence.[76] Marital conflict, frequency of the husband's drinking, traditional sex-role expectations about the division of labor in the relationship and the wife having higher educational attainment than the husband were four factors most often associated with abuse.[77]

A conclusion being reached is that in order to understand wife abuse, researchers should look at the behavior of the perpetrator rather than the characteristics of the victim.[78] If that is the case, perhaps we would be wise to take an even closer look at the batterers, their coercive techniques and their victims. That's exactly what is coming in the next chapter.

ROLES WE MAY PLAY IN UNHEALTHY RELATIONSHIPS

Of the following groups of statements—A, B, or C—which one set best describes you and the role you usually play in relationships?

Group A:

1. If I had to choose one emotion that best describes my innermost feelings as a child, it would probably be helplessness.

2. People sometimes accuse me of trying to lay a guilt trip on them in order to get my way.

3. Somehow, I always seem to wind up at the whim of others' behavior.

4. Some people might say I use weakness as a method of ruling others and getting what I want from them.

Group B:

1. People who know me well would describe me as a fighter, a debater.

2. I find great satisfaction in finding a fault, pointing it out and setting things right.

3. I'm the type who demands apologies and believes in inflicting punishment in return for wrongs and injuries.

4. If I had to choose one emotion that best typified

my innermost feelings during childhood, anger would be near the top.

Group C:

1. I find a certain amount of comfort, security and self-acceptance in managing the lives of others and taking care of them.

2. If I had to choose the one emotion I most remember from my childhood, it would probably be fear.

3. I seem to have a desperate need for control in my friendships, my family, and even in my career.

4. I need to be with people whom I can help in order to feel safe and in control.

As we learned in this chapter, Robin Norwood has defined three different roles women may play in unhealthy relationships with their men: rescuer, persecutor, or victim. In the above sentence sets, "A" describes the role of victim; "B" describes the role of persecutor; and "C" describes the role played by the rescuer. If you found yourself gravitating toward a set of statements describing one of those self-defeating roles, you may find it helpful to thoughtfully read aloud the following declaration, filling in the answers that apply to you:

I have a tendency to play the role of _____ (rescuer, persecutor, or victim) in conversations as well as in life. This tendency has helped prevent my focusing upon myself, and it has held me in my childhood pattern of _____ (fear, anger, or helplessness.)

I am beginning to realize that I cannot develop my potential as a fully developed human being, an adult who is in charge of her life, if I do not give up this restrictive role, this way of being obsessed with the others around me. I am also beginning to understand that as long as I remain caught in this role, this game, it will appear that another person is keeping me from my goal of happiness and that once I let go of the game, I will be left with total responsibility for my own behavior, choices, and life.

I now declare my desire and intention to let go of the game and stop playing the restrictive, self-defeating role of _____ (rescuer, persecutor, or victim). I will recognize and refuse feelings of _____ (helplessness, fear, or anger) when they seek to control me and shape my behavior. From this point on, I will refuse to allow myself to blame another person for keeping me from my goal of happiness. I now choose to assume total responsibility for my own behavior, my own choices, and my own life.

9

BATTERERS AND THEIR VICTIMS

*Sometimes the batterer attacks so subtly his spouse is scarcely
aware of what is happening. At other times he attacks openly.
But the object of his attack is always the same: Her self-esteem.*

IN HER BOOK, *The Battered Woman*, Dr. Lenore Walker has
identified these common coercive techniques used by batterers: (1)
physical abuse; (2) sexual abuse; (3) economic abuse; (4) disruption
through family discord; and (5) social battering. To conserve space,
I'll summarize these techniques while labeling and defining them
and the women's reactions to them as Dr. Walker has done in her
book.

IDENTIFYING THE BATTERER'S TECHNIQUES

Physical Abuse

All the women interviewed by Walker were surprised when their
husbands or lovers began to beat them. Even when their men had
been involved in violence before and they knew of it, these women
felt it couldn't happen to them.

Over a period of time, many of the women began to deny the
reality of the acute battering incidents. It seemed as though they

could not continue to think that their men, who said they loved them, could be as brutal as these incidents revealed.

In many ways, the denial served as a survival technique for those women who went back to live with their batterers. For example, the first day after the acute battering incident, the women remembered every detail clearly, and often with anger at their batterers. However, after the batterer began his phase-three loving and kind behavior, each of the victims became very certain that the incident had not occurred as she originally remembered, but rather as he told her it had occurred. She also began to assume much of the blame for the incident.[79]

Sexual Abuse

The batterer uses sex as an act of aggression against his partner. Sexual jealousy is also most universally present in the battering relationship. The batterer consequently accuses the woman of having affairs with other men and sometimes with women friends. Anyone who is kind to the battered woman, including her father, brother, boss, male co-workers, neighbors, supermarket clerk, or casual acquaintance, becomes a target of the batterer's jealousy.

In some cases, any man who glances at the woman in public becomes a potential target. Often this irrational jealousy spills over onto her woman friends, and she is also accused of lesbian affairs. As a result, battered women often begin to isolate themselves from other people, especially those for whom they really care.[80]

A battered woman is often told she is being sexually provocative.[81] The batterer may accuse her of flirting, wearing sexy clothing or acting seductively.

Drawing upon her experience with batterers and their victims,

Dr. Walker gives a very plausible reason why sexual jealousy is a common problem among batterers:

> The reported stories of sexual jealousy took on similar characteristics. In all cases, the batterer verbally harassed the woman with detailed fantasies of what form her sexual infidelities took...
>
> It is entirely possible that part of their sexual jealousy included projecting their own problems onto the woman. Many of these men were suspected of having sexual liaisons with other women, and in some cases it was confirmed. In others, they were actually having sexual affairs with men.[82]

Another characteristic in the sexual relationships of the battered women interviewed is the type of behavior in which the men forced them to engage. There is a significantly frequent mention of objects, third persons (usually other men), other couples, oral and anal sex and unusual positions in intercourse in battering relationships.[83]

Economic abuse

Economics can be used as a coercive tool in two ways in a battering relationship: One way is to trap the woman in the relationship through her fear of becoming poor. The second way is to use money as a coercive weapon.[84] Frequently, batterers become angry with their women and refuse to give them money to pay for necessary items such as rent or needed medicine. Women's fear of being cut off with no money for even the most basic necessities perpetuates this kind of psychological battering.[85]

Another unfair economic arrangement occurs when the man says he will take care of the bills, yet refuses to allot the woman enough spending money to buy the things she needs or wants. Since her judgment on how to spend money is constantly in question, she finds herself watching his moods, approaching him at the right time, then pleading or making excuses for the money she needs.[86]

Still another coercive economic situation occurs when the man does not work and the woman's income from a steady job she had held over the years keeps them economically stable. Many of the older battered women interviewed found themselves in this position as their partners became less able to perform a job because of flaring tempers or alcohol problems.

In several cases, the battered women inherited money. In these relationships, the women never controlled the inheritance. At best, it was shared, but usually the money went to support the batterer.[87]

As Dr. Walker summarizes:

> The use of economic deprivation as a coercive technique results in bargaining and trade-offs. Not only is the woman deprived economically, but also she is emotionally deprived as an adult. She has virtually no freedom. She is not permitted to learn how to manage money; or if she does, her abilities are discounted, and she is not allowed to make adult choices. Furthermore, when she realizes she wants something she then has to learn a whole range of manipulative techniques in order to get it...[88]

How can economic deprivation cease to be used as a coercive technique? Dr. Walker makes several practical suggestions: The woman must accept her right to economic freedom. The economic relationship between her and her partner must become a relationship of equality and fairness rather than superiority and control. Both partners need to contribute to decision-making and financial management, and each person must give the other person credit for work contributed in the relationship.[89]

Disruption through Family Discord

In the unhealthy atmosphere of the battering relationship, the family's function is also disturbed. The disrupted family structure can include the parents and relatives of both the battered woman and her batterer, their children, former spouses and stepchildren, and eventually even the children's spouses and their relatives and grandchildren.

Batterers are very accomplished at persuading their victims that the possibility of violence is always present. A climate of fear, maintained by the ever-present threat of extremely violent explosions, pervades the atmosphere.

Many of the battered women believe their men have extraordinary insight into their thoughts and actions. The men are seen as "omnipotent" in terms of their ability to survey their women's activities. Therefore, battered women feel as though their thoughts and behavior must be perfect or they may somehow trigger the inevitable acute battering incident.[90]

Threats of violence against the battered woman's family are also standard behavior for the batterer, who often describes exactly how he will torture and maim family members who get in the way. Since the woman knows her partner is capable of committing violence against her and the children, the very people he is supposed to love, she has no trouble believing the batterer will carry out his threats.

Therefore, she usually allows him to isolate her from her family; or in some cases, she visits her family without him. The woman is convinced that she cannot depend upon her family to protect her from him.[91]

Social Battering

Dr. Walker found that batterers in all social groups usually insist on approving, if not choosing, their wives' friends. Battered women are consistently isolated by their partners from women friends, especially those who are viewed as having some influence with the battered women.

But the batterer is adept at using other coercive techniques as well, in order to bring about the extreme social isolation he desires for his partner. For example, a batterer often uses social events as a weapon. If the woman is making plans to go somewhere, he may refuse to give her a firm decision as to whether or not he will attend. He may tell her that if she does something he wants, then he will go and will behave nicely. Very often at the last minute he will refuse to go, forcing her either to cancel or to make excuses when she arrives alone at her destination. Sometimes, he may attend the social function but behave obnoxiously. Other times, he will be charming and delightful. This behavior is successful because of its sporadic nature. The woman never knows when her partner will reward her by cooperating.[92]

TAKING A CLOSER LOOK AT BATTERERS

Although the majority of battered women do not come from violent homes, the batterers themselves generally do. In many cases, either these were beaten themselves, saw their fathers beat their mothers, or watched women and children treated with disrespect.

Descriptions of violent men indicate that there are enough similarities in their behaviors to suggest a violence-prone personality pattern, originating in childhood and becoming progressively more severe as the men practice aggression.

Researchers have also reported several other common characteristics of batterers pertaining to sex role, self-image and verbal skill deficits. Surprisingly, rather than displaying hyper-masculine, macho-man characteristics, abusers are more likely to score low in measures of both masculinity and femininity, suggesting poorly or inadequately developed sex-role identity. Second, a defective, vulnerable sense of self-esteem may motivate abusive behavior. An abuser is more apt to perceive or interpret some aspects of his spouse's behavior as somehow threatening or damaging to his self-esteem. Third, the verbal assertiveness skills of batterers may also be inferior to those of their wives. This skill deficit reduces the probability that batterers will confront their spouses concerning the abusers' feelings of jealousy, insecurity, and frustration. It also deprives their wives of opportunities to reassure their partners or clarify the facts. Instead, batterers tend to transform these and other feelings such as fear, sadness, hurt and anxiety into anger and violence. As a result, a batterer may resort to aggression in order to compensate for his verbal deficiency or as a response to his frustration.

Some researchers propose that the batterer, perhaps looking for the ideal mothering he never received as a child, may go into a rage when the nurturing, caring, or approval he expects from his wife falls short of his unrealistic demands. Then the batterer blames his wife for his actions.

The batterer may be very good at protecting his public image, lying to friends and relatives about what goes on at home and blaming his wife for their problems. It is not unusual for the batterer to be so convincing that relatives and friends believe him instead of her. This is understandable since victims often appear to be humorless, depressed, nervous, edgy, incompetent and unsure (especially in the abuser's presence), while batterers often come across as competent, smiling, and normal. At the other extreme, some abusers present themselves as helpless, pathetic victims while their actual victims may appear to play mothering roles.

Although the batterer can appear to be pleasant, charming and congenial in public, in private he becomes another person. The batterer, who is dependent and low in self-esteem, adopts a controlling, aggressive image with his wife to cover his lack of ego-strength and lack of inner control. Through berating, belittling and acts of aggression, he intimidates her into submission.

Sometimes he attacks so subtly she is scarcely aware of what is happening. At other times, he attacks openly; but the object of his attack is always the same: her self-esteem.

AN UNSPOKEN AGREEMENT

In her book, *Men Who Hate Women and the Women Who Love Them*, Dr. Susan Forward speaks of an unspoken agreement between the batterer and his partner. The agreement stems from their deep-seated needs and fears. The woman's part in the unspoken agreement may be: My emotional security depends on your love, and to get that I will be compliant and renounce my own needs and wishes. His part of the agreement may be: My emotional security depends on my being in total control.

The damage to the men and women locked in these destructive relationships is tragic enough, but what about the children? Does their presence affect the abuse in any way? What effects do all the confusion and pain have upon them?

CHILDREN AND BATTERING

The presence of children in the home affects the frequency of battering cycles. The number of acute battering incidents and the number of times the cycle occurs seem to increase at three distinct periods: When the woman is pregnant, when the children in the family are very young and again when they become teenagers. I should note, however, that age, not pregnancy, may be the determining factor of why pregnant women suffer so much abuse. Studies reveal that women under thirty-one years old are abused about twice as often as older women.

Women who have suffered battering when their children were small often cite the batterer's jealousy of the time spent with the children as the event triggering the abuse. Dr. Walker explains:

> Men who batter are extremely dependent individuals, constantly demanding a woman's undivided attention. Such a man is guaranteed to experience extreme frustration when his woman's attention is diverted from him and his needs; the presence of infants and children in the home ensures this will happen.[93]

About one-half of abusers batter their children as well as their wives.[94] However, whether or not children are physically maltreated by either parent in a battering relationship is less important than the psychological scars they bear from watching their fathers beat their mothers.

In her book, *Terrifying Love*, Lenore Walker reveals some of those scars.[95] I have taken the liberty of summarizing these psychological effects and listing them:

1. Children in battering relationships learn dishonesty and secrecy. They learn to become part of the conspiracy of silence. They learn to lie in order to prevent inappropriate behavior.

2. Since they know their own needs will rarely be consistently fulfilled, they learn to suspend fulfillment of their needs rather than risk another confrontation.

3. Like many children who suffer from overt physical abuse, these children learn to be accommodating and cooperative. They blend into the background.

4. They learn to deny anger rather than expressing it. They do not acknowledge tension.

5. They expend a lot of energy avoiding problems in general. They learn that confrontation is to be avoided at all costs.

6. They learn to manipulate.

7. They live in a fantasy world because it is much nicer than their real world.

8. When the screaming begins, they may stare transfixed, attempting to remain inconspicuous, watching in terror. Sometimes they turn up the television or music to block out the noise. Other times they fall asleep, pretending it is not happening.

9. When they are older, these child victims report enormous feelings of guilt because they chose

to conceal and deny these incidents rather than attempting to intervene.

10. They often assume responsibility for the beginnings of a fight.

11. Children often suffer from extreme learning problems in school and experience failure. Imagine trying to concentrate on schoolwork while wondering whether your mother will be alive when you return home.

12. Compliance and cooperativeness typify the children's behavior in school, though they may also experience conduct problems. Outside of school, these children are often impulsive, unruly and aggressive toward other children. They have learned many different coping mechanisms in order to spare being beaten themselves.

13. The children may experience anxiety disorders and depression.

14. The children exhibit a lack of ability to empathize with others.

Many batterers also display seductive behavior toward their children, especially their daughters. Many studies indicate a strong connection between battering and incest. Just as there is a high statistical incidence of boys who witness fathers battering their mothers becoming batterers themselves, there is also a high incidence of fathers and brothers committing incest with female children in those families where the father is a batterer.[96]

Children who grow up in battering households usually identify with one parent or another by around the age of ten or twelve. For example, when a woman's brother expressed outrage over the black eye and bruises she had received at the hands of her husband, a wealthy physician and respected leader in the church, their eleven-year-old son sided with his father. The boy explained calmly, "If Mother would only do what Daddy tells her, he wouldn't have to hit her."

It is not uncommon for children in the same family to be divided along different lines in regard to this identification, with one child siding with the abusive father and the other siding with the victimized mother.

Children also often identify with a father's coercive behavior. Seeing it as a method of gaining power and control, they begin to model their own relationship patterns along similar lines. According to Dr. Walker:

> In battered women's shelters, it is not uncommon to see children as young as two years old controlling their mothers by using the same language and mannerisms they've seen their fathers use. By the age of five, many children, particularly boys, want their father's approval so much they will do nothing to jeopardize it.[97]

Battered women in a research sample reported that their children chose one of two tactics; either they became supportive of their mother and attempted to stop the batterer from harming her, or they identified with the batterer and began to abuse their mother themselves.

But no matter which response these children choose, they have ambivalent feelings toward their mother. They both love her and hate her. They want to protect her, but they also feel that she deserves the abuse. In many cases, they are angry that she has abandoned them to meet the consuming needs of the batterer.

Dr. Walker concludes: "Children who grow up in abusive families are more likely on the giving or receiving end of abuse in the families they create as adults. In short, we are producing another generation of batterers and battered women."[98]

SOME WORDS OF HOPE

Not all men who witnessed or experienced parental violence as children become husbands who hit their wives. Not all abused wives or children abuse others. We should guard against jumping to the conclusion that once violence occurs in the family it will be passed on to the next generation.

Neither should we make the mistake of concluding that batterers are a homogeneous group, for they are not. All batterers do not conform to the stereotypical image of the sadistic tyrant who receives pleasure from brutalizing his loved ones.

Many abusers live with a deep sense of guilt and shame for their actions and long to be free from their fears, insecurities, uncontrollable rage, or addictions. These individuals may respond favorably in treatment programs where they are taught problem-solving skills, anger management, non-violent methods of dealing with conflict, communication skills, empathetic listening, sexual equality reflected by joint decision-making in the household and financial matters, and how to deal with insecurities and inferiorities. Some batterers may also need to receive help in overcoming drinking, drugs, and/or other addictive behaviors.

In cases where both partners are available and willing to participate, training the couple in appropriate time-out techniques may be useful. The procedure involves the systematic application of the following steps:

1. The abuser recognizes cues that signal the presence of anger.

2. He states that he needs to take a time-out, or simply makes a "T" sign with his hands without speaking.

3. He leaves the house for a specified period of time to cool down and collect his thoughts. Drinking, driving, or going to a bar are all discouraged. Many counsellors advocate seeking the support of a trusted, well-balanced Christian friend or fellow member of a support group.

4. He returns home at the specified time (up to an hour). This helps to establish contact, rebuild trust and discourage attempts to cope simply by avoiding the problem.

5. He then calmly states and discusses the issue related to his anger.

This strategy promotes rational problem-solving and provides a behavioral safety valve. However, careful attention should be given to avoid the possibility that this technique will be used to sidestep or ignore the other partner's concerns.

SOME WORDS OF CAUTION

Well-meaning friends and family members often advise a battered woman to leave her partner and start life over without him, but this may not be the best answer for everyone. Yes, when a woman's well-being, health or safety—or the lives of her children—are in jeopardy, she and any children involved need to get away from the danger. (During a bomb threat, people evacuate a building before an explosion.)

Whatever a woman's resources, those familiar with the growing body of research and statistics in the field agree that if there are threats or serious physical violence, the woman should get out, at least until the volatile situation stabilizes. A man's acts of violence or threats to get even or take revenge must be taken seriously. Therefore, it is essential that the woman line up basic resources, including a safe place for herself and her children to go, a way of getting there any time of the day or night, and some money.

However, I must stress this crucial point: the woman and the people who want to help her must understand that her being in a relationship with an abuser may not be the total problem, and her leaving the relationship may not be the total solution.

Once she is safe, the woman must be helped to understand the roots of any deeper, underlying problems. Unless she learns what it means to be a whole person, the woman could find herself in a situation that has gone from bad to worse. She might go back into the old relationship before she should. Or, as happens in many cases, she could eventually be attracted to another man who would mistreat her and begin a new, equally miserable and unhealthy involvement with him. There is truth in the statement: Victims attract victimizers. She needs to experience the joy and fulfillment that come from rebuilding her shattered self-esteem; restoring vital friendships; and regaining those parts of herself she may have relinquished in order to maintain peace.

If she is to experience healing and wholeness, the woman must learn to deal with her feelings of anger and guilt in regard to her batterer. Her devalued self-perception must be reshaped, and she must come to see herself as one who is of great worth and value to God. She must recognize that forgiveness does not mean excusing or condoning the abuser's behavior, but simply relinquishing him into the hands of God and giving up her right to retaliate for her pain and suffering.

A major factor which seems to determine wife abuse is whether or not the individual approves the use of violence against women. Therefore, one of the great benefits of becoming a whole, healthy person is that it gives the woman the chance to balance many of the warped messages her children have received about how men and women interact and to reverse negative role modeling her children have absorbed. As she develops into a happy, self-confident individual, the children's sense of well-being is enhanced and a powerful new role model is set up for them. Daughters learn that they, too, are of value and entitled to caring, sensitive treatment and that men can love women gently and without violence. Sons begin to see women as preciously unique, valuable and worthy of respect.

HAPPY ENDINGS TO A TRAGIC PROBLEM

Kay, whose abuse began a few months after she and Paul were married, endured verbal abuse, punches and shoves almost daily for fifteen years. Rather than becoming a financial and emotional burden on her aging parents, Kay made the decision to deepen her walk with God; make Him her source of security, peace and joy; and put her complete trust in Him. Kay learned to walk in close communion with the Lord, nourishing and strengthening her spirit through the Bible and in prayer. Crying out to God for wisdom and courage, in her quiet way Kay refused to become a doormat. Over the years, Kay's compassion, faithfulness and Christ-like spirit earned the respect of all those around her—including her husband.

As God supernaturally intervened, the physical abuse gradually stopped. Several times Kay watched in amazement as Paul's fist stopped inches from her face, and then dropped powerlessly at his side. Kay saw her husband begin a slow, but steady, growth in his relationship with God, herself and her children.

The path Kay chose is not the path God asks all his victims to walk. Remember, Esther, the psychologically abused wife I told you about earlier? Realizing that in an effort to keep the peace at any cost in her marriage she had carried selflessness and submissiveness too far, Esther began putting her foot down—gently, but firmly—one small step at a time.

First, Esther bought a new, becoming pair of glasses. Next, when she was able to fit it into the budget, she had her hair cut and styled. The transformation was astonishing, but month after month, Esther watched as her husband's condition deteriorated at an alarming rate. Realizing that he was a ticking time bomb that could be set off at the slightest tremor, Esther consulted several Christian advisors and made plans to separate from Larry. Those plans included setting aside money, finding a less expensive place to rent, learning how to have a restraining order placed on her husband should it become necessary, talking the situation over with her children and setting up a support system of Christian friends she could call on at a moment's notice. As the situation steadily worsened, Esther was forced to carry out her plans.

Eight years after she and Larry separated, Esther prayerfully decided to get a divorce in order to sever any legal ties with Larry where property, business dealings, and money matters were concerned. Realizing she needed a profession that would allow her to support herself and her children, Esther went to nursing school. She sacrificed for their future, living at near poverty level until graduation, but did so near the top of her class. Esther found employment in a profession she loved and eventually bought a home where she raised her children to serve God and live happy and emotionally healthy lives.

What should you do if you are a battered wife? I can offer no guaranteed formula. You and your situation are unique, and you must hear and obey God for yourself. You, not your advisors, are the one who will live with the consequences of your decision. Therefore, be sure you make that decision prayerfully and honestly, alone before God. He may lead you, as He did Kay, to stay. Or He may lead you as He led Esther. Whatever God tells you to do will turn out best for your personal situation as you continue to seek Him and follow His ways.

Remember this: Boys do not have to grow up to be abusive, and girls do not have to grow up to be victims. Women do not have to live out their lives in fear and misery. Batterers, if they are willing to repent, are receptive to counsel, instruction, and Divine help, can be totally free of every force and controlling compulsion and addiction in their lives.

We can do all that God asks us to do. We can be what God's Word says we can be. He is able—if we are willing. If we seek Him, He will give the grace, courage and wisdom to do what we should.

HOW TO RECOGNIZE A POTENTIAL BATTERER

Do certain signs warn of a man's potential violence? Dr. Lenore Walker lists the following characteristics that might identify a potential batterer. Please note: These clues do not prove conclusively that a man is abusive—only that the potential is there.

1. Was the man physically or psychologically abused as a child?

2. Was his mother battered by his father?

3. Has he been known to display violence against others?

4. Does he play with guns and use them to protect himself against others?

5. Does he lose his temper frequently and more easily than seems necessary?

6. Does he commit acts of violence against objects and things rather than people?

7. Does he drink alcohol excessively?

8. Does he display an unusual amount of jealousy when you are not with him? Is he jealous of other significant people in your life?

9. Does he expect you to spend all of your free time with him, or keep him informed of your whereabouts?

10. Does he become enraged when you do not heed his advice?

11. Does he appear to have a dual personality?

12. Is there a sense of overkill in his cruelty or kindness?

13. Are you fearful when he becomes angry with you? Does not making him angry become an important part of your behavior?

14. Does he have rigid ideas of what people should do based on male or female stereotypes?

15. Do you think you are being battered? If so, the probability is high that you are a battered woman and should seek help immediately.[99]

Are there other signs that may alert a woman to a potential bat-terer? The following are taken from a list of predictive behaviors in men that signal violence, published by the National Coalition against Domestic Violence:

1. Did he grow up in a violent family?

2. Does he tend to use force or violence to solve his problems?

3. Does he overreact to little problems and frustra-tions such as not finding a parking place?

4. Does he punch walls or throw things?

5. Does he have a tendency to be cruel to animals? (Such cruelty is a common behavior of men who are cruel to women and children.)

6. Does he abuse drugs or alcohol?

7. Does he think poorly of himself?

8. Does he guard his masculinity by trying to act tough?

9. Does he play with guns, knives, or other lethal instruments? Does he talk of using them against people or threaten to use them to get even?

10. Does he become angry if you do not fulfill his wishes, if you cannot anticipate what he wants?

11. Does he go through extreme highs and lows, as though he is almost two different people?

12. Does he treat you roughly? (Abuse during dating is a guarantee of later and more violent abuse.)

13. Do you feel threatened by him? Have you changed your life so you won't make him angry?

Ignoring or denying problems will not make them go away. The time to get help is now.

PART

ANGER, FEAR, confusion, shame, mistrust, hopelessness are the choking weeds and thorny problems that surround abuse. They seem to invade every aspect of a victim's life.

We've learned much about the destructive roots and poisonous fruits of abuse. Now it's time to begin the work of weeding, tilling, and sowing so that the unproductive soil of the soul can be reclaimed. Here are the issues we will address, one by one:

RECLAIMING
LOST GROUND

2

- » Discovering the power of forgiveness
- » Making offenses work for you
- » Overcoming rejection
- » Rebuilding shattered self-esteem
- » Exposing and breaking family curses
- » Conquering self-defeating fears and thought patterns
- » Overcoming destructive habits and behaviors

A fundamental law of the universe states: "Whatsoever a man sows that will he also reap," (Galatians 6:7, NKJV.) Take hold of the powerful seeds of truth shared in the pages ahead. Make them your own. Start sowing those seeds into the freshly tilled soil of your life, and never stop. In due season you will begin reaping an abundant, unending harvest!

❧ 10 ❧

DISCOVER THE POWER
OF FORGIVENESS

"He that cannot forgive others breaks the bridge over which he himself must pass if he would ever reach heaven; for everyone has a need to be forgiven."

GEORGE HERBERT

FORGIVENESS. Is it necessary? Some insist that it isn't.

Forgive? Ellen Bass, who with Laura David, co-authored the book, *Courage to Heal, A Guide for Women Survivors of Child Sexual Abuse,* says in her workshops: "Why should you? First they steal everything else from you and then want forgiveness, too? Let them get their own. You've given enough."[100]

The stance Bass and Davis assume on forgiveness is summarized in the following quotes:

> The only necessity as far as healing is concerned is forgiving yourself. Developing compassion and forgiveness for your abuse, or for the members of your family who did not protect you, is not a required part of the healing process...[101]
>
> Although there is a need for you to come eventually to some resolution—to make peace with your past and

move on—whether or not this resolution encompasses forgiveness is a personal matter. You may never reach an attitude of forgiveness, and that's perfectly alright.[102]

It is insulting to suggest to any survivor that she should forgive the person who abused her...[103]

Trying to forgive is a futile short-circuit of the healing process...It is not the grand prize. It is only a by-product. And it's not even a very important one. [104]

Are Bass and Davis correct? Is forgiveness simply an occasional, unimportant by-product of the healing process, or is forgiving my offender absolutely essential if I am ever to experience healing and wholeness? Centuries ago, Jesus set the record straight once and for all:

You have heard that it was said, "Love your neighbor and hate your enemy." But I tell you, love your enemies and pray for those who persecute you, that you may be children of your Father in heaven. He causes his sun to rise on the evil and the good, and sends rain on the righteous and the unrighteous. For if you forgive other people when they sin against you, your heavenly Father will also forgive you. But if you do not forgive others their sins, your Father will not forgive your sins. (Matthew 5:43-45; 6:14-15.)

Only if I have no need for forgiveness do I dare refuse to forgive another. When I refuse to forgive the person who wounded me, I break the bridge over which God's peace, wholeness and healing power must pass in order to get to me.

If forgiveness is so important to God, perhaps you and I had better find out exactly what it is, and what it is not.

WHAT IS FORGIVENESS?

Simply stated, forgiveness is giving up my right to hurt someone else for hurting me. Forgiveness, like the law of gravity, is one of the foundational principles God has woven into the fabric of our universe. We can choose not to forgive, just as we can choose not to ignore the laws of gravity, but we do so at our own peril.

Forgiveness means bestowing freedom instead of the punishment my abuser deserves. Forgiveness means giving love and understanding when the enemy expects only hatred and revenge. Forgiveness means turning over to God my desires to blame, defame and punish my offender.

I cannot be released from my offender or from the anger-arousing, shame-evoking, esteem-shattering memories connected with his/her offenses against me until I accept wholeheartedly God's way of forgiveness. Forgiveness is a releasing, transforming experience.

You and I cannot be transformed or truly separated from the past until we accept God's way of forgiveness. But what is God's way? The Apostle Paul, whose body was crisscrossed with scars from bloody beatings, who knew from firsthand experience what it was to be homeless, hungry, thirsty and unjustly imprisoned, exhorted:

> Bless those who persecute you [who are cruel in their attitude toward you]; bless and do not curse them. Bless those who persecute you [who are cruel in their attitude toward you]; bless and do not curse them. Do not let yourself be overcome by evil, but overcome (master) evil with good. (Romans 12:14, 17-19, 21, Amplified.)

What was Paul's motivation for forgiving? It was the example of Jesus Christ who bore the penalty for our sins. (See Colossians 2:14.) Therefore, "Be ye kind one to another," Paul pleads, "tenderhearted, forgiving one another, even as God for Christ's sake hath forgiven you," (Ephesians 4:32, KJV.)

As the beloved spiritual leader David DuPlessis loved to say, "God never gave us authority to justify anybody on earth, but He gave us full authority to forgive everybody."

FORGIVENESS IS NOT AN EMOTION

Forgiveness is not an emotion; it is an act of the will. Because if, even after having chosen to forgive someone, we still feel anger or pain, we mistakenly assume we have not forgiven.

If, after I choose to forgive, I do not feel as if I have forgiven, I must continue to keep my will set on obeying God. I must allow myself all the time and effort it takes to work through the stages of grief. Anger, for example must be acknowledged and dealt with, or someday it will surface in full force and deal with me. And I must choose daily to believe His Word and receive His grace and peace. Eventually, my emotions will fall into line with my decision to forgive.

FORGIVENESS IS NOT CHEAP

Because some may think forgiveness is cheap or free, victims may sneer at the idea of forgiving. But forgiveness is neither cheap nor free. If the offender is to be released from the penalty of his wrongdoing, someone must bear the loss.

The renowned theologian James Buswell summed it up when he said, "No one ever really forgives another, except he bears the penalty of another's sin against him."

Think of it this way: Let's imagine that you've just purchased an ancient, rare, and extremely valuable statue, and I bump into it and break it. You know I don't have the resources to pay for the shattered work of art, so you have one of two choices: You can demand I pay for it anyway—even if it means my mailing you $10.00 a month for the remainder of my life—or you can forgive the debt and bear the loss yourself.

Forgiveness is not free; someone has to pay. Either the offender bears the consequences of what he did (justice), or the offended bears the loss (forgiveness.)

FORGIVENESS IS A GIFT

Forgiveness is not something we can earn or for which we can work. It is a gift. If I hold back forgiveness until I think the offender deserves it, that is not forgiveness.

In *Courage to Heal*, Bass and Davis quote a victim of incest who angrily declared:

> I'll never forgive my father. It would be different if he had come to me at any point and said, "I'm sorry for what I've done. I've hurt you terribly. I'm going to get myself in therapy. I'm going to work this out." But he's never done that.
>
> He'd have to work awfully hard to get me to forgive him. He'd have to work as hard as I've worked from the time I was seventeen until now and he doesn't have enough time left in his life. He's going to die soon. So the chances of me forgiving my father are real slim.[105]

This woman is suffering from the mistaken notion that forgiveness is some sort of receipt for payment in full. But when we put off forgiving someone until we have collected the debt in full, complete with compound interest, we have not forgiven; we have simply gotten even.

UNFORGIVENESS DEFILES

Although a pity party feels good, we cannot afford the luxury of delaying forgiveness while we wallow in self-pity and coddle our hurt. Why? Because a seed of hurt does not lie dormant in the heart. If we do not forgive, thus killing the spark of life in the seed, it immediately begins sprouting, sending out a tenacious root of bitterness. (See Hebrews 12:15.)

Eventually that one root develops into an entire system that taps our peace, joy, and strength. As the root system develops, the seed surfaces and brings forth fruit that poisons us and everyone with whom we share it.

Time spent tending the foul crop of hatred, resentment and grudges is time spent in futile, senseless pain. So hurry to forgive as soon as you are offended, before the first root of bitterness begins to spread.

Even though you extend love and forgiveness to your offender, you have no guarantee that you will not receive evil in return. But Jesus commanded us to love our enemies, and love is not some temporary strategy or a clever form of manipulation. Love is supposed to be the Christian's way of life.

When we extend forgiveness and show love, we have no guarantee that our offender will repent or beg our forgiveness. But we are not responsible for the offender's actions. We are only accountable for our own.

FORGIVING DOESN'T MEAN YOU'RE A DOORMAT

Forgiving your offenders and returning good for evil is not the same as being naïve or a doormat. We must use wisdom when dealing with offenders. Christ taught us that different offenses require different responses:

> "You have heard that it was said, 'You shall love your neighbor and hate your enemy.' But I say to you, *love* your **enemies**, *bless* those who **curse you**, *do good* to **those who hate you**, and *pray* for those **who spitefully use you and persecute you**, (Mathew 5:43-44, NKJV, emphasis mine.)

Notice that the response should be tailored to the individual offense committed against us. For example, Jesus didn't say to keep giving to people who use us; He said to pray for them.

MUST THE OFFENDER MEET CERTAIN CONDITIONS?

If certain conditions are fulfilled, there is no limitation to Christ's law of forgiveness. The conditions for receiving Christ's forgiveness are repentance and confession. (See Luke 17:3-4.) However, even if our offender never repents or confesses, we can experience release from the offender and the offense by forgiving anyway and turning the person over to God.

Jesus was not teaching that we are to keep setting ourselves up in the role of victim. We forgive, yes, and we reap the benefits of that forgiveness. However, forgiving an unrepentant offender does not mean that we have to make him/her our bosom buddy or habitually socialize with that individual. As a matter of fact, the Bible teaches just the opposite. (See Matthew 18:15-17.)

FORGIVING CAN INVOLVE CONFRONTATION

When someone has wronged us and we are struggling with unforgiveness, the Word of God instructs us to go directly to the offender and confront him with the wrong committed:

> You shall not go up and down as a dispenser of gossip *and* scandal among your people, nor shall you [secure yourself by false testimony or by silence and] endanger the life of your neighbor. I am the Lord. You shall not hate your brother in your heart; but you shall surely rebuke your neighbor, lest you incur sin because of him. You shall not take revenge or bear any grudge against the sons of your people, but you shall love your neighbor as yourself. I am the Lord. (Leviticus 19:16-18, Amplified.)

Notice the purposes for this confrontation. First of all, by your silence the lives of others may be endangered (verse 16.) In addition, your failure to righteously deal with your anger resulting from the wrong done to you can eventually cause you to sin in at least four ways: You may become a dispenser of gossip and scandal in an effort to expose your offender and make him look bad (verse 16.) Secondly, you may hate the offender (verse 17.) Thirdly, you may take revenge upon the person yourself, rather than remembering that God has said vengeance is His and He will repay (verse 18.) And lastly, you may hold a grudge against the offender (verse 18.)

Why is the failure to confront and forgive such a serious matter? Because it results in hatred, and the end of hatred is spiritual death:

We know that we have passed from death to life, because we love the brethren. He who does not love *his* brother abides in death. Whoever hates his brother is a murderer, and you know that no murderer has eternal life abiding in him. (I John 3:14-15.)

However, confrontation should be redemptive, not retaliatory. Engaging in loving confrontation can lead to the offender's healing:

Brethren, if any person is overtaken in misconduct *or* sin of any sort, you who are spiritual [who are responsive to and controlled by the Spirit] should set him right *and* restore *and* reinstate him, without any sense of superiority *and* with all gentleness, keeping an attentive eye on yourself, lest you should be tempted also. (Galatians 6:1.)

FORGIVENESS DOES NOT MEAN DENYING OR SUPPRESSING ANGER

Sometimes we are ashamed to acknowledge that we are angry; but anger is a God-given emotion and is neither right nor wrong. It is the way we use anger that makes it right or wrong. (See Ephesians 4:26-27.) Instead of suppressing or denying our anger when we have been wronged, we must acknowledge that we are angry, take time to grieve and work through the anger and accept God's grace to channel it toward constructive ends.

Anger must be exercised in the right way, for the right reasons and against the right things. Anger can fortify our courage and convictions. It can challenge injustice and oppression. Anger when used correctly can incite us to set new goals, and it can strengthen our determination to persevere. Instead of using anger to strike out at others, anger should be used as God meant it to be.

FORGIVENESS AND FORGETTING
ARE NOT THE SAME

We must beware of pressuring ourselves or others to forgive and forget. Forgiving does not change the past. Facts are facts, events happened. The past cannot be altered, but when we truly trust God's promise that He makes all things work together for our good, the meaning of the past can be changed and the painful sting can be removed from our memories.

It is possible to so suppress the painful memories of the past that we forget them, at least for a time; but suppression is neither healthy nor productive in the long run. We must not struggle to hasten the process of healing by attempting to force forgetfulness. Neither should we expect a case of holy amnesia to strike our minds and obliterate painful memories.

Stubbornly insisting that forgetting must come first is like trying to pass the final exam before you have enrolled in the course. Constantly fretting and trying to forget just short-circuits and undercuts the healing process. Although God sometimes heals instantly, removing all the pain, guilt and grief in one miraculous moment, for most of us the healing process takes time.

As we grieve over the death of a dream or mourn a relationship as it should have been but never was, we begin to work through the various stages of grief: denial, isolation, anger, bargaining, depression, then acceptance, or as some prefer to list them: remembering, grieving, anger, and moving forward.

We should be aware that these stages do not always occur in the same order, that several may occur at the same time and that we may process our way through the cycle more than once. Forgiveness actually becomes a way of healing ourselves.

You and I can will ourselves to forgive, but only God can make us forget. And what is it that we forget? The memories themselves? Probably not. But God helps us forget the raw, stinging pain of those memories.

Gradually, the memories that pop into our minds begin to decrease in frequency and intensity. No longer do we constantly recall, rehash, and relive the events. Instead, as the healing process nears completion and the last of the poison is drawn from our souls, we find ourselves occasionally recalling the memories, but in a vague, detached sort of way, almost as if the experiences had happened to someone else. They no longer have the power to infect or agitate.

If you have been unable to escape the pain of the past, take a moment to meditate on these beautiful words from missionary Amy Carmichael:

> If I say, "Yes, I forgive, but I cannot forget," as though God, Who twice a day washes all the sands on all the shores of all the world, could not wash such memories from my mind, then I know nothing of Calvary love.[106]

Never doubt that God can perform that wonderful, cleansing work within you.

NO OFFENDER, NO ABUSER, IS UNFORGIVABLE OR UNLOVABLE

An adult survivor of child sexual abuse was quoted as saying:

> I don't forgive him. He was an adult. He is ultimately responsible. I can't forgive anyone who does a

thing like that to a child, particularly anybody who did it to me. If someone tried to do that to my kids, I would flat out kill them. He deserves to die a lonely, miserable man. Let it die with him. I'd be glad to see it kill him. It's not going to kill me.[107]

Perhaps you, like that troubled, bitter woman, angrily insist that you could never love or forgive the person who abused you. "I cannot love him; I cannot forgive her," you may say.

But before you make that final choice never to love or forgive your abuser, you owe it to yourself to stop, be honest and acknowledge certain fundamental truths.

First of all, when you say, "I cannot forgive," or "I cannot love," what you are saying is: "I will not forgive; I will not love."

God will give you the power and grace to do anything He asks you to do, but you must be willing to receive that power and grace. So stop lying to yourself. If you choose not to love or forgive your abuser, don't say, "I cannot." Admit rather, "I will not."

Second, remember that the unit of highest value in the entire human universe is the human soul (Mark 8:36-37.) Your abuser is of infinite, eternal worth.

Jesus Christ loved and valued your abuser more than He loved or valued His own life. He came into our world to save sinners, not perfect people. Jesus suffered and gave His live for your abuser, just as much as He suffered and gave His life for you. If Jesus loves the person who abused you, then Jesus can love him or her through you.

Martin Luther once explained it this way; "To love one's enemy does not mean to love the mire in which the pearl lies, but to love the pearl that lies in the mire."

But love for our enemies cannot be manufactured. Love is a gift of God, poured gently into our hearts by the Holy Spirit (see Romans 5:5.)

That divine love endows us with the ability to see the inestimable value of an individual's life and soul.

Here's a third fact to remember: If we set ourselves up as an individual's judge and jury, we close our heart's door of ministry. The opportunity to help heal another is lost when we allow that person's actions to determine our reactions.

Scottish theologian William Barclay lists three reasons why no human being is qualified to judge another:

1. We never know the whole story or the whole person. We cannot understand his circumstances or temptation.

2. It is almost impossible for any man to be strictly impartial in his judgment.

3. No man is good enough to judge any other man. Our own faults and inability to resolve them automatically disqualify us as fair critics.[108]

Another problem with judging is that we judge the other person's weakness from our point of strength.

When you or I reach the point in our lives where we are capable of paying the price of someone's sins, then we can judge him. Until then, we must learn to love others as God loves us—in our imperfection.

HAVE YOU FORGIVEN YOURSELF?

Forgiving ourselves can be the most difficult task in the work of forgiveness.

Sometimes when we fail God and fall far short of our own standards, we know in our hearts that God has forgiven us, yet we cannot seem to forgive ourselves. We wrestle with guilt, regret, and a never-ending host of what-ifs and if-onlys.

For some of us, the struggle does not end until we hear ourselves moaning, "How could I have done that?" And we are suddenly brought face-to-face with the fact that pride is the real enemy with whom we have been wrestling. It dawns upon us that if a perfect, holy God who never sinned has long since forgiven us, who are we not to forgive ourselves! We finally realize that our failure is not unique, for "No temptation has overtaken you except what is common to man..." (I Corinthians 10:13, NIV.) We tearfully admit that our own heart is just as deceitful and desperately wicked as any human heart (Jeremiah 17:9), and that if it were not for God's grace, our failure would have been far worse than it was.

For some of us, the guilty struggle ends through such confrontational, yet comforting, biblical revelation. For others, God Himself lovingly intervenes, using the ordinary, the commonplace, to convey the extraordinary.

In the story "The Jagged Memory," Lisa Wells Isenhower shared with Guidepost readers how God used a broken window to help her forgive herself for going against the Bible's teaching and against her own expectations of herself.

Because she was pregnant when Lisa married her husband, guilt had been a part of every one of their wedding anniversaries. Lisa dreaded the day when their oldest son would figure out that his father and mother were married only six and one-half months before he was born.

On the day of Bob and Lisa's eighth anniversary, burglars broke into their home through the bathroom window and robbed them. Since the glass shop was closed by the time Bob got off work, he had to tape up the gaping hole with cardboard and masking tape and wait until the following day to repair the broken window.

At daybreak the next morning, Lisa stood in the bathroom waiting for the water in the shower to run hot. Suddenly, she heard birds singing. Lisa realized that she was able to enjoy an early morning concert that she had missed for so long.

Says Lisa:

> The parallel was immediately apparent. My first pregnancy had been like the broken window that I had tried to cover it; a broken place I wanted to keep hidden. Yet the more I tried to hide my past, the more cut off I became from the beautiful music that God had for me.
>
> "Forgive yourself," God seemed to say. "Accept your broken places, and I will pour through them the music of healing and deep joy."
>
> Suddenly I felt a new closeness to God. I knew then the truth of the scriptural passage, "The sacrifices of God are a broken spirit; a broken and contrite heart, O God, You will not despise," (Psalm 51:17, NIV.)[109]

Are you still struggling with guilt over something that happened long ago? Stop trying to mask your jagged memories and shattered expectations.

DEALING WITH OUR BROKEN PLACES

For years I strove for perfection and performance in a painful, desperate effort to gain my father's approval and acceptance. Shamed by the rejection and degrading abuse I had received growing up and intimidated by my lack of education, I struggled to prove to my father and to myself that I was a person of value and worth, not a piece of garbage.

Like the seven-year-old boy from long ago who had proudly

shown his father the shiny jackknife he had found in the snow, I still longed to see a flash of pride on my father's face. Hungry for some small word of approval or just a faint smile of acceptance, I had proudly paraded my every hard-won accomplishment before him.

But as I lay in a cardiology ward at the age of thirty-two, God brought me face-to-face with my broken places. Tormented by fears of failure, ridicule and rejection, I had tried to be perfect in every area of my life: The perfect father, husband, even the perfect evangelist. The pressure of striving to be perfect absolutely broke me physically because there's no one perfect except Jesus. I worked so hard to keep up a front of perfection; but the shabby barrier of patched-up disappointments masked my weaknesses and carefully-covered failures I had erected between myself and everyone else. All the music of healing and joy had been shut out of my life.

As I lay on that hospital bed, God brought me to the place where I could be honest with myself and Him. I finally realized that I had to stop suppressing and hiding the past. As I admitted and accepted all my broken places and exposed them first to God and then to my dad the Spirit of God was released to perform a supernatural healing in my life and in the life of my father, as well.

If you are experiencing pain because of rejection and past hurts, please don't suppress them any longer. Take all your pain to Jesus. He understands. He allowed His body to be broken so that we, who are also broken, could be made whole.

MENDING THE BROKEN BRIDGE

An ancient verse from Hosea 4:6 says, "My people are destroyed for lack of knowledge." Not understanding what forgiveness is and what it is not is damaging and destroying the lives of many people. That is why I've given so much time and space to the subject.

If you are hurting and longing for healing, I think you know what may be blocking the way: A broken bridge of unforgiveness. Stop the hurting; start mending your bridge right now.

MENDING YOUR BROKEN BRIDGE

Shallow repentance is worthless; true repentance will set you free from unforgiveness and release you to God's highest and best. Where do you begin?

1. **Face it:** Who do you need to forgive?

   _____

2. **Confess it:** Release comes from confessing your sins to God. If writing out that confession will help you verbalize it in prayer, do so.

   _____

   _____

3. **Forsake it:** You must be willing to say good-bye to the old grudges, the smoldering resentment and the desire to punish your offender. The refusal to do this binds you to the offense and the offender; it keeps you in bondage to the past. Surrender every aspect of your sin.

4. **Live it**: Make forgiveness a way of life. Refuse to take up the old offense again. Refuse to allow the weight of new offenses to break the bridge over which God's peace, wholeness and healing power must pass in order to get to you. Learn to live in forgiveness.

❧ 11 ❧

MAKING OFFENSES
WORK FOR YOU

*"[God] has Himself gone through the whole of human experience,
from the trivial irritations of family life and the cramping
restrictions of hard work and lack of money to the worst
horrors of pain and humiliation, defeat, despair and death.
When He was a man, He played the man. He was born in
poverty and died in disgrace, and thought it worthwhile."*

DOROTHY L. SAYERS, *CREED OR CHAOS.*

WHY DOES GOD PERMIT PAIN and injustice in our lives? Mankind has struggled with this tough question since time began. For those who have been victimized and traumatized, the question becomes far more than just a stimulating topic for discussion. Driven by a desperate search to find truth and meaning, we eventually resolve the question one way or another. For some of us, the search leads to trust and faith. Others, too angry or anguished in spirit to continue the search, walk away empty.

Victims of abuse may never find all the answers to our questions this side of eternity, but in the midst of it all, if we find our all-wise, all-loving, all-powerful Heavenly Father, we have found enough. As a prisoner in a concentration camp explained, "It is far greater to know the Who of one's life than the why."

God is greater than our abusers. He can overrule and reverse the consequences of the offenses committed against us. He can give beauty for ashes. He can bring the miraculous out of the ridiculous. No life is too mixed up, no situation too tangled for Him. As one wise, elderly pastor expressed, "God can unscramble eggs."

JOSEPH'S INCREDIBLE STORY

The Old Testament Book of Genesis contains a story that rivals any current bestseller or famous classic for its suspense and attention-gripping plot. It is the incredible story of Joseph, a young man who victoriously overcame one injustice after another, any one of which would be enough to embitter or break the average person. It is also the story of Joseph's incredible God.

For years Joseph was the target of his brothers' vicious jealousy, hatred and rejection. Their father, Jacob, had never disguised the fact that Joseph was the favorite of his twelve sons. Because of their father's partiality, his ten older brothers hated Joseph so much that they couldn't speak a kind word to him. (See Genesis 37:4.)

There was another reason why Joseph's brothers hated him: Envy always hates the good and the blessings in the life of someone else.

Joseph had told them about two strange dreams he'd had in which his brothers bowed down to him and he reigned over them. The dreams made the brothers uneasy. What if this "master of dreams" as they mockingly called him, was marked for greatness after all? They could not bear the thought of their despised little brother rising to a position of prominence.

When Joseph was seventeen, his brothers' malevolent feelings reached the boiling point. Genesis 37 records the ugly scene. Instead of killing Joseph as they had planned, they threw him into a well in the wilderness, and then sold him to a band of traders whose caravan passed by. In Egypt, the traders sold Joseph to Potiphar, a high-ranking officer and chief executioner of the royal guard for Pharaoh, king of Egypt. Jacob's favored son was now a slave.

Let's look at what happened next:

> But the Lord was with Joseph, and he [though a slave] was a successful *and* prosperous man; and he was in the house of his master the Egyptian. And his master saw that the Lord was with him and that the Lord made all that he did to flourish *and* succeed in his hand. So Joseph pleased [Potiphar] *and* found favor in his sight, and he served him. And [his master] made him supervisor over his house and he put all that he had in his charge. (Genesis 39:2-4, Amplified.)

Things seemed to be looking up for Joseph. He had successfully adapted to a foreign culture, mastered a difficult language, and demonstrated impressive administrative skills. No wonder Jacob had loved this kid!

Unfortunately, Potiphar's wife was also impressed with Joseph. She threw herself at him day after day, but the handsome young man firmly resisted her advances. One day when she caught him by his coat and demanded that he lie with her, Joseph left his garment in her hand and fled from the house, refusing to hurt the heart of the God he loved or be disloyal to Potiphar.

Instead of rewarding Joseph for demonstrating such integrity, Potiphar chose to believe the hastily concocted story his wife told of attempted rape. He had Joseph thrown into the place where state prisoners were confined.

But God caused Joseph to prosper even in prison. The Lord had not left his special young man in Canaan to become a keeper of sheep, and He had no intention of leaving him in prison in charge of other inmates. God had marked Joseph for leadership of the highest sort. The prison, like the pit in the wilderness and Potiphar's house, was simply a place of passage for Joseph, not a place of permanence.

God did not waste Joseph's life, and He will not waste yours. He will place your talents and abilities where they are most suited and productive. But back to the story; I'll summarize for you.

Sometime later, Pharaoh's butler and baker offended the king. He threw them into prison, and they were placed in Joseph's charge.

One night each of the men had a dream which Joseph interpreted. Just as Joseph predicted, Pharaoh had the chief baker hanged, and the butler reinstated. However, instead of remembering his promise to appeal to Pharaoh on Joseph's behalf, the butler promptly forgot about the young man who had helped him.

Two long years later, when Pharaoh could find no one to interpret his strange, foreboding dreams, the butler suddenly remembered Joseph and recommended that the king send for him.

This is the place in the story where I hold my breath, hoping Joseph doesn't blow it. Too bad Pharaoh couldn't have met Joseph when he first arrived in Egypt as an optimistic, faith-filled seventeen-year-old. After all, for the past thirteen years Joseph had been the innocent victim of heartless cruelty, vicious lies and blatant injustice. Plus, he's been shut up in a dungeon with nothing but criminals and his own ruined reputation, tormenting memories, and shattered dreams for company. There's no telling the damage all that suffering had done to Joseph.

How will Pharaoh react if the guards haul in a thirty-something raving maniac with matted hair and filthy clothes? What if Pharaoh says, "I've had these dreams...," and Joseph curses and says, "Yeah, so what? I had some dreams myself once, and you see where they got me! God lied to me. My own brothers knifed me in the back. The boss I worked my fingers to the bone for believed the clever lies of his conniving wife and threw me into your stinking prison filled with human scum. Dreams! Dreams don't mean nothin' to me, man!"

I don't think I'm exaggerating. You and I both know people who've been broken and embittered by a lot less adversity than Joseph endured. So how did Joseph fare?

Thirteen years of some of the longest, darkest trials imaginable had neither embittered nor broken Joseph. His life serves as a strong reminder that it is not suffering itself, but our reaction to the suffering, that makes or breaks us.

Instead of allowing the offenses and injustices he experienced to drive him away from God, Joseph had chosen to draw even nearer to Him. During the most confusing, hopeless times of his life, Joseph had become intimately acquainted with the Lord's voice and His mysterious ways. Furthermore, he was not afraid to speak of his great God before a powerful pagan king.

First, Joseph effortlessly interpreted Pharaoh's dreams. Then this perfectly-poised slave articulately outlined a brilliant plan to save all of Egypt from the years of famine he had just foretold. No wonder Pharaoh instantly made Joseph second in command over all the land of Egypt. (See Genesis 41:40-41.)

How would you like to have been Joseph's older brothers when hunger forced them to go down to Egypt to buy grain and they found themselves bowing down before the little brother they had callously sold into slavery twenty-two years before? Surely he must hate them. What torturous means of death awaited them?

But Joseph could not restrain his tears as he made himself known to his brothers:

I am Joseph! Is my father still alive? And his brothers could not reply, for they were distressingly disturbed *and* dismayed at [the startling realization that they were in] his presence. And Joseph said to his brothers, Come near to me, I pray you. And they did so. And he said, I am Joseph your brother, whom you sold into Egypt! But now, do not be distressed *and* disheartened or vexed *and* angry with yourselves because you sold me here, for God sent me ahead of you to preserve life. (Genesis 45:3-5, Amplified.)

Then Joseph moved Jacob, his eleven brothers and their families, their flocks and all they owned to Egypt, gave them the best of the land and provided for them.

Now that's the story as it looked from the natural. But Psalm 105:16-24 records the story from God's point of view:

Moreover, He called for a famine upon the land [of Egypt]; He cut off every source of bread. *He sent a man before them*, even Joseph, who was sold as a servant. His feet they hurt with fetters; he was laid in chains of iron *and* his soul entered into the iron, Until his word [to his cruel brothers] came true, until the word of the Lord tried *and* tested him. The king sent and loosed him, even the ruler of the peoples, and let him go free. He made Joseph lord of his house and ruler of all his substance, To bind his princes at his pleasure and teach his elders wisdom. Israel also came into Egypt; and Jacob sojourned in the land of Ham. There [the Lord] greatly increased His people and made them stronger than their oppressors. (Amplified, emphasis mine.)

In the final analysis, it was a powerful, sovereign God, not Joseph's brothers, who sent Joseph to Egypt. But the Bible puts the responsibility for all the agony Joseph endured exactly where it belongs; not upon God, but upon the people whose offenses against Joseph caused his unjust pain and suffering.

The Bible also clearly reveals that God took the wicked injustices intended for Joseph's destruction and reversed them, making the offenses work together for Joseph's development and deliverance instead.

1. *Joseph's brothers sold him to Ishmaelite traders, intending to forever rid themselves of their brother and his lofty dreams.* The traders took Joseph to Egypt, exactly where God needed him to be in order to fulfill the dreams He had given Joseph and position him to save not only the nation of Egypt when the famine struck, but Jacob's entire household as well.

2. *Joseph's captors bound him with chains of iron.* However, as Joseph drew upon God's grace, God was able to use the painful, grueling experience to put "iron" into Joseph's soul, filling him with inner strength and perseverance. (See Psalm 105:18.)

3. *Joseph was sold as a slave to Potiphar.* But a sovereign God was setting Joseph for a series

of miracles. Potiphar, as Pharaoh's chief executioner, could have easily had Joseph put to death when his wife brought accusations against Joseph. Instead, he had Joseph incarcerated in the prison where the state prisoners were confined. When the right time came, Joseph was exactly where he needed to be to meet Pharaoh's butler.

4. *Once the butler was released from prison, he promptly forgot Joseph.* But God overruled the butler's offense of ingratitude. Two years later when the time was ripe, Joseph was strategically positioned so God could promote him directly from the prison to the palace as Pharaoh's right-hand man.

5. *During the thirteen years Joseph managed Potiphar's household and worked under the prison warden supervising all the other inmates, Joseph carried weighty responsibilities and difficult challenges.* But the problems and stresses Joseph confronted on a daily basis developed and matured his leadership and administrative skills. By the time thirty-year-old Joseph stood before Pharaoh, he was not only willing to accept the king's offer to rule all of Egypt, he was also thoroughly prepared.

I have belabored this point because it is so critical that victims of abuse come to understand, as Joseph did, that offenses and injustices do not come from God. The Bible makes clear God's position regarding people who abuse and misuse others:

> Then He said to the disciples, "It is impossible that no offenses should come, but woe *to him* through whom they do come! It would be better for him if a millstone were hung around his neck, and he were thrown into the sea, than that he should offend one of these little ones. (Luke 17:1-2, NKJV.)

It will be a fearful time when unrepentant abusers are called to stand before the Throne of God. Yet as we who have been victimized rightly respond to our offenders and to the sins they have committed against us, God can take those very offenses and injustices and cause them to work together for our good and for His glory. Joseph's life perfectly illustrates that fact.

A WALL, A WELL, AND THE WILL OF GOD

As Jacob lay dying, he called his sons around his bed and pronounced a blessing on each one. The beautiful blessing Jacob spoke to Joseph contained, in poetic form, a summary of the eternal principles which Joseph had discovered and staked his life upon: *"Joseph is a fruitful bough, a fruitful bough by a well (spring or fountain), whose branches run over the wall,"* (Genesis 49:22, Amplified.) Jacob's blessing was prophetic; it pictured Joseph as a tree planted beside a wall and a well.

A WALL

Joseph—the little tree—had been wrenched from his familiar, beloved surroundings and transplanted into a foreign land. The alien, godless culture was bad enough, but the little tree was also planted in the cold shadow of a massive wall. Sometimes a seemingly insurmountable problem comes into our lives. It is too large for us; it overwhelms and towers over us and shuts us in like a wall.

Tiny, struggling trees don't like walls. We fret and cry, "God is bigger than this problem; why doesn't He remove it?" But in some cases, God chooses not to remove our problem, but to use it.

Did the tiny tree, suddenly plunged into foreign soil, wilt in despair? Did the limbs of the little tree struggle for a time in the decision whether or not to stretch tall and straight toward the sun, or to droop dejectedly in self-pity? Was the fruit of the tiny tree consumed for a season by gnawing worms of rage and depression? Was its first crop of fruit hard and inedible as Joseph battled with bitterness and the desire for revenge?

I believe Joseph himself describes for us, by the use of the name he gave his first child, the tremendous battle he had fought and won with bitter, painful memories: "And Joseph called the firstborn Manasseh [making to forget], For God, said he, has made me forget all my toil and hardship and all my father's house," (Genesis 41:51, Amplified.)

Our part is to forgive. When we make the decision to give up our right to hurt others for hurting us, when we cease holding a grudge, God does His part. He makes us forget the toil, hardship, and pain of the past.

A WELL

"Joseph is a fruitful bough, a fruitful bough by a well..."
When God plants us by a wall, He also puts us beside a well. Have you found your well, or are your roots still running here and there along the surface, from puddle to puddle?

It may have taken a while for Joseph to notice the well. But at some critical point, Joseph discovered its life-giving waters and made the decision to force his roots down deep into God. As the tree drew upon God's abundant resources of grace, it started producing good, sweet fruit.

For a time, Joseph must have hated the confinement of the wall and despised its shadow. Why Egypt? Why slavery? Why prison? Along the way, Joseph discovered that the place had nothing to do with his happiness or fruitfulness; it was God's ever-available peace and presence that mattered more than anything. Maybe that's why Joseph called his second son Ephraim, meaning "to be fruitful,' for he said, "God has caused me to be fruitful in the land of my affliction," (Genesis 41:52, Amplified.)

Do you get it? God doesn't have to take us out of the difficult circumstances before our lives can begin to produce fruit. As we forgive our offenders and force our roots down deep into the waters of God's grace, we can be fruitful in our land of affliction.

Not everyone will believe your dream. Like Joseph's brothers, some people will try to take away your faith in your dream if you let them.

If you're not careful, you can begin to blame God and become bitter toward other people because the dream doesn't materialize on your timetable. But remember: It's God's dream. You didn't make the dream; it is the dream that will make you. God is putting iron into your soul through the painful situations you do not understand, so be patient.

In the middle of your darkest trial, keep seeking development as did Joseph. He learned to forgive. He learned to resist sin and serve God in a pagan society. He learned to defeat bitterness, loneliness and hopelessness and to persevere in faith and prayer. Like Joseph, you will discover that as you seek development, deliverance will come in God's appointed time.

THE WILL OF GOD

"Joseph is a fruitful bough, a fruitful bough by a well, whose branches run over the wall."

God is in control. There is no wall He can't topple anytime He wishes. So why doesn't God simply remove the wall? Joseph discovered why.

The little tree planted beside a wall and a well made the decision to stretch his limbs toward the sun and to push his roots deep into God. The tiny tree began to grow taller and stronger. It began to bud and blossom. Season after season, it just kept growing and blooming and bearing fruit where it was planted. And one day, its branches ran over the wall.

God wants us to grow straighter and stronger, taller until one day our fruit-laden branches cascade over the wall. The greatest joy we will ever know comes after we have grown bigger than the problem, and others—even our offenders—can come to us to find rest in our shade and be nourished and refreshed by the sweet fruit of victory in our lives.

After Jacob's death, his brothers, fearful that perhaps Joseph now would hate them and pay them back for the evil they had done him, fell down before him and said, "We are your slaves!"

> And Joseph said to them, Fear not; for am I in the place of God? [Vengeance is His, not mine.] As for you, you thought evil against me, but God meant it for good, to bring about that many people should be kept alive, as they are this day. Now therefore, do not

be afraid. I will provide for *and* support you and your little ones. And he comforted them [imparting cheer, hope, strength] and spoke to their hearts [kindly]. (Genesis 50:19-21, Amplified.

AN INCREDIBLE MAN OR AN INCREDIBLE GOD?

The purity and beauty of Joseph's character are almost intimidating. The man is so forgiving, so persevering, so loving, so completely Christ-like. We look at him longingly and say, "Could I ever be like that?"

The answer is yes. It was not that Joseph was some one-in-a-million, incredible man. It was that Joseph appropriated the grace of an incredible God. Instead of frustrating and annulling the grace of God by feeling sorry for himself or blaming others, Joseph discovered the secret of growing in grace. He learned to receive grace for his own sins and weaknesses, just as he learned to appropriate God's grace for the offenses committed against him.

REVERSING OFFENSES

Some of us haven't grown in twenty years or more because of something in our past—some shameful failure of our own, or some painful offense or injustice committed against us. We have allowed that thing to make us cynical, judgmental and dissatisfied. Because we have refused to appropriate God's grace we're not really going anywhere. We've reached our pinnacle. But if we will take whatever has offended us and bury it at the cross of Christ, we will begin to grow again. The very character and nature of Christ will begin forming in us.

Once you throw yourself upon God's grace and trust Him to

reverse your offenses, whether you are 16 or 96, there is more than heartache, more than sadness, more than the life of anguish and rejection you have known. There is hope!

When I was a brokenhearted, totally devastated eleven-year-old boy, the Lord Jesus walked into my room, stretched out His arms to me and said, "Son, I love you, and I have a wonderful plan for your life."

You may be crying, "If only God would make such a promise to me!" Let me tell you, He already has. And the wonderful promise is recorded in His Word: For I know the thoughts that I think toward you, says the LORD, thoughts of peace and not of evil, to give you a future and a hope, (Jeremiah 29:11, NKJV.)

God values you as much as He valued Joseph. Look to the cross.

God needs you as much as he needed Joseph. Look at your world.

And while you're looking, remember: *No wall, no matter how thick or high, can thwart His purposes for you!*

WALLS OR WELLS?

1. What is your wall?

_____

_____

_____

_____

2. What specific offenses are you asking God to overrule for your good and His glory?

_____

_____

_____

_____

3. God never allows us to be planted by a wall unless He also put a well nearby to nourish and sustain us. List some things you do, people you know and places you go from which you draw strength and nourishment.

_____

_____

_____

_____

12

OVERCOMING REJECTION

He is despised and rejected by men, A Man of
sorrows and acquainted with grief.

ISAIAH 53:3

THE CHINESE HAVE A SAYING: "In the broken nest,
there are no whole eggs."

My six siblings and I grew up in a broken nest—a dysfunctional
home in Massachusetts. We never knew what it was to be enveloped
in the warm security of a loving, nurturing family. Instead, our
fragile spirits were constantly exposed to the cold, fierce winds of
our father's violence and abuse; our fractured self-images oozed fear,
rejection and guilt.

In spite of all the physical battering and emotional damage, we
managed to survive. Most of us later experienced one or more severe
problems of our own: Abortions, divorces, addictions, involvement
in the occult and/or prostitution. One brother had a struggle with
compulsive gambling while another became a drug dealer to support
his own habit.

It's evident that there was a terrible problem in our home. As a
child, I didn't blame my father; I blamed myself. Perhaps the worst
part of it all was that I began to accept the names my father called
me and believed the awful things he said about me. Living in an

atmosphere permeated by my father's hatred and rejection, I picked up an image of myself that was not God's image of me.

I became very afraid, very shy, and would not look at people. Sometimes when I ate, my stomach would go into spasms. I developed a stutter and could hardly say my name the first eight years of my life. People laughed at me, so I wouldn't talk.

I was utterly starved for approval, but didn't know how to accept it, or feel deserving of it. Totally devoid of a shred of security or self-respect, I wrestled with fears that every person I met was either going to reject me or hurt me. I became adept at avoiding pain by blending into the background and doing nothing to attract attention.

THE INVISIBLE MAN

By the age of seventeen, after my father tried to choke me to death, I realized I had to get away from home before he killed me during one of his fits of rage. Knowing I'd have to trick him into signing the papers stating I had his permission to join the Army, I told my father that the recruiter wanted to talk with him about the possibility of my going into the service someday. Then I handed Dad the papers, casually explaining that he'd have to sign them in order to give the recruiter permission to visit. When my father signed the papers without even looking them over, I breathed a quiet sigh of relief. Now that I had his permission to join, all I had to do was pass the physical.

When I took the physical, I flunked because I was too skinny. At 5 feet, 11-1/2 inches, I weighed only 109 pounds but had to weigh at least 132 in order to pass.

The recruiter told me to eat bananas because they were fattening and would help me gain weight. So for thirty days, I ate hundreds of bananas. I ate one after another until the very thought of unpeeling another made me want to throw up. But by the end of the month, as far as I could tell, I hadn't gained an ounce.

Since eating bananas hadn't worked, I had to find another way to add weight to my skinny frame. Just then I remembered the sets of small two- and five-pound weights I had ordered from one of those "don't-be-the-skinny-boy-on-the-beach" ads in a magazine. Maybe I hadn't wasted my money after all.

Knowing the recruiter would make me walk to the scale in nothing but my shorts I found three plastic stretch belts and rigged up a harness. I put one belt around my waist and fastened the other belts to it so they'd fit between my legs. Then I carefully attached the weights to the belts, hoping I could wear them unnoticed beneath a pair of big, blousy boxer shorts.

Somehow I managed to make it to the recruiting station dressed in full gear. At one point, tears were running down my face, but I was determined. Stripping to my underwear, I walked to the scales like a little old Chinese man, praying all the way that the weights wouldn't clang together during the ordeal.

When I gingerly stepped on the scales, the guy who had weighed me before exclaimed, "Well, I can't believe it! You're up to exactly 132 pounds."

After lying my way into the service, I strove to avoid the pain of rejection during basic training by becoming the invisible man. I never let myself stand at the head of a line or at the end; instead, I learned to blend into the middle. I always searched for the path of least resistance and the comfortable security of anonymity.

I had no idea just how anonymous I had managed to become until the end of my twelve weeks of basic training at Fort Dix, New Jersey.

Although each of the other 244 men received an assignment to go to his next duty station, I didn't get one. When I came back after the weekend, the barracks were totally empty and the door locked, so I crawled through a window and went to sleep.

The next morning my drill sergeant came in and demanded to know what I was doing there. "This is my bed," I replied.

"No, it's not!" he retorted. "Who are you?"

Keep in mind that I was now over six feet tall and that this particular sergeant had worked with me every day for twelve weeks. Yet I had done such a good job of making myself invisible, the man honestly didn't even recall having seen me.

"Who are you?" he demanded.

"I'm Michael Evans, and this is my company."

"Nope, you don't belong to my company," the exasperated sergeant insisted. To prove his point, he went through the records and found absolutely no information on me. They hadn't even known I was there.

So, I gave him the date I'd arrived and the name of the courses I'd completed. The incredulous sergeant and his superiors kept me there two more months so they could create records for me before I was transferred to Korea.

Although I had studied a world map and had chosen Korea because it was the farthest spot from my home in Massachusetts, the thoughts and fears I longed to escape followed me.

I arrived at the army compound on Mount Wong Tong Ne in the winter of 1964, a few months before the war with Vietnam broke out. I loved the beauty and the quiet solitude as I walked across the mountain each morning for fourteen months, but far too often I found myself reliving the pain of my past.

I remembered the Christian woman in our neighborhood who asked Mother if she could take the children to a local vacation Bible school. Glad to get us out of the house for a few days and rationalizing that just one week of church couldn't hurt us, Mother had agreed. However, once she saw how much we kids enjoyed attending church, Mother told the lady she could take us each week.

When Father began attending church as well, things started turning around for him. He began his own construction company and moved us out of the run-down, government-subsidized housing projects and into a home of our own.

But something was very wrong. Although he attended church on Sunday mornings for several years and said he was a Christian, Father lived a double life. He forced us kids to go to church with him, carried a Bible around and had the Ten Commandments printed on the back of his business cards; yet he thought nothing of paying off city officials for business favors, getting drunk, or abusing us.

I vividly recall the day he came home and announced, "You @#$%^& kids are going to read the Bible and have devotions!" As we huddled around the table together in stunned silence with his open Bible before us, Father flew into a rage, beating first one and then another of us while screaming, "Read it! Read it out loud!"

I recalled the many times my father beat the "truth" out of me for one "crime" or another. Refusing to accept the facts, he slapped, kicked, threatened and questioned until I finally blurted out any lie that satisfied his vicious accusations.

You must be a terrible person, I'd sobbed to myself during those times when I wept all night long, hurting so badly, yet crying softly for fear he might hear and beat me again. *If you weren't such a horrible person, your father wouldn't call you names or do those things to you.*

Ever so gradually, the pain, the shame and the self-hatred spread through me in ever-widening circles like an overturned bottle of ink.

Tormenting fears and the dread of rejection stained all my perceptions and emotions.

All my life I had lived in a state of tension, constantly on guard. Everything and everybody seemed out to get me, eager to mock and inflict more pain. So on Mount Wong Tong Ne I made a decision: Never again would anyone hurt me as my father had. I would take karate and learn to defend myself.

Determined to achieve the only personal goal I'd ever set, I studied with a private instructor and channeled my determination and compulsivity into becoming an expert in the art of self-defense. Blessed with height and quick reflexes, I was a natural. In only six months I was eligible for a second-degree black belt. My abilities in karate seemed to earn admiration from my peers, as well.

But earning that black belt and the acceptance of my peers didn't turn my life around. When the Army transferred me back to Philadelphia to work as a recruiter, all my old fears and insecurities crossed the ocean with me.

To get ahead financially, I took a night job as a waiter in a Marriott Hotel restaurant to supplement my meager Army pay, and got myself a sparsely furnished room at the nearby YMCA. I also bought a car.

Before I could get my belongings moved into my room, someone broke into my car and stole the shirts and suits I'd had custom-made in Korea to fit my long arms and skinny frame. Then for good measure, they trashed the car, tearing the inside to pieces and ripping off the antenna.

Not long after that I'd met a young lady. I'd had only a handful of dates in my life, but this girl was really pretty. So summoning every ounce of courage I had, I asked her out—and she accepted!

I wanted to take her to a really nice place, but all I could manage was the restaurant where I worked. When I ordered a simple ground beef steak, the best I could afford, she laughed at me. Humiliated to tears, I realized the girl had agreed to a date with me, not because she liked me, but because she had assumed I was going to take her to an expensive place and show her a great time.

A day or so later my car still hadn't been repaired, so I was riding a city bus. Sitting beside an open window, I was staring into space as the bus slowed to a stop. I noticed some older kids standing near the corner. Assuming they were waiting for the bus, I slipped back into my reverie. Was I ever wrong! The boys were actually playing a rough game: When a bus rolled to a stop, they would find an open window, jump as high as possible and take a swing at whoever was sitting near the window.

I was staring straight ahead, my thoughts a million miles away, when a fist shot through the window and hit me squarely on the mouth. So great was the force that I fell out of my seat.

By the time I had picked myself up from the floor, the bus was moving again. I slumped dejectedly in my seat, mad at myself and the whole world, rehearsing the rejection and disappointments of the past few days: stolen clothes, a trashed car. Added to that was the first real date I'd had in years laughing at me as if I were an imbecile. And now the crowning insult: Mr. Second-Degree Black Belt, the one who had learned karate for self-defense, had just been hurt by a lucky shot from some street kid!

Back in my room my mind was stuck on my failures, replaying them again and again, like a phonograph needle bouncing back and forth on a scratched record. Realizing I needed something to help shake off my discouragement, I wandered downstairs looking for a book to read.

The title of a paperback caught my attention. It was *The Cross and the Switchblade* by some guy named David Wilkerson. Supposing it was a book on gang wars or street life, I took it back to my room.

But as I read about a skinny preacher sent by God to the streets of New York City to minister to drug addicts, run-aways, and prostitutes through a ministry called Teen Challenge, I sensed the Spirit of God speaking to my heart, dealing with me, reassuring me. God seemed to say, "You need Me. You need Me. I'm with you. I haven't left you since you were eleven years old."

I knew what He said was true. God really had been with me, protecting me, guiding me away from destructive forces and leading me ever closer to Him. I didn't drink or gamble; I'd had no desire to smoke or do drugs. Even in Korea, where all the villages near the Army compounds were filled with prostitutes, I had refused to touch a woman. As far as I knew, I was the only guy out of 245 men in our unit who didn't have a venereal disease.

I hadn't turned my heart away from God. I was still praying, but I sensed a deep, gnawing hunger for more of God and for fellowship with Christians. I had no real relationships to fill the vacuum in my life—no friend to talk with, to pray with, to keep me balanced. I was alone—terribly alone.

Not long after that I found myself on a bus traveling through South Philadelphia instead of having gone straight home from work to change from my Army uniform into street clothes. When I saw a church with a lot of cars in front, I got off the bus and slipped into a back pew.

That night a Christian businessman was giving his testimony, but I tuned him out. Instead of listening, I was thinking: *"You're not telling the truth. You're lying. My father was a 'Christian' businessman, and he was a hypocrite. He didn't care about my mother or us kids. All he cared about was making money and drinking booze, and I'll bet you're just like him!"*

By the end of the man's message, however, the Holy Spirit moved upon me so powerfully I ended up in the prayer room. After almost everyone had left, I was still on my knees weeping. The businessman knelt beside me and said, "It must be hard being a Christian in the service."

Wiping my eyes with the back of my hand, I answered, "I'm not sure if I really am a Christian." After all, I couldn't say I'd had the traditional "born-again" experience, although my encounter with Jesus years before had changed my life. The businessman prayed a simple prayer with me, and I caught a bus back to the "Y".

I spent the next week in my room, reading the New Testament from Matthew to Revelation and reserving the battered rocking chair in the corner for Jesus, just in case He wanted to visit me again.

At the end of that week, I returned to the church. This time I went to that altar at the conclusion of the service. A man I'd never seen before knelt and prayed with me a few minutes, then asked if I could loan him $25. That was a lot of money to me back then, and I didn't have that amount to spare, but I gave it to him anyway. (Gave is the right word. He never paid me back.) After he left, another man prayed with me, and I received the fullness of the Holy Spirit.

A cold, unfriendly wind drove stinging snow in my face and down my collar as I left the church that night. It was late and I'd missed the last bus, so I'd have to walk back to the "Y". As I bent forward, leaning against the wind and trying to ignore the icy numbness in my ears and the tip of my nose, people from the church honked and waved as they drove past.

"See," a whining, tormenting voice seemed to goad, "they still don't care." I just turned up my collar, shoved my hands deeper into my pockets and kept walking. A warm, comforting fire of joy had been kindled in my heart, and I was determined not to let self-pity smother it.

After that night, I began witnessing to people on the streets, telling them about Jesus. But I was still very much alone. A couple of weeks later as I was eating breakfast in a run-down restaurant, tears slipped down my face. "Lord Jesus," I prayed quietly, "I don't even know what an evangelist does, but I know You're calling me to be one. I'm just garbage, but if you can use garbage, I'll give You my life.

More quickly than it takes to tell it, I heard these words from I Corinthians 2:9 deep inside me:

> *"Eye has not seen, nor ear heard,*
> *Nor have entered into the heart of man*
> *The things which God has prepared*
> *for those who love Him."*

Then the Voice added: *"But I will reveal it to you by my Holy Spirit."* There it was again! In His brief appearance to me years before, Jesus had said, "I have a wonderful plan for your life." Now, in different words, He had reaffirmed that promise. Secret, wonderful things were being prepared for me. My part was to love God; His part was to bring it all to pass.

During the time I wasn't working for the Army or at the Marriott, I continued to walk the streets handing out tracts and telling people about Jesus.

Several months after being discharged in June of 1966 I was on the streets witnessing when I ran into some other young people who were also sharing Jesus with people. When they explained that they were with an organization called Teen Challenge and asked me to work with them, something clicked. Remembering how God had used David Wilkerson's book to speak to me, I accepted the invitation.

Not long after that, as the director of Philadelphia Teen Challenge and I were talking, I confided that God had called me to be an evangelist.

"If that's the case," he said, "you need to go to Bible school and prepare."

"But I don't know of any Bible schools."

"There's one in Minneapolis. Why don't you apply there?"

Following his counsel, I applied, and the college accepted me. However, one day in prayer I said, "Lord, I'm ready to go to Bible college in Minneapolis in September. Is that where I'm supposed to go?"

"No," I sensed the Lord saying, "You are to go south. You will not understand it now, but later you will understand the reason why."

So I went back to the director and told him what had happened. I asked if there were any Bible colleges in the south. The moment he mentioned Southwestern Bible College in Texas, I knew it was the place I was supposed to attend. Still, I was a little uneasy.

"Do they persecute Jews there? The gentiles in our neighborhood were really hard on our family. They'd throw tomatoes at our house, call my mother a 'Jew witch' and beat me up in school for being a Jew."

"No, no," the director replied with a chuckle. "You don't have to worry about that. They don't persecute Jews there."

I dreaded telling my parents God had called me to preach and I wanted to go to Bible college in Texas to prepare for the work He had for me. As I had feared, my parents told me I was absolutely nuts and tried everything in their power to keep me from going into the ministry. "You'll not receive a penny of support or an ounce of encouragement from us," they threatened, and they were true to their word.

At Southwestern, I attended classes by day and worked evenings at the freight docks in Dallas to supplement my veteran's benefits. I also picked up a few extra bucks teaching karate to some guys on campus. With the financial pressure off, I could concentrate on seeking God and learning His Word.

I looked forward to the uninterrupted hours I spent in prayer and fasting in the dormitory prayer room. "You need Me; you need Me," God had reminded me back in the run-down room at the "Y," so I sought Him earnestly—not just for more of His love and power, but for the healing of my insecurities and the tormenting pain of rejection.

I longed to know how it felt to experience true security, love and self-respect. Sometimes I felt like crying out, "I am hurting! Please recognize me; please accept me; please love me." But rather than finding a godly counsellor, pouring out my heart and sharing my fears and the pain of the past, I bottled everything up.

And I learned to play the "blame game." By judging and blaming others, I could keep my thoughts focused on their faults and problems instead of my own.

But mostly I blamed my father. My resentment against him smoldered inside me like a low-grade fever, sapping my energy and draining my spiritual resources. Although my heart knew I should forgive him, my mind continued to pile blame upon my father, dwelling on his failures, his cruelties. It was his fault that I hurt so badly inside; his fault that I couldn't trust anyone; his fault that I was so consumed by fear I couldn't even accept a compliment. His brutal rejection was the reason I was afraid to be myself or to risk letting anyone get close to me. Anyone, that is, except for Carolyn...

I met Carolyn when I first arrived at Southwestern and was immediately impressed by the tall, willowy girl with the soft, shy smile and long, beautiful hair. We didn't date, but I became her best friend. Then the guy she was engaged to broke the engagement thirty days before they were to be married. My heart went out to her because of all the pain and rejection I'd gone through as a child, though I'd never dared breathe a word to her about my past.

All summer I took Carolyn out and encouraged her—not to take advantage, but because I genuinely cared about her. I never even held her hand or kissed her; I just wanted to be there for her.

When she returned to campus in the fall, Carolyn asked me to tell her about some really dedicated guys at the college, so I recommended several. When a couple of those relationships didn't work out and she came to me in tears, I told her the same thing each time, "Carolyn, don't be discouraged. God has someone special for you."

About a year later, we each realized who that someone was, because no matter who Carolyn dated, she always wound up talking about me and our friendship.

We became engaged and later married Thanksgiving weekend of 1969. We took two days off from school, drove to Oklahoma City for our honeymoon, and made it back to college with $200 to spare.

Two months later, both Carolyn and I felt the Holy Spirit calling us to go to Arkansas to help begin a Teen Challenge program in that state. We spent the first year of our marriage in a house with twenty-two ex-convicts.

About a year later the Lord led us to Chicago where we worked with Jewish people. There God gave me a life-captivating vision of a world evangelism organization to touch Israel and the nations.

But when I shared my vision with some ministers, they rebuked me and told me I had a "David Wilkinson-type delusion of grandeur." I was told, "We've seen ministers like you before, and you're a dime a dozen. Repent and forget about this foolish vision you claim to have had."

Although I knew the vision was from God and was somehow central to the "wonderful plan" Jesus had promised for my life, the sharp rebuke reinforced my garbage mentality that had plagued me all my life. I had finally opened up to men I thought I could trust, and what had I received? Ridicule and rejection.

For some time I had allowed proud, perfectionistic workaholism to control my life. My heart had become divided: Part of me wanted to do the work of an evangelist and help people find God, but the wounded little boy inside longed for approval and the praise of people who seemed impressed only by how well I performed and how much I produced.

Without even realizing how contrary to God's Word my thinking had become, I built my life around three clever lies: (1) God will love me more if I do more; (2) it's more bold to work than it is to relax; and (3) I must never make a mistake, because mistakes are simply not acceptable.

Added to that unbearable weight was the inescapable fact that I had never truly forgiven my father. But good Christians are supposed to forgive, so I worked hard trying to prove to myself and to God that all was well. I hid my pain because I was on my way to becoming a big-time evangelist, and everybody knows that preachers of the Gospel aren't supposed to hurt.

All the time I was dying inside, living with the gnawing fear that every person I met was going to reject me or hurt me. I learned to look confident and smile widely in order to cover my lack of trust for others. But I couldn't fool everyone. Most people can sense when an individual is not being transparent. The person's conversation is shallow and cold because he holds back and doesn't really share his heart.

That's the way it had been with me year after year. The first link of the tormentor's chain around my neck had been forged in the fires of my father's rejection. Next came the link of bitterness, along with a sickening sense of hopelessness and defeat because I thought I had no self-worth. Wonderful opportunities and successes were coming to me in the ministry, but my sense of unworthiness and fear of failure kept me from enjoying them.

The weight of the chain was becoming more burdensome. You see, when a person doesn't have confidence or hope, he expects everyone to do something for him, and when they don't, in comes anger. I was angry about my past, angry with people who had disappointed me, angry about everything that could even remotely be interpreted as a form of rejection.

But as a minister, I wasn't supposed to be angry, so I had what you might call controlled anger. For the most part, I denied it and suppressed it. Sometimes I vented it on innocent, caring people who got too close.

The next link in the chain was a spirit of fear, because sooner or later, fear always attaches itself to rejection. I received death threats from some in the Jewish community, suffered through attacks from religious people and struggled with problems in my staff until a single day of peace and joy was a thing of the past. I thought everyone was out to get me.

Once the chain was complete, my emotions could be jerked up or down at the whim of the Enemy. A deep, tormenting depression settled on me. It got so bad that I'd have to stop preaching in the middle of a sermon and ask the congregation pray. After that happened almost a dozen times, I stopped preaching for about a year and refused to tell anyone why. I just hid. Eaten alive by fear, anger, rejection and bitterness, I'd sit on the stairs of our national headquarters after everyone had gone home and cry like the broken man I had become.

I don't know how long I would have gone on like that, burning the candle at both ends and wearing out my family and those around me. Mercifully, God drew the line, effectively saying, "That's enough! I have a wonderful plan for your life, but you're about to blow it. You have let unforgiveness and fear of rejection gnaw at your insides until there's only an empty shell left. Now will you deal with it, or shall I?"

That's when I found myself flat on my back in the cardiology ward at the age of thirty-two. *How could this be happening to me, God?* I cried. *What will people think when they hear about this?*

I could just imagine what everyone would say: "Did you hear about Mike Evans? Yeah, heart trouble, and he's so young. He must just be one of those who can't handle the pressure of stress. I wonder what will happen to his ministry; poor guy will probably lose everything. I'm sure the doctors will make him cancel his speaking engagements for months."

Fear washed over me. Fear of what people would say; fear of losing my health; fear of everything! That's when I called to confess my fears to author and friend Jamie Buckingham, and he prayed with me.

After that, God and I had a long heart-to-heart talk. I acknowledged my need to Him. I confessed the anger and bitterness I'd carried against my father for the senseless suffering and years of torment he'd put me through. And somehow as I did, something changed, something became right-side-up in me. God helped me view the injustices through the Cross. Instead of seeing my cruel father, I saw an opportunity to allow God to change me—not the man who had hurt me—but me.

It was a night of confession, a night of cleansing. I reached out to Jesus, and He took my hand and step-by-step began walking me out of the bondage of rejection.

Step One: Understanding What I Was Not and Who He is

At some point during that night in the cardiology ward, Jesus revealed to me the healing truth in a prayer the Apostle Paul had prayed: "that I may know Him and the power of His resurrection and the fellowship of His sufferings..." (Philippians 3:10, NKJV.)

"The fellowship of my suffering," Jesus whispered into my spirit, *"is understanding everything that you are not. The power of the resurrection is understanding everything that I am."*

I was finally beginning to comprehend what I was not: I was not perfect, and no amount of human striving could make me perfect. Nor was I a self-sufficient tower of strength; I was a fallible, frail human being.

Years before in my room at the "Y," Christ had said, "You need Me! You need Me!" And he was so right. I needed Him desperately, for everything I was not, Jesus was.

My fear of rejection had kept me from admitting, even to myself, what I was not. My stubborn pride and ignorance had prevented me from appropriating all that Jesus was.

I was weak and afraid, but that night I drew from Jesus the strength and courage to share with Carolyn—for the first time in our eleven years of marriage—the carefully guarded secrets of my past.

Thankfully, I did not stop there. From that point forward I have continually striven to exchange what I am not for what He is. As Paul wrote in I Corinthians 1:30, "Christ Jesus...became to us *wisdom* from God, and *righteousness* and *sanctification*, and *redemption*." (NASB, Emphasis mine.) Whatever I am not, whatever I need Jesus is.

Step Two: Seeing Myself as God Sees Me

Everyone has his or her favorite Bible character, but for me, Jacob is one of the all-time greats in the Bible. Jacob took advantage of his brother, Esau's, weakness and hunger to cheat him out of his birth-right—the rights of a firstborn son. (See Genesis 25:29-34.) Jacob also tricked his blind, elderly father into giving him the blessing that rightfully belonged to Esau. (See Genesis 27.) As a reward for his deception, Jacob had to leave his home, his parents and every-thing he held dear to keep Esau from killing him.

Face it: This was not a perfect man by any stretch of the imagination. Yet, just look at what God said about Jacob in Isaiah 43:1-3, NIV:

> But now, this is what the LORD says—
> he who created you, Jacob,
> he who formed you, Israel:
> "Do not fear, for I have redeemed you;
> I have summoned you by name; you are mine.
> When you pass through the waters,
> I will be with you;
> and when you pass through the rivers,
> they will not sweep over you.
> When you walk through the fire,
> you will not be burned;
> the flames will not set you ablaze.
> For I am the LORD your God,
> the Holy One of Israel, your Savior;
> I give Egypt for your ransom,
> Cush and Seba in your stead.

And God addressed the wonderful words in verse four to the same man:

Since you are precious and honored in my sight,
and because I love you,
I will give people in exchange for you,
nations in exchange for your life.

How could God say that to a man who had tricked his twin brother and deceived his father—a man who had always counted on his cleverness, work, status and power to give him identity and fulfillment? God could say those things because, after years of conniving and manipulating, Jacob had an encounter with God:

> And Jacob was left alone, and a Man wrestled with him until daybreak... Then He said, Let Me go, for day is breaking. But [Jacob] said, I will not let You go unless You declare a blessing upon me. [The Man] asked him, What is your name? And [in shock of realization, whispering] he said, Jacob [supplanter, schemer, trickster, swindler]! And He said, Your name shall be called no more Jacob [supplanter], but Israel [contender with God]; for you have contended *and* have power with God and with men and have prevailed, (Genesis 32:24, 26-28.)

God had always been aware of the weaknesses in Jacob's character, but He had also seen what Jacob could be. Therefore, in His love, God brought Jacob to a place of desperation, a place of decision, a place of self-discovery.

You and I, like Jacob, must come to that place where we wrestle with God—bringing our questions to Him, making room for Him, refusing to let Him go until He blesses and changes us. Only in God's presence will we come to know our identity—not just the person we have been, but the person we can become.

God is the one who has redeemed us, called us by name and claimed us as His own. Only through a dynamic encounter with Him can we discover ourselves and our true mission in life.

The God who encountered Jacob in a barren wilderness and brought him face-to-face with himself, used a cardiology ward to help bring my identity and purpose into focus. Don't be afraid of God, for your ultimate good brings you to your own personal place of desperation, decision, and self-discovery. If you will wrestle with Him there, if you will refuse to release Him until He blesses you and reveals your true identity and purpose, you will eventually win your battle with rejection. Your old opinions of yourself and the opinions of others will matter less and less as you come to believe that you are what God says you are: Redeemed; called by name; His very own; Precious in His sight; honored, beloved!

Step Three: Confessing Faults, Concealing our Virtues

For many years I remained locked in a struggle with two false, unrealistic images of myself.

One image, formed in the early years of my childhood and constantly reinforced during the seventeen years I lived at home, had been shaped by what my father thought of me. To him I was an illegitimate (or so he thought) piece of garbage that did not deserve to be loved. I was an unwanted chunk of subhuman scum that would never amount to anything. This Mike Evans was an inadequate, unlovable, inferior, under-educated failure who would be viewed with disgust and disappointment by anyone who really got to know him.

But I had also carefully shaped a fantasy image of myself, a totally unrealistic idol of the superhuman person I longed to be. And along with that idol I had inscribed a list of goals so impossible I could never achieve them. This Mike Evans was the perfect husband, perfect father, the perfect evangelist. He never had a failure, never made a mistake. Although he was not faster than a speeding bullet and could not leap tall buildings in a single bound, he could solve any problem and master any opponent.

"Mr. Perfect" with all his remarkable virtues was the image I sought to present to others. "Mr. Inferior Failure" was the Mike Evans I kept hidden away under lock and key.

Through years of practice, I had become very skillful at concealing my weaknesses, fear and failures while broadcasting my virtues and successes. But this was exactly opposite of what Jesus taught us to do.

Jesus told us to conceal our virtues (giving, fasting, praying, winning people to God, acts of mercy) and to confess our faults. Why? Because of Solomon's words in Proverbs: "As a man thinketh in his heart, so is he" (Proverbs 23:7, KJV.)

Psychologist O. Hobart Mowrer summed it up for us when he said that we become what we conceal. Did you get it? Whatever is hidden in our hearts eventually becomes our self-concept.

No wonder I felt inferior, rejected, and inadequate. Every weakness or failure that pointed in that direction I had carefully concealed. Now I was realizing the importance, the priceless value, of the New Testament command: "Confess to one another therefore your faults (your slips, your false steps, your offenses, your sins) and pray [also] for one another, that you may be healed *and* restored [to a spiritual tone of mind and heart], (James 5:16, Amplified.)

But does that mean we are to confess our faults indiscriminately, to just anyone who happens along? No. James directs us to confess our faults to a godly person to whom we can be accountable, a person who cares about us enough to pray earnestly for our healing. However, the Word of God also teaches that if we have hurt or disappointed an individual, we must be willing to make ourselves vulnerable, go to them and confess our wrong, then ask their forgiveness.

I had always been too proud of my weaknesses to ask another for help. I was too hungry for acceptance and approval to admit the mistakes I'd made. I told you in Chapter One how Jesus enabled me to go to my father and open my heart to him, admitting my mistakes, confessing my failures and begging his forgiveness.

The presence of God came upon my father as he sobbed out to me that he should have been imprisoned for the things he had done to me. And then my father confided that he, too, had been abused as a child. He also told me that as a young man, he had served God and even been called into the ministry, but had turned his back on God and His calling.

I will never forget those minutes when my father and I confessed our faults one to another and wept and prayed together. Unfortunately, the story does not end with "and they lived happily ever after." That's for fairy tales, not real life.

COPING WITH ONGOING REJECTION

I always hate to talk about this because I'm concerned it will discourage people, but I make myself say it anyway. It's a lot better to know up-front that even after you have forgiven your abuser, even though he/she may also have asked your forgiveness, the pain and rejection may not be over.

Some abusers want to change, but they simply don't know how. They're afraid that if they ever break down, admit their failures and make themselves vulnerable, they will be rejected.

On the other hand, some abusers are perfectly content to stay the way they are. They do not wish to change. They do not want to see their blind spots. They do not care about the way you feel, and have no interest in communicating with you. They simply want it their way. Therefore, you are the one who has to learn to do things differently.

These methods of handling hurt and rejection are a waste of time: Arguing, defending yourself, threatening, screaming, sullen silence, trying to force the person to see it or do it your way, pouting, self-pity.

The Bible says it this way:

> Never return evil for evil or insult for insult (scolding, tongue-lashing, berating), but on the contrary blessing [praying for their welfare, happiness, and protection, and truly pitying and loving them]. For *know that* to this you have been called, that you may yourselves inherit a blessing [from God—that you may obtain a blessing as heirs, bringing welfare and happiness and protection], (I Peter 3:9, Amplified.)

My relationship with my father has gone through many ups and downs in the years since the Lord sent me to confess my faults and ask his forgiveness. I love my father, and have truly forgiven him. However, sometimes I wonder if he had trouble forgiving himself.

Early in 1991, I called my father just to say, "I love you." His response caught me totally off-guard.

"You're a hypocrite, just like some of those other guys who've been caught in sin!" he screamed angrily.

"Dad," I gasped, "what have I done? Tell me and I'll repent."

Every syllable dripped with sarcasm as he retorted, "I don't know your specific sin, but I'm waiting for you to get saved."

I was too stunned, too emotionally drained, to respond.

"Do me a favor," he continued acrimoniously, "when I die, don't come to my funeral. I don't want any hypocrites there."

I said good-bye and hung up the phone, struggling to hide my ragged emotions. Feeling sick and shaken, I buried my face in my hands and cried, "When, God? When is this rejection going to end? In all these years my father has never so much as sent a birthday or Christmas card to me or one of my children. He's never visited in our home. And now, for no reason, he calls me a hypocrite and orders me not to come to his funeral."

The next morning I was really hurting—not just for myself, but for my father—so I decided to take my son, Michael, fishing. Maybe the fresh air and some fellowship with my bubbly, chatty six-year-old would help soothe the tenseness and pain inside.

I showed Mikey where to cast his hook, then deep in thought I settled back to soak up the warm sun. Eventually, he got his line tangled in a nearby tree. Still subdued, I worked the line loose and gave it back to him. I was unaware that my silence was troubling to him until Mikey stared up at me and asked, "Daddy, are you mad at me?"

"No, son," I assured him, patting his shoulder. "Daddy's not mad at you."

A while later Mikey's hook snagged on something else. As I quietly worked it free and handed it back to him, he again asked, "Daddy, are you mad at me?"

Squatting down so I could look in his eyes, I answered, "No, no, Michael, Daddy's not mad at you. I've just got a lot on my mind this morning."

He nodded, and I assumed he understood. But a few minutes after we'd returned home, Mikey brought me a tightly folded sheet of yellow paper he had torn from one of my notepads. I unfolded it and saw that he had drawn a big, lopsided heart. Inside the heart were little stick figures of himself and me holding hands and carrying fishing poles. On my pole Mikey had drawn a big fish and on his pole, a little fish. Carefully tucked inside the folder paper was $1.29 in change that he had earned doing small chores around the house. I knew it was all the money the little guy had in the world.

"Puzzle?" I said, "I really like the picture, son, but what's your money doing in here?"

"I want to give it to you, Daddy," he replied solemnly.

Tears welled in my eyes. "Mikey, I can't take your money." He insisted, "That's all the money I have, and a dad is worth more than $1.29."

Forgetting about trying to hold back the tears, I grabbed Michael and pulled him tightly against my chest. God was talking to me through a six-year-old boy, and He had my undivided attention.

Like little Mikey, I would gladly give everything I owned in exchange for my father's love and acceptance and approval. But money and material things couldn't buy what it would take to touch my father's heart and make it whole so he could love. Only God could do that. Until that happened, it was my business to love my father, unconditionally. It was God's business to change him.

For years, I paid my father's house and car payments without any thanks from him. This was nothing new, as I had never had a word of affirmation from him. At some point, we reached an uneasy truce, and in the last weeks of Dad's life, he willed all of his belongings to me—everything he owned. Because God's favor on my life has been so bounteous I was able to in turn give his entire estate to my six siblings. I spoke at his funeral and talked about his record as a war hero and how much he loved his mother. Sadly, those were the only good things I could say about him.

Since it is the truth that sets us free, every day I attempt to apply the truth God has taught me by:

1. Understanding what I am not and who He is.

2. Seeing myself as God sees me—redeemed, called by His name, His own, precious, honored and beloved.

3. Confessing my faults and concealing my virtues.

How can one overcome rejection? I know this: It can't be accomplished by will power, human effort, or the mere passage of time. Time doesn't heal—Jesus does. So keep your heart focused upon Him.

A WORD FOR WOUNDED SPARROWS

Do you know what it is to be despised and rejected? Are you one of those fragile little eggs that somehow managed to hatch, even in a broken nest? If so, let me assure you that the Lord's loving eyes are upon every wounded sparrow that has fallen to the ground.

You don't have to be perfect. You don't have to perform. But if you ever want to fly, you must release the painful weights of the past and spread the wings of your soul to embrace the healing, renewing winds of the Holy Spirit. Once you've done that, then get ready, little bird—you're about to soar!

REPLACING LIES WITH TRUTH

Many childlike perceptions and beliefs are inaccurate and must be revised. For example, you don't still believe in Santa Claus, the Tooth Fairy, or the Easter Bunny, do you? Yet many adults continue to believe the old lies they heard as children from their abusers.

Instead of seeing abuse or rejection as something done to us, the little child inside still sees it as something we caused by our own faults and failures.

Are you still tenaciously clinging to old perceptions and beliefs about yourself that need to be revised? If so, the following exercises may help lift the burden of self-blame and self-rejection you accepted from your abuser.

1. On a separate sheet of paper, list all the bad things your abuser told you about yourself over the years. Bring them out into the open and look at them in the light.

2. List all the bad things you say to yourself when you fail or feel insecure.

3. Destroy those lists in whatever manner you wish—tear them into pieces; burn them; dig a hole and bury them.

4. Now write a letter to the little child within you, focusing on the loving, tender things you, as an adult, would say to a child who has been abused as you were. Say the things you wish you could have heard as a small child.

❖ 13 ❖

REBUILDING SHATTERED
SELF-ESTEEM

*"We are haunted by an ideal life, and it is because we have
within us the beginning and the possibility of it."*

BISHOP PHILLIPS BROOKS[110]

HOW DO YOU SEE YOURSELF? That's your self-image.
How do you feel about yourself? That's your self-concept. What
value and sense of worth do you possess internally? That's your
sense of self-esteem.

EVALUATING YOUR SELF-ESTEEM

Before we talk about self-esteem, perhaps you would like to evalu-
ate your own. The checklist below may provide some interesting insights and help you determine specific areas on which you
need to work. Use the following key to rate yourself: U=usually;
S=sometimes; and R=Rarely

_____ My childhood was marked by one or more of the following:
parental abuse, parental neglect, overbearing parental
authority.

_____ I fear opening up and being real with others; I'm afraid they
will reject me.

_____ I get discouraged easily because I don't have confidence in my ability and I'm afraid I might fail if I try something new.

_____ I rarely trust my own judgment when making decisions, so it takes me a long time to make up my mind.

_____ People sometimes think I'm arrogant because I have trouble admitting that I'm wrong or asking for forgiveness.

_____ I find it difficult to forgive others.

_____ A deep need for approval and personal worth drives me to be a high achiever.

_____ I habitually over-schedule because I'm afraid to say no.

_____ I believe my significance and security have to be earned by performance and production.

_____ I seek the praise of others in order to affirm my own worth.

_____ I feel acceptable only when I achieve and perform.

_____ I often put others down in an attempt to lift myself up. I critically pass judgment on how things are done or handled.

_____ As a child, I was often told that I could do better if I would only try harder.

_____ Looking for acceptance compels me to be a perfectionist.

_____ I work hard and accomplish much, but am rarely satisfied with that work. If I perform up to my standards, I quickly raise the bar even higher.

_____ I have fallen into the trap of seeking the approval and compliments of others by criticizing myself.

_____ I find that I try to escape reality through television, drugs, compulsive shopping, or overeating.

_____ I seek identity through association with successful, important people.

Study the responses marked with "U." Which two or three areas tend to be major struggles for you? In this chapter as we discuss the formation of self-concept and the effects of high or low self-esteem, you may find helpful insights into your problem areas. You will also learn how a positive sense of self-esteem can be developed.

HOW THE SELF-CONCEPT IS FORMED

A human self-concept consists of two ingredients: a sense of identity answering the question, "Who am I?" and a sense of self-esteem answering the question, "What am I worth?"

At birth, a baby has no sense of identity or self-esteem. Only as the infant begins interacting with others does he acquire a sense of who he is and what he is worth. A child's self-concept is shaped by what he believes his parents or primary caretakers think of him. In the early, formative years—between three and five years—the child's self-concept comes into focus. His view includes impressions, thoughts and feelings which have accumulated in his mind since birth and have, for the most part, grown out of his interaction with those responsible for taking care of him.

THE EFFECTS OF POSITIVE SELF-ESTEEM

Our self-esteem and our evaluations of others play a crucial role in our happiness, effectiveness and interactions with others. For example, individuals who possess a firm self-identity, a clear concept of themselves, tend to be better able to cope with the world around them. People who possess an overall positive evaluation of themselves are more open to relationships and are more likely to participate in a group to which they belong.

In the late 1960s, Developmental Psychologist Stanley Coopersmith conducted a well-known study of self-esteem and its development using a sample of ten- to twelve-year-old boys. Coopersmith found that the boys with high self-esteem were active and expressive individuals who tended to do well both academically and socially. They were eager to express opinions, did not avoid disagreement, and were not overly sensitive to criticism. These boys were optimistic about their abilities, set high goals for themselves, and generally achieved those goals.[111]

THE EFFECTS OF POOR SELF-ESTEEM

Insecurity, fearfulness and poor self-confidence are just some of the attitudes that can result from low self-esteem. For example, boys with low self-esteem in Coopersmith's study presented a picture of discouragement, depression and anxiety. In social situations they did not express or defend themselves. They avoided exposing themselves to attention and shrank from contact with others. The boys had little faith in their abilities and rarely met with success.[112]

In the mid-1960s, sociologist Morris Rosenberg studied self-esteem. He concluded that, generally, the individual with a poor view of himself:

> » Is more vulnerable in interpersonal
>   relationships;
> » Is deeply hurt by criticism;
> » Is more awkward with others;
> » Finds it hard to make conversation;
> » Does not initiate contacts;
> » Assumes others think poorly of him or do not
>   particularly like him;
> » Feels relatively lonely and isolated.[113]

Later investigations have obtained similar results.

Another symptom of low self-esteem is fearfulness in expressing love. A person whose self-worth is extremely low may be unable to love himself. When self-love is difficult, loving someone else is also difficult. Even if they feel love, people with low self-esteem may have difficulty expressing it, since they believe they have little love to give and that their expressions of love have no worth.

DEVELOPING A CHILD'S SELF-ESTEEM

How can the development of self-esteem in children be encouraged? Experienced counsellors and studies conducted by Coopersmith and others have identified several principles important to the development of a child's internal sense of worth and value.

1. Demonstrate Genuine Interest in the Child

In judging ourselves, we often do so from the perspective of the important people in our lives. Our self-concept is greatly determined by the views others have of us.

In Coopersmith's study, a boy high in self-esteem had parents who showed a great deal of interest in him. They knew their son's friends and spent time discussing problems and engaging in joint activities with him. These parents clearly indicated that they regarded their son as a significant person, worthy of their interest. As a result, the boy came to regard himself in a favorable light.[114]

On the other hand, parents of a boy low in self-esteem demonstrated less interest in the boy's welfare, were less likely to spend time with him, were less likely to know his friends or activities, and rarely considered his opinion in family decisions.

2. Set Consistent Standards for Behavior

Coopersmith found that parents of the boy high in self-esteem set high standards for their son's behavior and were consistent in enforcing the rules.

Parents of the boy low in self-esteem tended to be permissive, having no clear-cut, consistent standards for his behavior, yet dealing out harsh punishment when he gave them trouble.[115]

3. Provide Regular Feedback on Importance & Value as a Person

Coopersmith's stucy revealed that low self-esteem boys did not receive daily feedback about their importance as persons. As a result, they came to have doubts *about their own value and effectiveness.*[116]

4. Provide Positive Day-to-Day Personal Relationships

On the basis of his findings, Coopersmith pointed out the fallacy of a number of ideas about what contributes to self-esteem. Surprisingly, a positive self-image did not seem to be related to physical attractiveness, height, social class, or an outstanding ability in a particular area.

Coopersmith concluded that a good opinion of oneself does not require external signs of success such as appearance or material possessions. Instead, it stems from our day-to-day positive, personal relationships with parents, teachers, and peers.[117]

5. Develop a Strong Emotional Bond Between Child and Parents

Many clinicians believe the emotional bond between child and parent is the most important factor in the development of a child. Emotional bonding is certainly a vital factor in the development of a positive self-concept. Children who are denied a strong emotional bond with their mother and father must go through life compensating for this lack. Many experts believe that the most extensive problem for both boys and girls is the lack of a strong emotional bond with their father.

6. *Meet the Child's Emotional and Relational Needs*

Traditional masculinity can be devastating on men's relationship with their children. A father may rely on his wife to relate to the children for him. Whatever closeness he has with his daughter is more likely to be based on illusion and image than on actual information about himself, and his relationship with his son is often surrounded by competition. The message too often conveyed by such a father is: It's not who you are as a person, what you are inside, or establishing meaningful relationships that counts; it's how much you produce, how well you preform; how "macho" you are.

Unfortunately, a boy's lessons in emotional inexpressiveness and competition come early. Boys are taught verbally, or by example, that the one who comes first, who is born first, who earns more, or who scores higher is better. But what if a boy doesn't happen to fit one or more of those categories? What happens to his fragile sense of self-esteem?

On the basis of an in-depth study of 370 men over a period of time, Samuel Osherson, author of *Finding our Fathers: The Unfinished Business*

of Manhood, concludes: "Boys grow into manhood with a wounded father within, a conflicted
inner sense of masculinity rooted in men's experience of their father's as rejecting, incompetent,
or absent."[118]

Many fathers have little or no problem in fully committing themselves to a lifetime of hard work in order
to support their families economically. But what they do
have trouble doing is meeting the relational and emotional needs of their wives and children.

Trying to achieve the unrealistic standards of hyper-
masculinity cripples men emotionally. It prevents them
from establishing bonds of intimacy with their children,
with their wives, and with their male friends. Their
masculine restrictiveness does not allow them to love
or relate fully.

Osherson believes that as a result of a distant relationship with their fathers:

Men carry around as adults a burden of vulnerabil-
ity, dependency, or emptiness within themselves, still
grieving, reliving a time when going to Mother for
help as they wanted to do was inappropriate, and they
wouldn't or couldn't go to Father with the confusion,
anger, or sadness they felt. When men are put in touch
with their pain today, they respond ambivalently—with
rage or shame, attempting to prove their independence,
as well as with curiosity and a desire to deal with the
wounds they feel.[119]

If we are honest, most of us would have to confess
that the majority of parenting we see around us—even

in the church—is, in reality, mothering. Fathers and mothers need to be involved jointly in rearing their children; however, the father's contribution must not be merely on a surface level. It must be significant enough to establish deep emotional bonding with his children.

But fathers must understand that deep emotional bonding means more than saying, "I love you," or "I'm proud of you." A verbal expression of love without a corresponding investment of time in the relationship comes across as superficial. Such shallow expressions of love are difficult for children to believe and accept.

Grandfathers, male relatives, men in the church, and other godly role models can be called upon to help fill the gap in the hearts of children when a father's influence is missing. And remember, if you are a single mom, you have the pledge of God's own overshadowing presence and protection. Take this promise and make it your own:

> A father of the fatherless, a defender of widows, *Is* God in His holy habitation. God sets the solitary in families; He brings out those who are bound into prosperity; But the rebellious dwell in a dry *land,* (Psalm 68: 5,6, NKJV.)

7. Develop a Relationship of Trust

Parents must also learn to trust their children. A child who does not experience trust can develop a negative self-image—"I am a person who is not to be trusted."

Parents who do not trust their children will seek to maintain control over them. On the other hand, the trust parents place in their children will encourage them to be trustworthy. Eventually, the children will learn to trust themselves and others.

PRINCIPLES FOR BUILDING SELF-ESTEEM IN ADULTS

We have examined factors important to the development of a positive self-esteem in children. But what about adults with low self-esteem? Can a low level of self-esteem in an adult be altered? Thankfully, the answer is yes.

Now, let's talk about you: Did your parents, for whatever reason, fail to help you develop a positive sense of self-esteem? If so, here are four basic practical steps you can take to raise your self-esteem:

1. *Stay Away from Negatives*

The pages of the Bible are filled with stories of beautiful friendships. However, the Scriptures also describe relationships that were weakened or had to be totally dissolved: Abraham and Lot, Samuel and Saul, Paul and Demas to name a few.

The Bible gives clear-cut guidelines as to the types of people we should choose as close friends as well as characteristics of friendship we should avoid. For example, Psalm 1:1 warns us not to walk in the counsel of the ungodly, stand submissive and inactive in the path where sinners walk, or sit down to relax and rest where the scornful and mockers gather.

Proverbs 13:20 declares that if we walk with wise men we shall be wise, but if we associate with fools we will become fools. Proverbs 20:19 counsels us not to associate with those who reveal secrets and talk too freely. Proverbs 22:24-25 urges us not to make friends with people given to anger, lest we learn their ways.

Although it can be a difficult process, reevaluate your friendships. Ask yourself the following questions which may help determine whether certain relationships are having an adverse effect on you:

1. Is my friend more critical than complimentary?

2. Does this individual habitually judge and criticize others and laugh at their dreams?

3. Does the person always seem to be siphoning my energy and time through useless talk?

4. Does the individual frequently take advantage of my kindness or generosity, use me, belittle me, or treat me disrespectfully?

5. Does the person lead me closer to God or farther away?

6. Is this person given to gossip, bursts of temper, and to stirring up strife and discord between others?

7. If I were to rate our friendship on a scale from one (negative: tears me down and brings out the worst in me) to seven (positive: strengthens me and brings out the best in me), would I have to give the relationship a rating of four or less?

If, after answering those questions, you realize that a friendship is constantly breaking you down instead of building you up, choose the option best for you. You can set limits and learn to say no, realigning the friendship according to biblical standards and principles, while continuing to stay in occasional contact. Or you can get out of the relationship altogether and begin developing other quality friendships.

Never hesitate to minister to hurting people as God leads, but discern the difference between ministry and being in covenant with someone who has a bad spirit. Negative relationships can keep you bound to the past, sap your strength and joy, and damage your growing sense of self-esteem.

In addition to negative relationships, what other negatives are tearing down your self-esteem? Negative environments? Negative books, magazines, television shows or movies? Negative music? What about those junk foods in the pantry or refrigerator that drain your energy, put on the extra pounds and make you feel bad about yourself? That's a big negative to avoid.

You see, when we talk about building our self-esteem, it doesn't do any good to wander off into some idealistic, philosophical never-never land. When it comes to building self-esteem, there are few, if any, shortcuts. It's hard work, but the results are worth it!

2. Stop Comparing

One of the central tasks of life is to value and accept ourselves, even as we try to improve. This helps to keep our self-esteem high.

An important secret to self-acceptance and over-coming the inferior, guilty feelings that go with low self-esteem is found in the Parable of the Talents taught by Jesus in Matthew 25:14-20. Three servants were entrusted with various sums of money, "each according to his ability."

Through wise investments, the servant who received five talents and the one who received two talents doubled their master's money. But the servant who received only one talent dug a hole and hid the money.

The Bible makes it clear that the master knew each of his servant's abilities. He was very much aware that this third servant wasn't a financial wizard, and he didn't expect him to be. The master simply gave the servant the amount of money he was able to handle.

Yet because the servant didn't feel he had the financial skills the other two servants had, he let feelings of inferiority and fear of failure prevent him from doing even as simple and safe a thing as putting the money in the bank and allowing it to draw interest.

Where did the servant make a mistake? Actually, he failed on two accounts: First, he saw the master as a hard, demanding, unfair man. Secondly, the servant made the mistake of comparing himself to others and envying what they had instead of accepting himself for what he was and using what he had. Because he was not a five-talent or two-talent servant, the one-talent servant buried his talent and made no gain or improvement whatsoever. He refused to try to accomplish anything just because he didn't have the ability to do everything.

Someone put it like this: "The five-talent or the two-talent man is tempted to try to do it all; the one-talent man sits back and lets them do it all because he has only one talent."

Do you know what God's Word says about people like the one-talent, bury-your-gift-in-the-dirt servant? "When they measure themselves with themselves and compare themselves with one another, they are without understanding and behave unwisely," (II Corinthians 10:12, Amplified.)

Comparing ourselves with others is a useless, frustrating, paralyzing path that will lead us straight to an inferiority complex. The point of the parable is that we are to live in reality, be grateful for what God has given us and use our abilities to glorify Him. Only when we accept ourselves for what we are, do we become real people.

There's a second point to the Parable of the Talents: Use it or lose it. When the unfaithful servant confessed that he had dug a hole and hidden his talent, the angry master ordered:

> "You wicked, lazy servant! So you knew that I
> harvest where I have not sown and gather where
> I have not scattered seed? Well then, you should
> have put my money on deposit with the bankers,
> so that when I returned I would have received it
> back with interest," (Matthew 25:28, NIV.)

Because of her feelings of inferiority and a series of disappointments, an extremely gifted young soprano stopped singing. After several sad, unfulfilling years, she said, "People always told me if I didn't use my talent, God would take it from me. I don't know about that, but I can tell you this: I may have not lost my talent to sing, but I lost my song."

If you want to develop a positive sense of self-esteem, you must stop comparing. As blind and deaf Helen Keller said, "So much has been given to me I have no time to ponder over that which has been denied."

3. Start Forgetting

If you want to develop a positive sense of self-esteem, start forgetting. You must leave the things that are behind before you can reach ahead. Paul said, "Forgetting what lies behind and reaching forward to those things which are ahead, I press toward the goal..." (Philippians 3:13.) But how can you forget the past?

Actually, in Philippians 3:13, the word *forget* (epilanthanomai) is better translated "neglect." Paul is speaking of forsaking and willfully neglecting the past, not laboring to wipe it from your mind. Forgetting the past isn't a matter of not remembering the hurts or failures; it means to no longer allow old hurts and failures to rule you.

Like an emotional pack rat, have you allowed your soul to become crammed with useless fears and rusty old hurts that should have been discarded long ago?

If your heart is cluttered and constantly concerned with former things, something new and wonderful can be ready to spring forth and you won't even know it or be ready for it because you're so preoccupied with the past. As God commanded through Isaiah the prophet:

"Forget the former things;
do not dwell on the past.
See, I am doing a new thing!
Now it springs up; do you not perceive it?
I am making a way in the wilderness
and streams in the wasteland,
(Isaiah 43:18-19, NIV.)

Do you want God's new thing? New relationships, new dreams, new attitudes, a new you? Then forget the past. Refuse to allow old hurts, memories and fears rule you any longer.

4. Simply Admit and Ask

Are you struggling to rebuild shattered self-esteem and find purpose and direction in life when everything seems to be spiraling downward? Admit that you're too weak to fight alone. Ask God to take over.

If you and I are to experience healing and wholeness, our self-perception must be reshaped from one who has been devalued to one who has value in the sight of God. But to reach that goal, we need more than a strong will and faith in ourselves. We need God to take us by the hand and walk us through the rough places and the smooth places. We need a heavenly Father to encourage us, instill confidence and a sense of self-worth in us and believe in us.

If it's hard for you to believe in a God like that, admit your unbelief. Tell God exactly where you are in your struggle to know and trust Him. Ask for His help. When you do, the greatest, most powerful, most loving

Father in the universe will begin revealing Himself to you. And once you begin to understand who He really is, you will never, ever be the same.

BUILDING YOUR SELF-ESTEEM

1. Remember the "Evaluating your Self-Esteem" checklist at the beginning of the chapter? Of the questions you marked "Usually," list three or four that have been major problem areas for you in the past:

   a. _____

   b. _____

   c. _____

   d. _____

2. We talked about four steps for building your self-esteem: (a) Stay away from negatives; (b) Stop comparing; (c) Start forgetting; (d) Simply admit and ask.

Take a moment to look over the three or four major problem areas you listed above. Which of the four steps can you take to deal with each problem area? In order for you to take that step, what specific actions must be taken, what specific changes must be made?

   a. Problem area: _____

   Step to take: _____

   Specific Action or Change: _____

   _____

   b. Problem area: _____

   Step to take: _____

   Specific Action or Change: _____

   _____

c. Problem area: _____

  Step to take: _____

  Specific Action or Change: _____

  _____

d. Problem area: _____

  Step to take: _____

  Specific Action or Change: _____

  _____

Take a moment to bow your head and ask God for the courage and strength to take those steps and make those changes in your life.

❦ 14 ❦

FINIDNG A GOD YOU
CAN BELIEVE IN

To the question, "Where is God when it hurts?"
author, Dr. Paul Brand replied, "He is in you, the
one hurting, not in it, the thing that hurts.[120]

ALL HUMAN BEINGS have three basic needs: 1) self-worth,
2) intimacy with others, and 3) intimacy with God. However when it
comes to number three, many survivors of abuse end up with a very
fragile faith—or horrifyingly, no faith at all.

As one victim explained:

> I was in a very conservative religious group for
> twenty years. For a long time I thought Jesus could heal
> me. When I was thirty-eight, I went to hypnotherapy
> as a last resort to cure the intense migraines I suffered.
> That's when I began to remember the sexual abuse. The
> first thing I thought was "What kind of God have I been
> believing in?"
>
> A little girl had been beaten and raped and God did
> nothing about it. I got really angry. So I went to my min-
> ister and he gave me this cock-and-bull story about how
> God wasn't responsible. It was all man's badness. He
> told me I shouldn't be angry at God.

The more I remembered, the more I realized that God didn't care about me at all. And if He didn't care, He wasn't who I thought He was. Then, who was He?

It's been an incredible loss. The spiritual side of me, which had been nurtured all my life, doesn't have a place to go. It's been very painful. I lost my sense of roots, my sense of purpose. All my friends in the church rejected me. I haven't been able to find a God I can believe in.[121]

So much senseless suffering; so many unanswered questions. It's like trying to put together a 10,000-piece jigsaw puzzle with no picture for reference. Tired of trying and sick of simplistic explanations, some hurting people angrily shove the puzzle aside, turn their backs and stalk away.

But life's complex puzzle does have a "picture guide" to go by. What is that guide? A God we can believe in! Once we discover Him, all the other pieces begin to make sense and begin to fall into place.

WHAT DOES YOUR GOD LOOK LIKE?

Noticing how busily her little boy was coloring, a mother asked, "What are you drawing, honey?"

"I'm drawing a picture of God."

Suppressing a chuckle, the mother asked, "But how can you draw God's picture? No one knows what He looks like."

Coloring furiously, the boy replied, "Maybe so, but they're sure gonna know when I get through with my picture."

If you were to draw a picture of God as you perceive Him, what would your God look like? Which of the following descriptions would most clearly resemble God as you picture Him?

» An angry giant with a hammer in his hand.

» A smiling shepherd with a lamb on his shoulder.

» A doddering old man dozing in a rocking chair while all around the helpless and innocent are starving, suffering and dying.

» A giant thumb flattening a helpless ant.

» An open hand with a tiny sparrow calmly perched on the thumb, cheerfully pecking away at a bread crumb.

» A cosmic scientist in a white coat, taking careful notes as he peers curiously through a microscope at ant-sized human beings suffering all sorts of atrocities.

I asked you to participate in that little exercise for three reasons. First, it is important for you to be aware of the mental picture you have of God because of the major role the image plays in the purpose and meaning you attribute to life and in the way you interpret its tragedies, trials and triumphs. A healthy view of God prepares you to respond to all the events of your life—the good, the bad, and the ugly—in the most constructive way possible.

Second, the impression you have of God is very important since the way you picture Him determines how you will relate to Him. Your concept of God shapes your basic emotional attitude toward Him: trust, love, anger, fear.

Third—and equally important—your picture of God also determines how you believe He relates to you.

YOUR GOD-CONCEPT

The view you have of God, the way you picture Him in your mind, is called your God-concept. It is a composite of mental images, thoughts and feelings which have accumulated in your mind since birth. These images, thoughts and feelings give you your understanding of God.

Although there may be no evidence of religious thinking during the first two years of life, a baby develops religious-like attitudes and behaviors in his relationship with his parents during this time that he will later transfer to God—behaviors such as trust, awe, fear, comfort and joy.

All of a child's impressions, thoughts and feelings of a religious nature interact with his views of his parents to form his God-concept. Your image of God will probably reflect your parents' own concept of God. In addition, the way you view your parents—especially your father—will help shape your God-concept.

Stop for a moment and answer this question: What is the first thing that comes to mind when I think of the word "father?"

Do you know what I used to think? I thought of anger, rage, bitterness, rejection, condemnation, ridicule. Why? I never knew acceptance of love from my father. I never heard those words used in relation to me.

When I think of the word "father," certain memories always push to the forefront of my mind: Like the time I soiled my pants when I was three years old, and he beat me, and beat me, and beat me.

Or I recall those freezing cold winter evenings when I was nine or ten years old and my father sent me out at night to shovel snow in the shopping centers where his construction company had jobs going. I remember shivering and asking myself, *Why is he making me do this?* I always knew that in the morning my father would curse me and knock the living daylights out of me because I hadn't done the job well enough to suit him.

I remember how I worked three jobs when I was fifteen and

sixteen and made $200 each week. I took every dime I had and gave it to my parents, brothers and sisters. I didn't want to have bitterness in my heart toward anyone. I just wanted love and acceptance.

I recall my father following me down the street when I left home at seventeen to join the Army. He screamed curses at me. The last words I heard him yell as I turned the corner were, "You punk! You'll be in the stockade within six months."

I remember asking the recruiter to send me to the worst place in the world. I wanted so desperately to prove to my father that I was tough like him and that I wasn't the cowardly weakling he said I was. I was willing to die just to gain some approval and acceptance from him. But all my life, no matter what I did or how hard I tried, I could never get my father to say, "I'm proud of you. Son, I love you. Mike, you're special."

As an adult, I found myself addicted to achievement, still struggling to gain my father's acceptance and approval and the approval of my heavenly Father as well.

Do you see how our concept of our parents can affect our image of God? If we see them as cruel, hard and punishing, we will tend to see God the same way. And we will respond to Him in anger and fear. On the other hand, it we are parented properly, we will tend to view God as loving, wise and compassionate. We will trust Him and learn to rely on His help and comfort.

YOUR GOD-CONCEPT AFFECTS YOUR SELF-CONCEPT

Like our self-concept, the concept we formed of God early in life can be highly resistant to change. However, many people have been enabled to change their negative self-concepts by first transforming their negative God-concepts. As we discover what God is really like and realize how much He loves us and how precious and important we are to Him, we can learn to love and value ourselves as He does.

HAS SOMEONE TOLD YOU LIES?

In the late 1970s, the well-known lecturer and author Ian Thomas spoke at an ethics class at Southwestern Baptist Theological Seminary in Fort Worth. The students privileged to be present that day have probably never forgotten an analogy he used.

"Imagine," said Thomas, "that you and several other beings from another plant have been entrusted with the mission to travel to a tiny planet called Earth in order to observe its inhabitants. Thousands of years before, word had spread through the universe that on this unique planet lived human creatures that the God of the universe had created in His image, in His likeness. In your planet's desperate search to know the true God, you and your comrades have been ordered to observe, and then return and report to your people.

"'When you see Earth's inhabitants who were created in God's likeness, you will know what God is like,' explains your superiors, 'so observe carefully. Then come back and tell us.'

"After an incredibly long journey you arrive on Earth. You disguise yourself to look like humans and walk around the streets of its great cities. You read its newspapers, watch its movies, listen to its music, and view its newscasts. And you are utterly appalled by what you see: murder, deception, rape, robbery, violence, greed, disease, perversion, wars...

"Sad and totally disheartened, you and your companions make the long, treacherous voyage back through space to your planet and sadly relate all you have seen.

"'If that is what God is like,' your superiors conclude, 'we have no need of Him. We will not serve Him.'"

Too absorbed in the thought-provoking analogy to comment, the ethics class sat transfixed as Thomas asked and then answered his own question. *"Do you know what sin is? Sin is the lies man tells about His Maker!"*

I'd never thought of sin exactly like that before, but Ian Thomas was right. When preachers and other Christian leaders sin, they are telling crushing, disappointing lies about the One they have been called to represent. And when a child's parents—those in authority over him and closest to him—sin by abusing that child, treating him harshly and unfairly or withholding love and acceptance, they are lying to the child, poisoning his God-concept. Their actions are saying, "This is what God, your ultimate authority, is like."

FINDING A GOD YOU CAN BELIEVE IN

Pastor Jack Hayford, founder and former pastor of The Church on the Way in Van Nuys, California, sometimes relates a two-part illustration shared by one of his Bible school professors many years ago to explain this point more clearly. The first part of the professor's illustration goes like this:

> "My wife and I have come to your orphanage because we want to adopt a child." The orphanage director beamed at the couple seated in his office. They seemed ideal in every detail. All their paperwork was in order, and their references were impeccable.
>
> "But we don't want to adopt just any child," the husband continued. "We want to adopt the child that has been the most difficult for you to place, the child no one else wants."

"That's a most unusual request," the director replied. "Most of our applicants want just the opposite—the brightest, the best, the most beautiful—"

"Oh, no!" the wife interrupted, "We're really serious about his. We want to adopt the child who has the most problems."

Without hesitation, the director pulled a dog-eared folder from the stack of files on his desk. "That would be Bobby," he said. "He came to us when he was almost two years old, and he's seven now. If you want problems, Bobby's got them."

The couple leaned forward in their chairs, their eyes devouring every word on the pages before them.

"Let's see," muttered the director as he skimmed page after page in the folder. "Little Bobby has all sorts of fears and he's terribly insecure. He's very introverted and withdrawn. And ever since Bobby came to us, he's had a problem with crying and screaming out in the night. Some sort of terrible nightmares, I suppose."

The man looked at his wife, smiled and nodded.

"Oh yes, there's something else I should tell you," said the director, hardly daring to look up. "The boy was born with a very bad clubfoot. He walks, of course, but with a very awkward limp."

"Yes!" exclaimed the husband and wife simultaneously. "Bobby is the boy we want."

Not too long after all the legalities had been completed, the couple picked up the little boy and the brown paper sack that signified all his earthly belongings—a few tattered bits of clothing—and drove him home.

"This is where you will live, now," said the man. "Hurry up, grab your stuff and come on inside. Your mother and I need to talk to you before you meet the rest of your new family."

The little boy picked up his sack and hobbled behind the man and woman as they led him into the house and then into the living room.

"You sit over there," the father ordered, pointing to a straight-backed chair. "Now," he said as his wife sat beside him on the sofa, "we need to get several things straight from the very beginning."

The little boy nodded apprehensively.

"My wife and I have a twelve-year-old son and a ten-year-old daughter. Don't expect us to love you the way we love them. They're our flesh-and-blood children, and you're not. But as an example to our children and to the community, we wanted to do something for someone less fortunate."

Bobby bit his lower lip to hide the quivering.

"And about your clubfoot," the man continued. "Don't think you'll receive special treatment because of it. You'll be expected to excel in anything you attempt. We want you to grow up to be strong, independent, and self-reliant. We have very high standards in this house, and you're not going to use your disability or your unfortunate background as an excuse not to measure up. Do we understand each other?"

The boy gulped and nodded.

"And there's one more thing. The director at the orphanage told us that you cry and scream out in the night. There will be no more of that. You're safe here, so make up your mind right not to get ahold of those silly fears and quit all that crying and screaming. Is that clear?"

Let's stop here for a moment. If Bobby is like most children reared in harsh conditions, he will tend to fear that God has the same personality as his parents—the primary authority figures in his life. To Bobby, God will be harsh, stern, demanding, perfectionistic, cold, aloof, and uncaring. Bobby will fear that God's love and acceptance will be withdrawn any time his performance does not measure up to the idealistic standards set for him. He will mistakenly learn to mistrust God and His motives, just as he is learning to distrust his new parents and their motives.

Now let's go back to our story. The second part of the scenario is identical up to the part where the car pulled up to the front of the couple's home and stopped.

As the father helped the little boy out of the car he said, "Bobby, we're so glad you've come to live with us and be our son. Mama and I can hardly wait for you to meet your older brother and sister. They're excited to meet you, too, but we asked them to play with Grandmother in the backyard until you, Mama and I have a chance to talk for a few minutes. Okay?"

Bobby nodded and reached for his sack. The mother put her arm around his thin shoulders and shortened her steps to his as they walked up the sidewalk to the front door. "Don't worry about your things. Dad will take care of them for you. And I've got a surprise. Next week, Dad and I are going to take you shopping so you can choose some new outfits! Okay?"

The man and his wife took Bobby into their living room and sat him on the sofa between them. "Son," said the father taking the boy's hand, "I can't tell you how pleased and thankful we are that you belong to us now. You're the other son we've always wanted. We chose you especially! Now you're part of our family, just like our daughter and other son."

"Bobby," the mother added, "We know you must be awfully tired of limping and having to wear that heavy old shoe. Dad and I have been talking to lots of doctors. We found one very special doctor in the city. He has operated on many small children with clubfeet just like yours. Now they can walk and run just like other kids. They don't limp or have to wear special shoes any more. When you tell us you're ready, Daddy and I would like to take you to that doctor and let him fix your foot just as good as new. Okay?"

The boy nodded, his eyes shining.

"And, son," the father said quietly, "the director at the orphanage told Mama and me that you get scared sometimes at night and cry and scream out. But you don't have to worry about that. We're putting you in the bedroom right beside ours, and we had a door cut in the wall between the two rooms. That's so if you have a bad dream or get scared, Mama and Daddy can get to you to let you know you're safe."

The woman smiled and squeezed the little boy's knee. "Bobby, we love you with all our hearts. Pretty soon, you're going to be so happy here and feel so safe, all that old fear and those scary dreams will go away and never come back. Now, sweetheart, let's meet the rest of your new family."

YOU NEED A GOD WHO GIVES YOU SECURITY

I've loved Jack Hayford's illustration from the first time I heard it because it gives us a tiny glimpse of what our heavenly Father is really like. God knows that you and I can't rid ourselves of deeply rooted fears by simply willing them to go away. Only the certainty and security of knowing that we are perfectly loved by a perfect heavenly Father can banish that type of fear. As we begin to comprehend how completely and unconditionally God loves us, our hearts cannot help but love Him in return. That's what God is teaching us in I John 4:18-19:

> There is no fear in love [dread does not exist], but full-grown (complete, perfect) love turns fear out of doors *and* expels every trace of terror! For fear brings with it the thought of punishment, and [so] he who is afraid has not reached the full maturity of love [is not yet grown into love's complete perfection]. We love *Him*, because He first loved us, (Amplified.)

You will find security when you find a God in whom you can believe.

YOU NEED A GOD WHO OFFERS ABUNDANT LIFE

You need a God who gives you security. You need a God who is so pure, so compassionate and so loving, He is irresistible. You need a God who uses His power to empower you, not to dominate you. And you need a God who offers you an abundant, fulfilling life, not just a bleak existence.

Jesus Christ came to empower others to have what He called "abundant life." Contrary to much popular teaching today, abundant life means more than having all our personal needs met. The abundant life Jesus talked about means knowing a God who is bigger than your past and your problems. A God who loves you so much that He gave His only Son to die for your sin so you might receive free, full forgiveness for your sin and have eternal life; a God who offers freedom from shame, guilt and every addiction known to mankind.

The abundant life Jesus spoke of leads us to maturity and unconditional love because He gives us something bigger than ourselves for which to live. As we learn to submit to one another, to forgive, love, serve and value each other, to pour out our own lives for others, we find true abundant life.

YOU NEED A GOD WHO IS IRRESISTIBLE

Several years ago, a handsome young athlete lay alone in a hospital room. His efforts to build a strong, muscular body by taking steroids had backfired; now he was dying.

One day his attention was drawn to the Gideon Bible on his bedside table. Having nothing better to do, he opened it to the New Testament and began to read about the life and ministry of Jesus. Absolutely awestruck by what he saw, the young man continued to read until he had read not only the book of Matthew, but Mark, Luke, and John, as well.

"I saw Jesus as He really was," the young man explained later, "and He was irresistible!" Weeping unashamedly, he bowed his head and gave what was left of himself to God.

The doctors had said some of his major organs were so badly damaged he could not possibly live, but God had other plans for that young man's life. Completely restored to health, he began to minister to students on a college campus.

I agree with that young man. The happy-eyed Christ who walked into my bedroom years ago—the Jesus Christ I see revealed in God's love letter, the Bible—is irresistible.

YOU NEED A GOD WHO USED HIS POWER TO EMPOWER YOU

Power—the ability of one person to influence or affect another—is an element found in all human relationships. But power must be handled responsibly, for it has the potential to shape or shatter another person's identity and self-concept. Legitimate power is authority. Illegitimate power is dominance.

Power is a highly valued commodity in our culture, and some individuals will resort to trickery or manipulation in an attempt to gain it. Several years ago a bestselling book claimed that a person without resources or skills could gain power through intimidating others. The author offered suggestions designed to give an individual the upper hand. These included controlling the situation by arranging to meet people on your own turf, deliberately making people wait several minutes for an appointment, making previous arrangements with a secretary to interrupt the appointment time so guests could see how powerful and important one is. As victims know so well, abusers are an example of individuals who have learned to use their positions of power in order to control others. They love to intimidate, dominate, and manipulate.

Although many individuals in our society will go to any length to obtain power, the concept of empowering has been neglected. Empowering is the process of instilling confidence, of strengthening and building up others to become more powerful and competent.

One of the characteristics that makes Jesus so irresistible to me is the way He handled power during his life and ministry on earth.

Christ could have used His miraculous power to become wealthy. He could have acquired massive palaces by the sea, servants to attend to His every whim, stables of horses and jewel-studded chariots. Instead, the empowering He modeled for us involved serving others. He emphasized this principle in His teachings:

> But Jesus called them to *Himself* and said to them, "You know that those who are considered rulers over the Gentiles lord it over them, and their great ones exercise authority over them. Yet it shall not be so among you; but whoever desires to become great among you shall be your servant. And whoever of you desires to be first shall be slave of all. For even the Son of Man did not come to be served, but to serve, and to give His life a ransom for many," (Mark 10:42-45, NKJV.)

Christ used His power to empower others. He helped them mature and develop their full potential. Rather than dominating and dictating, He encouraged learning through dialogue, discussion and participation. Jesus built others' confidence and encouraged them to undertake and carry out tasks and responsibilities. He knew when to back off and allow His followers to learn through trial and error, while offering support and encouragement when needed. Jesus not only taught proper behavior toward the weak, poor and powerless, He also modeled it.

Are you using power to control others or to empower them? Like Jesus, we can use power to serve others. We can love God and our neighbors as ourselves. Instead of merely concentrating on our own needs and interests, one of the main thrusts of our lives can be helping others achieve a sense of wholeness and self-esteem.

As someone said, "True significance is found when we invest in a cause that will outlive us."

Jesus Christ, the greatest "Empowerer" this world has ever known, put it this way:

> For whoever desires to save his life will lose it, but whoever loses his life for My sake will save it, (Luke 9:2, NKJV.)

Will your life end in disappointment, self-hatred and despair? Or will you close your eyes with a smile on your lips because you found a God you could believe in, and learned to live a life of wholeness and fulfillment?

PUTTING IT ALL TOGETHER

I realize this chapter has included a ton of facts and information. You may feel frustrated, confused or overwhelmed.

> As Philip Yancey says in his book, *Disappointment with God*, "Knowledge is passive, intellectual; suffering is active, personal. No intellectual answer will solve suffering."[122]

Hearing the truth will increase our faith, but it is *knowing* the truth that sets us free. (See John 8:32.) But what does it mean to know the truth? It means "to know through experience, a knowing that comes from an active, firsthand, personal relationship between the one who knows and the person or thing known." It is a knowledge gained through personal acquaintance with God, a relationship of intimacy with Him.

And that brings us full circle: How can we have, or even desire to have, an intimate relationship with Someone we have trouble loving and trusting? Someone we always felt was angry with us or demanding that we be perfect? How can we make the God-connection when we're still living in the past—when our hurts, disappointments and anger with God still hold sway over us? How can we find a God in whom we can believe?

EXPERIENCING GOD FOR YOURSELF

Several years ago I had the unique privilege of climbing Mount Sinai in the starlight. It's difficult enough to climb the rugged mountain during the day in the blistering desert heat, but at night when the wind is blowing and it is freezing cold, the climb can seem really rough.

Although I was dressed in parka and earmuffs, I was shivering with cold. That's why I thought I must be hallucinating when about halfway up the mountain about fifteen men raced by me wearing nothing but shorts. No shirts, no shoes—just shorts!

By five o'clock in the morning I had made it to the summit and was huddled in a little hut with Jamie Buckingham and a half-dozen other men. Suddenly, above the howling wind, I heard men singing to the tune of "Amazing Grace," but in a language I didn't recognize.

Stepping out of the hut, I was surprised to see the group of half-clothed men who had run past me during the early-morning hours. They were standing there with a man that I later learned was a missionary. As I walked toward them, the man smiled and stepped forward. He explained in English, "These men are all heads of villages in New Guinea. Let me introduce you to the chief who is the leader of the group. He has eleven wives and twenty-three children, and has become a Christian."

The chief smiled, revealing teeth that had been sharpened to points. "Their people were headhunters before they became Christians," said the missionary, "and it was their practice to sharpen a tooth each time they ate human flesh."

I flashed a broad smile at the chief, fervently hoping he hadn't acquired a taste for tall, slim Americans.

The missionary explained, "After I led these men to Christ and began teaching them the Scriptures, they had trouble believing that some of the places they had heard about from the Bible actually existed. They'd ask questions such as, "Is there really a Mount Sinai? Is Jerusalem a real city? So, I finally got them here so they could see for themselves and go back and tell their people."

I blinked back tears as former headhunters stood with bare feet firmly planted on the top of Mount Sinai, weeping and singing "Amazing Grace" in their native tongue.

When it comes to believing in a loving, all-wise, all-powerful God, a lot of us are like those New Guinea natives. "Is there such a God?" we ask in disbelief. "Does He want me with all my faults and failures? Can I really trust Him? Do I dare tell Him how I really feel? What if He becomes angry and rejects me?"

You don't have to journey all the way to the Holy Land to find a God in whom you can believe. You don't even have to make some giant leap of faith. Just dare to be as honest as the man in the Bible who came to Jesus and cried, "Lord, I believe. Help Thou my unbelief. I want to know you personally, intimately. Please reveal yourself to me."

The lies of the past have plagued you long enough. You'll never be totally healed; you'll never find your true purpose in life until you come to know God for yourself and begin to see Him as He really is.

You don't need relief; you need release—release from anger and bitterness; release from your own sins and failures and from the pain of the past; release from the lies that have smeared and distorted your concept of God; release into a fulfilling, meaningful, abundant life. You will find all these things and more as you come to know the magnificent, irresistible God of the Bible as He really is. He's a God in which you can believe!

GETTING IN TOUCH WITH YOUR CONCEPT OF GOD

Taking time to answer the following questions thoughtfully and honestly will benefit you by: 1) helping you sort through and identify your feelings; 2) enabling you to recognize many of the roots from which your pain and confusion have grown; and 3) helping to replace your distorted concepts of God with truth.

1. Has my concept of God been influenced and distorted by sins others committed against me—by the lies others have told me about Him?

2. Do I feel bitterness or anger toward God because I blamed Him for allowing the abuse?

3. Is it possible I have repressed my true feelings (of hatred, anger, mistrust) toward God, yet indirectly expressed those feelings toward Him by turning them on myself or others?

4. Has my hatred or anger toward God ever taken the form of outright defiance or flagrant violations of His moral laws and scriptural principles?

5. When feelings of mistrust, rage or hatred toward God have surfaced after being hidden for years, have I stifled those feelings because a well-meaning person advised me to or because I did not realize that frankly acknowledging such intense

emotions was a vital part of forgiveness, allowing me to be reconciled to Him?

6. Have my past efforts failed because I have tried to rush the healing process?

   a. Have I fully acknowledged and frankly expressed the emotions I feel?

   b. Have I identified and expressed my feeling about the abuse and the abuser?

   c. Have I made the decision to forgive but failed to realize that healing emotional and spiritual brokenness takes time, just as healing a badly broken bone takes time?

7. What problems in my Christian walk may be related to my feelings about God?

8. Because I have been damaged emotionally and spiritually, do I find myself selecting or focusing on Bible passages emphasizing punishment, wrath, and the unpardonable sin?

9. Once my God-concept was distorted, did that become a pattern of life? Do I suffer from spiritual paranoia? Do I take the most loving, affirming statements (even in the Bible) and twist them into insults, rejections or threats?

10. Do I need to balance my view of God and enhance my relationship with Him by focusing on scriptures that emphasize God's love, compassion, mercy, and grace?

15

EXPOSING FAMILY CURSES

"God doesn't arbitrarily condemn some people to a lifetime of sin and hardship and disappointment. Evil doesn't come from God; it comes from the Devil, and it comes also from the twisted world we live in. It comes as well from our own hearts, because by nature we resent God and want to run our own lives. The Bible says, "Each one is tempted when, by his own evil desire, he is dragged away and enticed" (James 1:14).

—DR. BILLY GRAHAM

THE SOUND OF MY PHONE ringing startled me from sleep. I squinted at the clock on my nightstand as I groped for the receiver. *Who on earth is calling me at this hour?* I wondered sleepily. *It must be an emergency.*

"Hello...?"

"Michael? Hello, Michael?"

It took a moment for me to recognize the voice of my Uncle Michael as the man sobbing into the phone on the other end of the line.

"Yes, Uncle Mike, it's me."

"Michael, something is happening to me. All hell has broken loose in my life. I feel like I'm cursed! I've gone to the best psychiatrists and doctors that money can buy. A lot of people are telling me this is strictly emotional, but whatever it is, it's killing me. I'm dying!"

Uncle Mike was beginning to calm down a bit and I realized he just needed to talk.

"Michael, I've thought about all of this, and the amazing thing is that almost everything I've experienced happened to my father and to my grandfather. What do you think, Michael? Could it possibly be in my genes?"

ARE CURSES REAL?

Uncle Mike didn't know that scripturally, he was right on target. There is such a thing as a curse; it is the opposite of a blessing. Both blessings and curses are major themes of Scripture. For example, the words "blessing" and "bless" are in the Bible over 400 times, and the word "curse" in its various forms, occurs about 230 times.[123]

Many people believe in blessings; however, when it comes to curses, a lot of people refuse to believe they are real. But just as opposites such as hot and cold, good and evil, day and night, up and down are real, so are blessings and curses.

How does a curse work? As Merrill F. Unger who compiled *Unger's Bible Dictionary*, explains, a curse carries with it its own power of execution:

> These divine maledictions are not merely imprecations, nor the expressions of impotent wishes; but carry their effects with them, and are attended with all the miseries they denounce or foretell. Curses delivered against individuals by holy men are not the expressions of revenge, passion, or impatience; they are predictions, and therefore, not such as God condemns.[124]

Blessings and curses both take the form of words and may be written, spoken aloud or uttered inside. However, blessings produce good effects and curses produce evil effects. Here's a New Testament example of a curse pronounced by Jesus:

> Now the next day, when they had come out from Bethany, He was hungry. And seeing from afar a fig tree having leaves, He went to see if perhaps He would find something on it. When He came to it, He found nothing but leaves, for it was not the season for figs. In response Jesus said to it, "Let no one eat fruit from you ever again." And His disciples heard *it*. Now in the morning, as they passed by, they saw the fig tree dried up from the roots. And Peter, remembering, said to Him, "Rabbi, look! The fig tree which You cursed has withered away," (Mark 11:12-14, 20-12, NKJV.)

Jesus never touched the fig tree, but His words, spoken in the power of the Spirit, were as swift and sure as the blow of an axe to the root of the fig tree.

Once they are spoken, blessings and curses tend to continue through time until they are cancelled or revoked. For example, the Bible records a curse pronounced by Joshua, a man of God, after Israel had destroyed the wicked city of Jericho:

> Then Joshua charged *them* at that time, saying, "Cursed *be* the man before the LORD who rises up and builds this city Jericho; he shall lay its foundation with his firstborn, and with his youngest he shall set up its gates," (Joshua 6:26, NKJV.)

Around 500 years later, a man rebuilt Jericho. What happened?

> In his days Hiel of Bethel built Jericho. He laid its foundation with Abiram his firstborn, and with his youngest *son* Segub he set up its gates, according to the word of the LORD, which He had spoken through Joshua the son of Nun, (I Kings 16:34, NKJV.)

Why did those ancient words come to pass? Because, as we see in the above verse, they were not just something that Joshua dreamed up or called out in anger or frustration; they were supernatural, self-fulfilling words of God spoken through Joshua. Curses are very real.

CAN THERE BE FAMILY CURSES?

My Uncle Mike was correct in believing that curses are real. He was also correct on another count: There is such a thing as a family curse. The Word declares:

> You shall not bow down yourself to them or serve them; for I the Lord your God am a jealous God, visiting the iniquity of the fathers upon the children to the third and fourth generation of those who hate Me, But showing mercy *and* steadfast love to a thousand generations of those who love Me and keep My commandments, (Exodus 20:5-6, Amplified.)

Hating God, turning one's back on Him and rebelling against Him brings a curse. Notice that the effects of this curse can come not only upon the person who commits the sinful act, but also upon the individual's children, grandchildren, and great-grandchildren.

MY FATHER'S WORLD

The earth is the Lord's, and the fulness thereof,
Formed by the hands of His Infinite Love.
A home for God's children, artistically planned,
with broad boundless oceans surrounding the land.

An house of rare treasures, that only His mind
Could conceive with magnificence, vast and sublime
He hangeth the earth, so the Scriptures declare,
Upon nothing, a sphere which revolved in mid-air.

The sky which surrounds it is jeweled with stars,
Old Saturn and Jupiter, Venus and Mars,
And great constellations He tossed into space;
By power of His Word they are held in their place.

Reflecting God's Glory, the sun is our light
By day, with the stars and the moon for the night
The snowy capped mountains which tower to the sky
Stand guard o'er the plains as the ages pass by.
                                            adorn
The lakes like blue sapphires, the mountains XXXX
Reflecting God's smile in the sunlight at morn,
The rivers, bright silver strands, wending their
                                            way
Through canyons and valleys, like children at play

The Pines of the forest, tall, fragrant and green
Sway gently to music of breezes serene.
The grass as a carpet has flowers of all hue,
A pattern of yellow and purple and blue.

The L ark and the Mocking Bird, mounting in
                                            flight
Fling sky-ward their song both by day and by night
The deer in the forest and fish in the seas,
The butterflies, fowls, and hard-working bees.

The orchards and vineyards and fields of rich
                                            grain,
Are nourished by mother earth, sunshine and rain.
Deposits of silver and gold and rich ore
God placed ' neath the surface for man to explore

The grand scenic wonders, a thrill to behold,

A wall of pure granite, so high and so bold.
The water-falls foaming and dashing its spray,
Tossing and tumbling and making its way

From tops of the mountains to valleys below,
And then toward the ocean to peacefully flow.
Supplying with moisture the low-lands and plains,
And serving to carry the excess of rain.

The earth is the Lord's, and the fulness thereof,
Formed by the Hands of His Infinite Love,
Oh, who can declare it, His glory and fame?
The Great Master Builder, the LORD id His name.

However, read that last verse again: "But showing mercy *and* steadfast love to a thousand generations of those who love Me and keep My commandments."

An individual's sin can affect his or her descendants for three or four generations, but an individual's love and obedience to God can affect his or her descendants for a thousand generations.

> But where sin increased *and* abounded, grace (God's unmerited favor) has surpassed it *and* increased the more *and* super-abounded, (Romans 5:20, Amplified.)

Does this mean that you and I are a spiritual garbage dump for all the accumulated sins of our forefathers, and that we are accountable and responsible for the sins they committed? Definitely not! You and I are born with a propensity to sin, but we are not born with the responsibility for sins committed by someone else. However, we can certainly be affected by the careless, selfish sins of our ancestors. Take the pitiable little babies born to drug-addicted mothers. In much the same way, the effects of curses can continue from generation to generation until the door opened by the Enemy is slammed shut.

WHO IS YOUR ENEMY?

Never forget: God is not your enemy! Our own sinful choices open us up to the attack of our real enemy—Satan. If we choose to serve other gods—whether idols of stone or idols of power, money, ambition, or lust—God will allow us to make that choice. If we do not wish to serve and obey God, if we do not desire to walk in covenant with Him or enjoy His blessings and protection, He will not force us or violate our wills. He simply withdraws His protection from us and excludes us from His covenant. (See Leviticus 20:1-6, for example.)

On the other hand, if we choose to reverence God and walk in His ways, this is what He promises:

> For I will be leaning toward you with favor *and* regard for you, rendering you fruitful, multiplying you, and establishing *and* ratifying My covenant with you, (Leviticus 26:9, Amplified.)

God allows us to make the choice between life and death, blessing and cursing. (See Deuteronomy 30:15-16, 19-20, Amplified.)

Perhaps your father, a grandmother, or great-grandfather chose sin, the curse of death instead of obedience, blessing and life, and you still feel the effects of that choice today. Although you do not bear the guilt of their sin, you are suffering the consequences of their sin.

We see a similar principle in effect when individuals break God's natural laws by abusing drugs, alcohol, tobacco, and sex. Not only do they harm their own bodies, but they can harm the bodies and minds of their descendants as well. If such a thing is possible in the natural, physical realm, can you see how it is possible to harm ourselves and our descendants in the spiritual realm?

Ask yourself: Am I making bad, sinful choices that will bring harmful consequences upon me and my descendants? Or have I made up my mind that I will choose life and blessing? If you choose to obey God and walk in His way, the family curse can be broken and its harmful effects halted once and for all—not only in your life, but in the lives of your descendants.

As believers in Christ, we are not placed under the law as a covenant of works. We are under grace. But sin can give Satan a foothold in our lives or cause us to become caught in one of his traps:

Be angry, and do not sin: do not let the sun go down on your wrath, nor give place to the devil, (Ephesians 4:26-27, NKJV.)

...not a novice, lest being puffed up with pride he fall into the same condemnation as the devil. Moreover he must have a good testimony among those who are outside, lest he fall into reproach and the snare of the devil, (I Timothy 3:6-7, NKJV.)

God has given us commandments to follow for our good and for the good of others. He has also given us a free will, and we may choose life or death, blessing or cursing. Sinful choices open the door to Satan's vicious attacks, and he shows no mercy. We may exercise our authority over Satan and his works and defeat him, or we can forfeit our authority, choose the curse and live in defeat because of our sin and selfishness.

HOW DOES A CURSE BEGIN?

After describing the wonderful blessings that will come on those who obey and worship God, Deuteronomy 28 also describes in great detail the terrible curses that will plague those who refuse to follow and serve Him. The root cause of all curses is found in Deuteronomy 28:15:

But it shall come to pass, *if you do not obey* the voice of the Lord your God, to observe carefully all His commandments and His statutes which I command you today, that all these curses will come upon you and overtake you: (NKJV, emphasis mine.)

Did you notice that we do not have to pursue curses or blessings either, for that matter? All we have to do is fulfill the conditions, either negative or positive, and either blessings or curses will overtake us.

In explicit detail, Deuteronomy 27: 15-26 lists various sins that spring from one root cause: Deliberately disobeying God's commandments. Each of these sins can become the breeding ground for the transmission of family curses. They fall under four main categories:

1. Idolatry, false gods, and the occult

Although many people do not realize it, dabbling with the occult is linked with worshipping false gods since it involves going to those who serve them for help or hidden knowledge. Involvement with idolatry and the occult exposes one to satanic influence. (See Deuteronomy 18:20-14; I Corinthians 10:19-22.)

2. Wrong attitudes and actions toward parents

Deliberately dishonoring, showing contempt for and rebelling against one's parents can cause one to be cursed. (See Matthew 15:4.)

Children, obey your parents in the Lord, for this is right. "Honor your father and mother," which is the first commandment with promise: "that it may be well with you and you may live long on the earth." And you, fathers, do not provoke your children to wrath, but bring them up in the training and admonition of the Lord, (Ephesians 6:1-4, NKJV.)

This does not mean we are to obey a parent if we are asked to do wrong, or that we must allow a parent to abuse us. It does mean that if our attitude toward a parent is wrong, we need to repent and adjust our attitude and—as much as depends upon us—our relationship with the parent. Then the full blessing of God can come upon us.

3. Unnatural or illicit sex

Curses can accompany such sinful acts as adultery, fornication, incest, homosexuality, and bestiality.

4. Injustice to the weak or helpless

In our day this sin includes preforming and procuring abortions and committing abuse of all types, including child sexual abuse. Abusers must recognize this curse, repent, turn to God for mercy, and accept His forgiveness and transforming power.

The Bible also reveals other common causes of curses:

> a. Relying upon ourselves rather than God (Jeremiah 17:5-6)
> b. Stealing and perjury (Zechariah 5:1-4)
> c. Breaking a vow to God (Malachi 1:14)
> d. Withholding tithes and offerings due to God (Malachi 3:8-10)
> e. Curses from people representing Satan (Deuteronomy 18:10-12)

HOW TO RECOGNIZE A CURSE

Please don't think I'm saying everything harmful or bad that has happened to you is the result of a curse. Many things we go through are simply the natural consequences of our own or someone else's willfulness, ignorance or foolishness. For instance, selfishness, stubbornness and indifference destroy more marriages than curses do. Proverbs 14:1 says, "A wise woman builds her house, while a foolish woman tears hers down by her own efforts," (Living Bible.)

If your friend jumps off the roof of a three-story building and breaks his leg, he is not the victim of a curse. He foolishly defied the natural law of gravity and lost.

Drunkenness and gluttony bring their own natural punishment because violating laws of nutrition, growth and health bring physical deterioration and death, whereas obeying those laws brings strength and life.

As a final illustration: If a farmer ignores God's law of the seasons by planting all his seed just as winter is approaching and the freezing temperatures kill all the seedlings, he can't blame his losses on a curse.

As one man observed, "At times, when we are going through sorrows, pressures and problems, we look about us and realize we are walking through the ripened field of wild oats we sowed in the past."

To summarize, many of our problems are simply the consequences of poor choices and wrong decisions or the breaking of natural laws. In such cases God hasn't punished us or cursed us, we have punished or cursed ourselves.

The point is clear: If we want to reap the blessings of God, we must obey His natural and spiritual laws. But how can we tell if a curse is actually at work in our lives? There are four guidelines that may help:

> 1. A curse is something like a dark shadow or
> an evil hand from your past—oppressing you,

pressing you down, holding you back, ripping you up and propelling you in a direction you do not wish to take. It is like a negative atmosphere that surrounds you and seems to be stronger at some times than at others, but from which you are never totally free.

2. If a curse is operating in your life, it is very probable that you have been struggling against something which you have never been able to master or overcome. Yet if you look for a cause in your own life, you may not be able to find it.

3. Frustration seems to be a key word in describing your life. For example, you reach a certain level of achievement or progress in your life and you seem to have all the needed qualifications for success, yet something goes wrong. You start over, reach the same level, then something happens yet again. This seems to be the pattern for your life, yet you can find no obvious reason for it.

4. You may be vaguely aware that this frustrating pattern did not begin in your own lifetime. The same thing may have happened to one of your parents, or you may be aware of similar patterns in the life or family of a grandparent.

5. This pattern may occur in various areas: business, personal relationships (especially marriage and family), career, finances, health, and other areas. In all probability, that dark shadow or evil hand you sense at work in your life, perhaps goes back several generations.[125]

WHAT ARE SOME SPECIFIC FORMS CURSES MAY TAKE?

Deuteronomy 28 summarizes the blessings God will send upon those who obey His voice and walk in His ways: God's favor and exaltation, health, prosperity, victory and reproduction in every area of one's life. In verse 13, we have this promise: And the LORD will make you the head and not the tail; you shall be above only, and not be beneath, (Deuteronomy 28:13, NKJV.)

Next, the curses that will come upon the disobedient are listed. The disobedient can include an individual, family, community, nation, or even an entire civilization. As we would expect, the curses are essentially the reverse, the opposite of blessings. Verses 15-21 list definite manifestations that these curses may assume:

> Curses in the city,
> Curses in the fields,
> Curses on your fruit and bread,
> The curse of a barren womb,
> Curses upon your crops,
> Curses upon the fertility of your cattle and flocks,
> Curses when you come in,
> Curses when you go out.

> For the Lord himself will send his personal curse upon you. You will be confused and a failure in everything you do, until at last you are destroyed because of the sin of forsaking him. He will send disease among you until you are destroyed from the face of the land you are about to enter and possess, (Living Bible.)

Deuteronomy 28 speaks about the curses in more detail, so take time to read the entire chapter. Carefully study and meditate upon it and notice several specific things the curses entail: Humiliation, failure to reproduce, mental and physical sickness, family breakdowns, defeat, poverty, failure, oppression and God's disfavor.

Below is a list of seven common indicators of curses, linking most with corresponding phrases from Deuteronomy 28:

1. Mental and/or emotional breakdown; key words—confusion and depression. (Verses 20, 28, 34, and 65.)

2. Repeated or chronic sicknesses, especially if they are hereditary or without clear medical diagnosis—key words, plague, incurable, extraordinary, fearful, prolonged and lingering. (Verses 21-22, 27-28, 35, 59, and 61.)

3. Barrenness, repeated miscarriages or related problems. (See verse 18.)

4. Breakdown of marriage as well as family alienation. (Verse 41.)

5. Continuing financial insufficiency, especially where the income appears to be adequate. (Verses 17, 29, 47-48.)

6. Being accident prone.

7. A history of suicide or unnatural deaths in the family. (Numerous references are made to unnatural or untimely deaths in Deuteronomy 28.)[126]

CURSES AND DEMONIC ACTIVITY IN OUR TIME

Many sincere Christians in our day know very little about Satan and the demons who serve him. While some deny his existence, others scoff at the mention of demonic activity, chalking it up to folklore or fanaticism. How dangerous it is to try to solve great problems with small answers.

A Sunday school teacher conducted an experiment to discover how well his class of boys was informed on the subject of Satan. The responses were both interesting and revealing:

"Satan has bright red skin, a long tail with an arrow-shaped tip and hoofs for feet."

"He has horns like a goat."

"His wife is very pretty, but she's pink, not red like he is."

Satan doesn't mind such misconceptions. Neither is he upset by those who deny his existence or remain ignorant of his methods. False ideas such as those allow him to work undetected.

The radiant victory of beloved Corrie ten Boom, even in the midst of her imprisonment in a German concentration camp, inspires those who read her wonderful book, *The Hiding Place*. Corrie gives some of the wisest, most thought-provoking insights I have ever heard in regard to our enemy Satan and those who serve him. Although I could share examples of satanic power and demonic curses from many sources, because of her worldwide reputation for integrity, truthfulness, and scriptural balance, I have chosen to quote from some of Corrie's writings and personal experiences.

In her informative book, *Defeated Enemies*, Corrie frankly discusses the danger involved in consulting a fortune-teller:

> After the war in Germany, there was among many
> people great uncertainty about the soldiers that were

missing. Were they still in Russian concentration camps, or had they died during the fighting? This uncertainty caused great suffering among their relatives, and many people went to fortune-tellers to find out about their loved ones. I don't know whether they got any real information, but this I know, many came to me and told me about permanent darkness in their hearts and an urge to commit suicide. This symptom is always a sure evidence of demon influence.[127]

Corrie also tells the story of May, an intelligent girl in England, who told Corrie that she longed for peace in her heart, but every time she made a decision to accept Jesus, something kept her back from that step. As she questioned the girl, it didn't take Corrie long to discover the root of May's problem:

Think back over the events in your life and tell me if you have ever been to a fortune-teller. Do you know that when you do such a thing you fall under the curse of it, so that the way to God becomes blocked for you? Yes, even the way to conversion! Such a spell may ensnare you even if you have just allowed yourself to be treated by a [hypnotist.] Very often such people are also on the wrong side and that may be a great danger.

After hearing Corrie's warning, May laughed mockingly and admitted that she had gone to a fortune-teller years ago, but that she only did it for fun and didn't believe in it.

Corrie's wise reply wiped the look of amusement off the girl's face:

May, suppose you were a soldier during war, and you had to reconnoiter certain terrain. By mistake you fell into the enemy's hands by entering his territory. Do you think it would help if you then said, "O excuse me, please, it was not my intention to come here; I just came by mistake?" Once you are on their terrain, you are at their mercy. Though you did not know it, a demon has taken possession of your heart, and your life has fallen under his spell. When you want to be converted, he comes in between. You don't understand the significance of it, and that's why it is so dangerous. Paul says in Ephesians 6:12, NKJV: "For we do not wrestle against flesh and blood, but against principalities, against powers..."

Seeing the fear on May's face, Corrie hastily added:

I'm not telling these things to make you afraid, May. If I had no more to say than this, it would have been better to keep silent, but the first step towards victory is to know the enemy's position. And the wonderful thing about it is that Jesus is victor. He is far stronger than all the powers of Hell. What you have to do is close the door exactly where you opened it. I mean this. Think of some Scripture passages which speak of forgiveness.

May thought for a moment and replied, "In whom we have redemption through His blood, the forgiveness of sins," (Colossians 1:14, NKJV.)

Corrie nodded. That is right. Now ask the Lord

Jesus to go back with you to that very moment when you committed that sin. Confess your sin, ask forgiveness and give thanks for it (forgiveness), because the text which you quoted is true. Then the door is closed, and you are free. Then you are no longer at the demon's mercy.[128]

Corrie also describes various ways demons can manifest themselves through human beings they torment and seek to control. Some of the manifestations she mentions include:

- » The urge for murder or suicide
- » Ever-recurring fears of various forms
- » Abhorring the name of Jesus and cursing or reacting negatively when the name or blood of Jesus is mentioned
- » Strong dislike of the Bible
- » Physical symptoms such as grotesque movements, strange voices speaking through the person—often with a sound that differs from the person's normal voice; shrieking; paralysis of one or more parts of the body; convulsions; the person being thrown to the ground; wild or fearful expressions in the person's eyes; a strong smell[129]

There was a time in my life when I would probably have been hesitant when it came to talking about curses or demonic influences. But my years of ministry in the United States and in countries around the world, as well as my experiences in counselling with hundreds of people, persuaded me that we cannot ignore such a serious problem. Watching the painful battles that members of my own family have fought in this arena only strengthened my resolve to discuss this dangerous problem frankly and openly.

As I've already told you, because of our dysfunctional family and the abuse to which we were all subjected, most of my brothers and sisters have struggled with one or more serious problems in their adult lives: Divorce, abortion, gambling, dugs, and immorality. I believe these manifestations were the result of the curse that sin produced in our family.

I can assure you that no curse of Satan can stand against the power of God. No matter how deep-seated it may seem to be, a family curse must yield to the name of Jesus.

WHAT DOES YOUR FAMILY TREE REVEAL?

Prayerfully examine your family tree to help uncover generational curses and their roots. First, chart your family tree from as far back as you can remember. Include the ancestors of your parents, your aunts and uncles, brothers and sisters, and children, if any.

Next, beside each person's name, write any facts that may be significant in your search. For example: committed suicide, rebelled against parents, never married, divorced, died by accident or unnatural death, lived in poverty, family fell apart, no children, miscarriages, alcoholic, adulterer, criminal, had abortion, sickly, occult involvement (fortune-telling, palm reading, Ouija board, horoscopes and others), follower of a false religion, miserly, obese, abuser, victim of abuse, and any other factors you can recall.

Now examine what you have written, looking for specific sins that could have bred a curse and for repeating patterns that may signal the effects of an ongoing curse.

With that information in hand, it's time to continue to Chapter Sixteen: Breaking Family Curses.

✤ 16 ✤

BREAKING FAMILY CURSES

So if the Son sets you free, you will be free indeed.
JOHN 8:36, ESV

HOW CAN YOU MAKE the transition from curse to blessing? In the case of a family or generational curse, you need to discover the cause or source of the curse. Prayerfully go back over the nine main causes of curses that we discussed in detail in the last chapter:

1. Idolatry, false gods, and the occult
2. Wrong attitudes and actions toward parents
3. Unnatural or illicit sex
4. Injustice to the weak and helpless
5. Relying upon ourselves instead of God
6. Stealing and perjury
7. Breaking a vow to God
8. Withholding tithes and offerings due to God
9. Curses from people representing Satan

Did you find any of these causes present in your family tree?

FOUR PRELIMINARY STEPS

Before you come to God and claim your release from the curse or curses operating in your family, you need to take four preliminary steps:[130]

1. Recognize

In his book, *The Father Heart of God*, pastor and author Floyd McClung helps individuals diagnose the exact nature of the problem by distinguishing between *sin, an emotional wound*, and *bondage*. For sin there needs to be forgiveness; for an emotional wound there needs to be healing; and for spiritual bondage we need to be set free. Sometimes we need help in all three areas.

You cannot confess a wound as if it were a sin, because a wound is not a sin. Yet if, as a result of being hurt, you have developed a sinful attitude or response, even if others are to blame, God still holds you responsible for your response. In fact, God does not see it as a matter of the other person being 80 percent to blame and you 20 percent; both you and the other person are 100 percent responsible for your own actions. Until you accept total responsibility for your own attitudes and actions, healing is hindered. Why is that? If your attitude is one of resentment, bitterness or unforgiveness, God's healing and forgiveness are blocked.[131]

You need to recognize the true nature of your problem, and if possible, identify the source or the cause of the curse; that is, the sin or problem through which it originally entered.

If you can pinpoint the exact cause or causes of the curse in yourself or in your family, that's wonderful. But if you cannot, don't worry. God knows the root of the curse. As Corrie ten Boom once told people, "I am so glad that God does not ask us to give a clear diagnosis. We may simply act on His Word, and we experience that God 'watches over His Word to perform it.'" (See Jeremiah 1:12.)

Once you have recognized that the effects of a curse are operating in your family and, if possible, have identified the specific cause or source, you're ready to take the next step.

2. Repent

Repent of whatever initially exposed you to the problem, whether it was your own sin or the sin of your ancestors. If it was your sin, in your mind go back to the place where the sin opened your heart to the influence of the powers of darkness. Confess your sin to Jesus and ask Him to blot it out with His holy blood. Then ask Him to close the door you opened to the enemy.

As one woman took this step, in her mind she suddenly saw the blood of Jesus being sprinkled on ground where ugly weeds and thorny plants were growing. As the blood touched them, they instantly withered away, and the ground was purified so good seed could be sown and thrive.

3. Renounce

To renounce means *to declare that one gives up, to cast off; refuse to recognize as one's own.* You must renounce the sin or problem, saying, "It no longer belongs to me. I do not accept it. Through Jesus I have the right to be free from it. It's not my problem any longer."

4. Resist

Take a very definite stand against the power of Satan. First, submit to God. Then you can resist the devil and he will flee from you. (See James 4:7.)

In summary, after you have identified the root cause or source of the curse, you must recognize, repent, renounce, and resist. Then you are ready to come to God and claim your release and deliverance from the curse through a very specific prayer.

BREAKING THE CURSE

Jesus describes how an unclean spirit, after it has gone out of a man, walks through dry places seeking rest and finds none:

> Then he says, 'I will return to my house from which I came.' And when he comes, he finds *it* empty, swept, and put in order. Then he goes and takes with him seven other spirits more wicked than himself, and they enter and dwell there; and the last *state* of that man is worse than the first. So shall it also be with this wicked generation, (Matthew 12:44-45, NKJV.)

How is it possible that a house that is swept, empty and garnished can once again become a stronghold for the devil? To comprehend this, we must understand that the word empty in the Greek means "to take a holiday, be at leisure." Swept means "to brush lightly," and garnish means "to trim." The picture is of a clean, nicely decorated house, but the problem is that the house is unoccupied. Jesus Christ is not Lord and Master of the house and it is not guarded and kept by His power. When the evil spirit decides to return and bring seven more wicked spirits with it, all they have to do is walk right in the front door.

Human beings cannot afford to deal lightly with the devil. It doesn't matter how wealthy, intelligent or powerful we are by human standards, without Jesus Christ we are no match for Satan and the evil spirits who serve him. Tacking up a few pretty pictures and sweeping our sins under the rug won't keep the devil from our doorstep. A little slap on the wrist or meekly pleading, "Now devil, won't you please stop bothering me?" won't get the job done, either.

The Scriptures warn us to be ever on guard against Satan:

> Be well balanced (temperate, sober of mind), be vigilant *and* cautious at all times; for that enemy of yours, the devil, roams around like a lion roaring [in fierce hunger], seeking someone to seize upon *and* devour. Withstand him; be firm in faith [against his onset—rooted, established, strong, immovable, and determined]...(I Peter 5:8-9, Amplified.)

Do you remember the story of Cain, Adam, and Eve's oldest son? He became angry with his brother Abel and with God because God accepted the sacrifice Abel offered in obedience and rejected the sacrifice Cain made. Unlike his brother, Cain flippantly offered a sacrifice of his own choosing and tried to approach God on his own terms, rather than following God's explicit directions. Genesis 4:5-7 describes what happened next:

> But for Cain and his offering He had no respect *or* regard. So Cain was exceedingly angry *and* indignant, and he looked sad *and* depressed. And the Lord said to Cain, Why are you angry? And why do you look sad *and* depressed *and* dejected? If you do well, will you not be accepted? And if you do not do well, sin crouches at your door; its desire is for you, but you must master it, (Amplified.)

Like a hungry lion, sin crouched outside the door of Cain's heart. He could have driven it away; instead, he opened the door a few inches and tossed a few tasty morsels at the lion's feet. Pretty soon, he had the lion eating out of his hand. Cain thought the lion was tamed, that it was a pet with which he could play and lead around on a leash. But the savage lion conquered him instead, and Cain wound up deliberately murdering his own brother.

You cannot play with sin. When someone agrees with you in prayer, helping you to bind the lion and drive it away from your door, you must refuse to allow it to return. You must not feed it tidbits from your table or set out a bowl of milk for it. That lion is your enemy, and if you do not master it and drive it away once and for all, it will master you. You and I cannot afford to deal lightly with the devil.

Satan has authority over the disobedient, unbelieving and unsaved. But the Word of God reveals that through the blood of Jesus, we can have our sins forgiven, be redeemed from the curse and be delivered from Satan's authority. If you sincerely want your curse-breaking prayer to have the authority of the Word of God and the power of the blood of Jesus behind it, you must recognize the issues God sets before you and base your faith on God's Word, refusing death and curses and choosing life and blessings.

Take a moment to meditate upon the following verses:

> Christ has redeemed us from the curse of the law, having become a curse for us (for it is written, "Cursed *is* everyone who hangs on a tree"), that the blessing of Abraham might come upon the Gentiles in Christ Jesus, that we might receive the promise of the Spirit through faith, (Galatians 3:13-14, NKJV.)
>
> He has delivered us from the power of darkness and conveyed *us* into the kingdom of the Son of His love, in whom we have redemption through His blood, the

forgiveness of sins, (Colossians 1:13-14, NKJV—also see Ephesians 1:7.)

For this purpose the Son of God was manifested, that He might destroy the works of the devil, I John 3:8, NKJV.)

Behold, I give you the authority to trample on serpents and scorpions, and over all the power of the enemy, and nothing shall by any means hurt you, (Luke 10:19, NKJV.)

Once you have grasped these scriptures as realities for yourself, you are ready to claim release from any curses over your life. The Bible declares in Matthew 12:29, NKJV:

Or how can one enter a strong man's house and plunder his goods, unless he first binds the strong man? And then he will plunder his house.

You may find it helpful to ask a strong, trustworthy Christian who is filled with the Holy Spirit to agree with you in prayer, binding the powers of darkness that have plagued you and denouncing each root of the family curse as the Spirit of God reveals it to you.

What are the steps you should take in claiming your release?

1. Confess your faith in Christ and in His sacrifice on your behalf

Confess with your mouth your faith in Christ and the power of the blood He shed for you on Calvary. This releases Christ to operate in the supernatural realm in your behalf as your Savior and Deliverer. As Revelation 12:11, Amplified, reminds us:

And they have overcome (conquered) him by

means of the blood of the Lamb and by the utterance of their testimony, for they did not love *and* cling to life even when faced with death [holding their lives cheap till they had to die for their witnessing].

2. Repent of all your rebellion and sins, committing yourself to obedience

In order to remain free from the curse once you are released, you must commit yourself to hear and obey the voice of God.

But the word is very near you, in your mouth and in your mind *and* in your heart, so that you can do it. See, I have set before you this day life and good, and death and evil. [If you obey the commandments of the Lord your God which] I command you today, to love the Lord your God, to walk in His ways, and to keep His commandments and His statutes and His ordinances, then you shall live and multiply, and the Lord your God will bless you in the land into which you go to possess, But if your [mind and] heart turn away and you will not hear, but are drawn away to worship other gods and serve them, I declare to you today that you shall surely perish, and you shall not live long in the land which you pass over the Jordan to enter and possess. I call heaven and earth to witness this day against you that I have set before you life and death, the blessings and the curses; therefore choose life, that you and your descendants may live, (Deuteronomy 30:14-19, Amplified.)

3. Claim forgiveness of all sins

The great barrier keeping God's blessings out of our lives is unforgiven sin. God has already made provision for our sins to be forgiven, but He will not do this until we confess them. (See I John 1:9.)

It may be that the sin of your ancestors, not some sin of your own, exposed you to the curse. You are not responsible or accountable for the sin of your ancestors, yet your life and well-being have been affected by them. (See Leviticus 26:40.) Therefore, in order to deal with your sin or the sin of your ancestors that exposed you to the curse, ask God to blot it out.

He who covers his sins will not prosper, but whoever confesses and forsakes them will have mercy, (Proverbs 28:13, KJV.)

The exercise at the end of Chapter Fifteen (What Does Your Family Tree Reveal?) may have aided you in discovering specific sins or areas of weakness that have exposed you and other family members to Satan's attack. If you feel that certain sins committed by you or by your ancestors were exposed, confess your sins and ask God to release you from the consequences of your ancestors' sins.

4. Make a clear-cut decision to forgive all other people who have ever harmed or wronged you

Unforgiveness, bitterness or resentment can keep God's blessings out of our lives. They are also barriers to our prayers. Those sinful attitudes will keep us under the curse. If we want total forgiveness and deliverance, we must extend total forgiveness to others. Here are some simple words you can use: "By a decision of my will, I forgive all those who have harmed or wronged me, just as I want God to forgive me." (Name any person or persons you need to forgive.)

5. Renounce all contact by you or your ancestors with anything occult or satanic

Get rid of any objects that are in any way associated with idolatry, the occult or secret societies. You cannot expect deliverance from the curse if you keep an accursed object in your home.

You shall burn the carved images of their gods with fire; you shall not covet the silver or gold *that is* on them, nor take *it* for yourselves, lest you be snared by it; for it *is* an abomination to the LORD your God. Nor shall you bring an abomination into your house, lest you be doomed to destruction like it. You shall utterly detest it and utterly abhor it, for it *is* an accursed thing, (Deuteronomy 7:25-26, NKJV.)

And many who had believed came confessing and telling their deeds. Also, many of those who had practiced magic brought their books together and burned *them* in the sight of all. And they counted up the value of them, and *it* totaled fifty thousand *pieces* of silver, (Acts 19:18-19. NKJV.)

6. Bind any demonic spirits that are influencing or troubling you, command them to leave you and not return. Loose the

grace and power of God upon your life. Then declare in the name of Jesus that you are now released from the curse.

And it shall come to pass *That* whoever calls on the name of the LORD Shall be saved, (Joel 2:32, NKJV.)

"Assuredly, I say to you, whatever you bind on earth will be bound in heaven, and whatever you loose on earth will be loosed in heaven," (Matthew 18:18, NKJV.)

When you take these steps with a sincere, obedient heart, you can rest assured that the doors that once stood open to the past will be shut by the mighty hand of God.

THE PRAYER OF RELEASE

Remember, true effective prayer is not formulaic. It is talking to God out of a sincerely earnest heart. Therefore, in order to have a better understanding of how to pray, first read through the following prayer. It is simply a guideline, a model pinpointing specific points with which you need to deal. Feel free to modify it to fit your personal situation. Remember that when you add faith and firm obedience, these are not just empty phrases. On the other hand if the words are prayed from an insincere, uncommitted heart, they will have no value. When you are ready to pray this prayer of release, pray it with faith and authority:

Dear Lord Jesus,

I believe you are the Son of God and the only way to God. I believe You died on the Cross for my sins and that You rose from the dead. I believe that You were made a curse in order that I might be redeemed from the curse and receive Your blessings.

I trust You now for mercy and forgiveness. I commit

myself to You and receive Your grace to follow and obey You from this moment forward.

I ask You to forgive and blot out any sins committed by me that exposed me to a curse. (Name any specific sins of which you are aware.) Jesus, I ask you to walk back into my past and shut once and for all the door that sin opened to the Enemy.

I forgive people who have harmed me or wronged me. In the name of Jesus, I break the spirit and power of my abuser over me. God, I totally, wholeheartedly forgive those who have offended and abused me. (Name the people.)

I renounce all contact with Satan, occult practices, false religions and unscriptural secret societies. If I have any objects that link me to these things, I promise to destroy them. (Name any of the above in which you were involved.)

Upon the authority You have given me as a child of God, I claim full release. I bind the powers of Satan over my life. I revoke every curse. I declare that Satan is a defeated foe, that all his claims in my life have been cancelled by the shed blood of Jesus Christ. I declare that I now am free from every curse that has ever come upon me or affected me in any way. I release the full abundant blessings of God in my life.

In the name of Jesus I pray, Amen.[132]

As soon as you finish the prayer, by faith receive your release. Accept it as an accomplished fact. Begin to thank God for freeing you from the curse. Thank him that the curse in your family has been broken. Thank Him that He has promised to reverse the curse and show His mercy and steadfast love to a thousand generations of those who love Him and keep His commandments.

> You shall not bow down to them nor serve them. For I, the LORD your God, *am* a jealous God, visiting the iniquity of the fathers upon the children to the third and fourth *generations* of those who hate Me, but showing mercy to thousands, to those who love Me and keep My commandments. (Exodus 20:5-6,NKJV.)

And remember:

> You are of God, little children, and have overcome them, because He who is in you is greater than he who is in the world, (I John 4:4, Amplified.)

GOD BREAKS THE POWER OF CANCELLED SIN

In Israel, I once watched an old shepherd remove the hide from a little dead lamb and lay it on an orphan lamb. Within minutes an amazing thing happened. The mother of the little lamb that had died began to sniff the orphan. When she smelled the scent of her own baby, the ewe took the orphan lamb, fed it and made it her own.

That's what Jesus did for us. The sinless Lamb of God suffered and shed His blood for us. When we come to God for cleansing and the blood of His Son is applied to our hearts, God no longer sees our sin, our imperfections or our past failures. He "smells the scent" of

His precious Son upon us and accepts us as His very own. The power of sin is broken in our lives, and we are free!

But that's not all. Jesus not only sets us free from the curse of sin, but He can keep us free. We, our children and our children's children need never experience the wickedness, darkness and the destructive effects of a curse.

LIKE FATHER, LIKE CHILD

Read the following statements and if they apply to your life, allow the truths they contain to sink deeply into your heart:

> Just because I was abused does not mean I will become an abuser.
>
> Just because my parent, grandparent, or other person in my life divorced, had a poor relationship, committed suicide, or abused someone, does not mean that I must.
>
> Just because my parent, grandparent, or other person in my life was addicted to alcohol, drugs, or pornography does not chain me to that addiction.
>
> I am not doomed to become like my father, mother, or any other ancestor.
>
> God is my Father. He is my inheritance, and I can become just like Him.

> O Lord, You are the portion of my inheritance and
> my cup; You maintain my lot. The lines have fallen to
> me in pleasant places; Yes, I have a good inheritance.
> (Psalm 16:5-6, NKJV.)

17

CONQUERING THE
TIGER WITHIN

Say to those who have an anxious heart, "Be strong; fear not!
Behold, your God will come...He will come and save you."

ISAIAH 35:4, ESV

MANY YEARS AGO in ancient Persia, a king and his ministers were debating whether mental or physical sufferings were the most severe. To settle the dispute, one minister proposed an experiment. He took a lamb with a broken leg and shut it up in a cage with plenty of food and water. He then took a perfectly healthy lamb and enclosed it in a big cage with a tiger. The tiger was bound by a strong chain so the beast could spring near the lamb, but could not possibly touch it.

The next morning the king and his ministers arrived to view the results of their experiment. The lamb with the broken leg had eaten all the food and was resting comfortably. The other lamb lay dead from fright.

I think I know how that frightened lamb felt. For eight-and-a-half agonizing years I shared an inescapable cage of emotional suffering with a drooling, razor-clawed tiger. It threatened to devour my peace of mind.

From early childhood my head had tilted to one side and my penmanship was horrible. Even in the Army, my superiors criticized my practically illegible handwriting. But in 1982, a strange and perplexing problem began to attack me. Whenever I felt tense or under unusual pressure, my neck began to spasm. My head would shake uncontrollably as if I had palsy. Time after time as I'd walk to the pulpit and open my Bible to preach, the terrible jerking would start. I don't remember how many times I had to stop and ask the congregation to pray for me before I could continue.

Overwhelmed by fear and embarrassment, I went to numerous doctors seeking help. Each one told me the same thing: "It's an emotional disorder stemming from the abuse you suffered as a child."

An emotional disorder! What more humiliating affliction could a minister of the Gospel have? Here I was preaching to others about peace and joy while my head felt as if it would shake right off my shoulders.

As time passed, the tormenting jerking spells attacked with greater frequency and fiercer intensity, and so did the relentless tiger of terror. "You're having a nervous breakdown," it would snarl in my ear.

Sometimes after everyone had left our ministry headquarters building for the day, I'd sit alone on the stairs as tears streamed down my face. Fear of rejection, fear of failure, fear of inadequacy seemed to attack from every side. The anger, pain and unforgiveness bottled up inside like a monstrous abscess were coming to a head. Too proud to confide in anyone, I felt as if my heart would burst.

Then in 1989 came the most totally humiliating attack of all. Ted Koppel invited me to appear as a guest on his television show, *Nightline*, to discuss the storm of controversy swirling around televangelist Jimmy Swaggart.

I was accustomed to sitting under hot lights and staring into a camera because our ministry had won several Angel Awards for prime-time television specials. But this time, just as my face appeared on screens nationwide, the tiger pounced. Awful neck spasms and head shaking began and did not stop. At one point, the tremors became so violent that I, in desperation, attempted to steady my neck and chin with my hand.

All the way home my mind replayed the humiliating scene. Here I was, a minister of the Gospel, in front of ten million people, appearing on the verge of collapsing with a nervous breakdown—or something.

When I unlocked the door of our home and stepped inside, I found Carolyn crying. As I hugged her, she sobbed, "Please promise me you'll never do another television show."

How could I promise such a thing? I simply could not roll over, play dead, and let the tiger win. The Word of God I had preached and believed for more than twenty years was true. I knew it was! Somewhere, somehow, I would find a way to slay the voracious beast.

I saw doctor after doctor and each time was told the same old thing; but I was determined not to give in to the dreadful fear constantly prowling in the shadows of my mind.

In 1990 Ted Koppel invited me for a return engagement on *Nightline*. Carolyn prayerfully agreed with me that the Lord would fill me with peace and assurance and that God would receive glory from all that was said. Miraculously, I experienced no tremors or spasms; the interview went very well.

Finally, in 1991, after visiting almost fifty doctors over an eight-year period, I walked into the office of the physician who was to discover the answer to my problem. First he subjected me to a series of the most thorough physical examinations I'd ever had. Then he asked a battery of questions concerning symptoms and my history. He even inquired about my ancestors and wanted to know from where they came. Finally, the doctor delivered his diagnosis:

"You're not struggling with an emotional disorder," he reassured me. "You are suffering from a rare neurological disease—spasmodic torticollis. It's caused by an inherited defective gene and primarily affects the Ashkenazi Jews in Russia—your mother's ancestors.

I wanted to laugh, cry, and jump for joy. At last the terrifying tiger had a name. But as I was soon to discover, my foe was still very much alive.

The only effective treatment for the disease was surgery. Because the defective gene was sending signals to three nerves in my neck which caused the spasms and tremors, the nerves would have to be removed during a nine-hour operation at the University of Florida Medical Center.

To prevent air from traveling from my neck into my heart, the operation had to be performed with me sitting upright. For thirty minutes before the actual surgery, I was conscious on the operating table with a tube inserted into my heart.

But it wasn't the tube or the physical discomfort that frightened me: It was the fear that the worst would happen—a fear that had tormented me from my childhood. Only moments before I slipped into unconsciousness, I suddenly felt overwhelmed by a dark and foreboding dread. It was as if I could see all the mocking, rejecting faces from my past hovering in a circle around the table where I would recline during the surgery. "We've got you now," they seemed to sneer.

But from years of spiritual warfare, I continued to battle Satan inwardly, instinctively pleading the blood of Jesus over my life. Then I slowly slipped into a peaceful calm.

When I awoke, faith and perseverance had won. The tormenting tiger had been vanquished.

CONQUERING PARALYZING FEARS

Do you know what it is to live with self-defeating thoughts and feelings? Do paralyzing fears stalk you night and day? How can you stop the tiger before it destroys you?

You may have heard the phrase "the paralysis of analysis." Some are good at analyzing all the drawbacks in a situation and thinking of everything that could possibly go wrong. However, when it comes to actually getting busy and solving the problem, we find that we're paralyzed by one fear or another. It is fine to analyze, but it must be channeled into constructive action.

What do you do when confronted by an anxiety-provoking problem? How do you cope? Do you immediately set out to solve the problem, or do you allow fear to paralyze you into inaction?

Family therapists tell us that most of our coping behaviors, whether functional or dysfunctional, effective or ineffective, are learned from the established patterns in our families.

Have you assessed your personal coping style? In not, here's your chance.

RATE YOUR PROBLEM-SOLVING SKILLS

Circle the letter that best describes your response:

1. Whenever I am confronted with a threatening, fear-provoking situation:
   a. I am quick to perceive it as a problem.
   b. I'm likely to deny the seriousness of the situation because I lack confidence in my ability to deal with problems.

2. If I believe a situation is a problem:
    a. I make the decision to try to resolve it.
    b. I work harder to avoid the problem by ignoring or forgetting the situation, distorting the meaning of warning messages or minimizing the severity of the problem through wishful rationalization as the stress increases.

3. Once I've determined to attack the problem:
    a. I search for information relevant to solving the problem, and then from that information, I decide which option is the most effective way to take care of the situation.
    b. I settle for the solution that requires the least expenditure of time, money, energy, and resources.

4. Once I've tried my selected solution:
    a. I evaluate its effectiveness to determine whether I should continue with the strategy, revise it, or discard it in favor of an alternative solution.
    b. I get tired of the stress while I'm waiting and don't allow my chosen solution sufficient time to work.

5. In this final stage of the problem-solving process:
    a. I either accept my original solution or I return to the second stage, once again deciding whether or not to attempt to solve the problem.
    b. I am so out of touch with reality, I'm incapable of perceiving whether the problem is being solved, gauging the problem accurately, or making necessary changes.

As you may have already guessed, "a" is the response selected by effective problem-solvers. Any "b" answers you may have selected reveal weaknesses in coping and problem-solving skills. Study your answers to help recognize weak coping skills the next time a problem arises.

CONVERTING DESPERATE FEARS INTO SOLVABLE PROBLEMS

Let's look at another weapon you can use in conquering paralyzing fears. How can you resolve your worst fears?

First, you should define your most desperate fears, putting them into words. Next, convert your paralyzing fears into solvable problems to which you can find practical, workable solutions. Here's how it works:

> PARALYZING FEAR
> I'll never be able to find a better job.
>
> SOLVABLE PROBLEM
> I may not get the greatest job at first, but I'm willing to work hard, persevere, and develop my abilities. When a better opportunity comes along, I'll be prepared.

Solvable problems not only restate desperate fears in such a way as to make them less terrifying, but the restatements create some solutions and new perceptions as well.

What paralyzing fears are tormenting you and holding you back? Perhaps you'll want to take time to list the two things of which you are most afraid. Then you can reshape those fears by rewording them as solvable problems to which you can find workable solutions.

Paralyzing Fear:

1. _____

2. _____

Solvable Problem:

1. _____

2. _____

Transforming paralyzing fears into manageable thoughts and solvable problems helps you concentrate on finding solutions and alternatives. You will discover that the process also decreases some of your dread of the unknown.

DOING THE THING YOU FEAR
Please answer the following questions:

1. Do you try to dodge challenges or opportunities that would expose you to the attention of others or make you more visible? ___Yes ___No

2. Do you retreat from one-on-one contact with others? ___Yes ___No

3. Do you seek to avoid unfamiliar routines and surroundings or situations over which you have little or no control? ___Yes ___No

4. Do you instinctively avoid any relationship or situation in which you might feel threatened or vulnerable? ___Yes ___No

If you answered yes to question after question, you probably have allowed fears of pain, rejection or failure to squeeze your life into a dull, predictable rut.

The Apostle Paul wrote to Timothy:

> For God has not given us a spirit of fear, but of power and of love and of a sound mind, (I Timothy 1:7, NKJV.)

One way to break free of fear's domination is to read the Scriptures and remember that God has set us free from the spirit of fear. Another is to do the thing you fear. For example, how does a professional skier or skater react to a fall? The athlete gets up and tries again.

As I related earlier, I felt like a miserable flop after my first Nightline appearance. But I knew I did not dare give in to the fears that told me I would fail again and open myself up for more ridicule and rejection if I ever received another invitation from Ted Koppel. An inner wisdom told me that if I trusted God and forced myself to do the thing I feared most, I could conquer the problem.

What are your two greatest fears?

1. _____

2. _____

What would you do in each of those situations if you were not afraid?

1. _____

2. _____

If you will take your fears one at a time and confront them head-on, acting as if you are not afraid, in time your feeling will align with your actions. Gradually, you will begin to gain a sense of confidence, and you will begin to walk in faith as the old fears are shed.

PRESCRIPTION FOR CONQUERING PARALYZING FEARS

How can we handle our paralyzing fears more effectively? Let's summarize what we've learned. First, we must recognize and reject our weak coping skills and replace them with effective problem-solving techniques. Second, we should define our desperate fears, putting them into words. Next, those fears should be restated as solvable problems for which we can find workable solutions. Finally, we must begin doing the thing we fear as we walk in the power and strength of our Lord Jesus Christ.

CONQUERING SELF-DEFEATING THOUGHTS AND FEELINGS

Sometimes you and I can be our own worst enemies. We allow negative thoughts and feelings to defeat us at every turn.

The following exercise will help you get in touch with your feelings. Please answer each question with a yes or no:

Yes No   My Feelings

___ ___   1. I feel sad the majority of the time.

___ ___   2. I often feel frustrated.

___ ___   3. I feel self-hatred.

___ ___   4. I feel frightened.

___ ___   5. I feel bewildered and confused.

____ ____   6.   I feel very angry much of the time.

____ ____   7.   I feel overwhelmed about many things

____ ____   8.   I feel guilty. I'm always in the wrong.

____ ____   9.   I feel hopeless.

____ ____   10.   I feel weak and powerless.

____ ____   11.   I feel stupid and incompetent.

____ ____   12.   I feel useless and without purpose.

If you experience other strong feelings that are not listed here, write them down also. If you answered yes to even a few of these questions, you are obviously experiencing some emotional pain and distress. However, it is possible to make changes in your feelings and, therefore, in your life through learning to conquer and control defeating, destructive thoughts. You can actually learn to master the negative thoughts and feelings that have sabotaged your judgment and reason, making your life miserable.

THOUGHTS COME BEFORE FEELINGS

Our thoughts—what we say to ourselves—clearly play an important role in controlling our lives. Did you know that most emotional responses, for example, are not the result of external events, but of what we tell ourselves about the events?

For example, my emotional response to flunking a test will be different depending on what I tell myself about it. Do I say to myself that the failing score proves I am stupid and should drop out of class, or do I say to myself, "Don't let it get your down. Keep working hard and you'll do better next time."

Because most of us have no idea that our feelings are a direct result of our thoughts, we tend to blame our feelings on external events. What someone said; what someone did; pressures, problems. Recognizing the impact our negative thoughts are having on our feelings can help us gain more control over what we are thinking and feeling.

DISTINGUISHING BETWEEN THOUGHTS AND FEELINGS

The following exercise can help you clarify the connection between your thoughts and feelings. The feelings listed are the same for those contained in the questions you answered in the last exercise. See if some of the thoughts that go along with the feelings seem familiar to you.

Feeling: I feel sad a majority of the time.
Thoughts: What have I got to live for? Life is miserable. Are my struggles worth it?

Feelings: I feel frustrated.
Thoughts: Nothing I do makes any difference.

Feelings: I feel self-hatred.
Thoughts: I'm a piece of junk. My life's a wreck, and it's my fault. I'll never amount to anything.

Feelings: I feel frightened.
Thoughts: Something bad is about to happen. When things don't work out, what will I do then?

Feelings: I feel bewildered and confused.
Thoughts: Why does this always happen to me? What did I do wrong? How can things that seem so right turn out so bad?

Feelings: I feel very angry much of the time.
Thoughts: I'd like to hit and scream and tell them exactly what I think of them, if only I weren't so scared.

Feelings: I feel overwhelmed about many things.
Thoughts: Nothing I do works. Someone else is always smarter, better looking or luckier than I am. They get all the breaks.

Feelings: I feel guilty and always in the wrong.
Thoughts: It's my fault; if only I were a better person.

Feelings: I feel hopeless.
Thoughts: Who am I kidding? Things are never going to change. There's no way out of this.

Feelings: I feel weak and powerless.
Thoughts: Nothing I can say or do will make a difference. Nobody listens to me anyway.

Feelings: I feel stupid and incompetent.
Thoughts: I can never win; I'm a born loser. I always find a way to mess things up. I can't do anything right.

Feelings: I feel worthless and without purpose.
Thoughts: What am I good for, anyway? Life has no meaning. Nobody needs me. I could drop off the face of the earth and no one would miss me.

Feelings: I feel isolated and lonely.
Thoughts: People usually think poorly of me and don't particularly like me, so why bother trying to make friends?

Feelings: I feel like a miserable failure.
Thoughts: If it involves a change or a challenge, I avoid it. Why set myself up for more shame and frustration?

Did any of those thoughts resemble some of yours? Are you beginning to realize how negative thoughts may influence your feelings?

Making the critical distinction between thoughts and feelings requires honesty and discernment. Recognizing destructive, defeating thoughts and replacing them with constructive, conquering thoughts takes practice. Changing ingrained habits and responses takes time. But if we are determined and if we persevere, we can learn to isolate thoughts from feelings, choose constructive reactions and change our behavior. As the Word reminds us:

> Brethren, whatever is true, whatever is worthy of reverence *and* is honorable *and* seemly, whatever is just, whatever is pure, whatever is lovely *and* lovable, whatever is kind *and* winsome *and* gracious, if there is any virtue *and* excellence, if there is anything worthy of praise, *think on and weigh and take account of these things [fix your minds on them]*, (Philippians 4:8, Amplified, italics added.)

MY, WHAT BEAUTIFUL WINGS YOU HAVE!

As a child, you may have had no other alternative than to accept the picture of yourself that your parents or authority figures handed you. Because you had no clear image of yourself, if you were told that you were worthless, hopeless, to blame, and other negative things, you tended to believe what you were told. Soon you transformed those negative beliefs into punishing, self-defeating thoughts, feelings and actions.

But you do not have to remain a twisted image of someone else's cruel lies and distortions. God longs to enable and empower you to be more than you ever hoped or dreamed.

It took years to establish that warped concept of yourself, and it may require years of struggle to establish an accurate image of the special individual God created you to be. But as John Garlock, a gifted and inspiring Bible teacher, shares in the following illustration, the struggle is itself a vital part of the success.

Louis Agassiz, the famous American naturalist, was interested in the metamorphosis that occurs as a caterpillar becomes a butterfly. He found a chrysalis on a branch one day. Being careful not to disturb it, he cut the branch and carried it inside to his desk. Day after day, he watched it, waiting for the chrysalis to split and the butterfly to emerge. Finally, a crack appeared. And little by little, he could see the struggling creature inside, breaking the strands wound around it one by one. The creature would struggle and struggle—then fall back, exhausted. Then it would struggle again.

Finally, only a few strands of the cocoon still held the butterfly in prison. Agassiz, having compassion, reached into his desk drawer and took out a pair of scissors. Being careful not to touch the butterfly, he snipped those last few strands. The cocoon fell open, and out crawled the butterfly.

To his dismay, the butterfly never flew. It crawled all its life. In discussing this circumstance with another naturalist who had conducted a special study on butterflies, Agassiz asked why the butterfly didn't fly. His friend explained, "You doomed it to the life of a cripple by sparing it from struggle. The butterfly requires the intense struggle of breaking out of the cocoon to initiate circulation in its wings. By removing the struggle, you doomed it to an unfulfilled life."[133]

Most of us wish that God would simply zap us with a bolt of holy lightning and instantly transform us into a whole, perfect person. We grow weary of struggling to change and grow. The battle against paralyzing fears and self-defeating thoughts and feelings seems too much for us at times. But we can change. We can overcome.

You are not the hopeless, helpless victim of either your heredity or your environment. Your struggles, like those of the weary butterfly in its confining cocoon, are creating strength. They are preparing you for the day when you will stretch your beautiful wings and soar!

✤ 18 ✤

OVERCOMING DESTRUCTIVE HABITS AND BEHAVIORS

*Therefore if any person is [ingrafted] in Christ
(the Messiah) he is a new creation (a new creature altogether);
the old [previous moral and spiritual condition] has passed away.
Behold, the fresh and new has come!*

II CORINTHIANS 5:17, AMPLIFIED

Autobiography in Five Short Chapters

I. I walk down the street.
> There is a deep hole in the sidewalk.
> I fall in.
> I am lost...I am helpless.
> It isn't my fault.
> It takes forever to find a way out.

II. I walk down the same street.
> There is a deep hole in the sidewalk.
> I pretend I don't see it.
> I fall in again.
> I can't believe I'm in the same place.
> But, it isn't my fault.
> It still takes a long time to get out.

III. I walk down the same street.

There is a deep hole in the sidewalk.
I see it is there.
I still fall in...it's a habit.
My eyes are open.
I know where I am.
It is my fault.
I get out immediately.

IV. I walk down the same street.
There is a deep hole in the sidewalk.
I walk around it.

V. I walk down another street.[134]

CHANGING DESTRUCTIVE HABITS AND BEHAVIORS

Why do we drive ourselves toward unattainable goals? Why do we push for perfection? Why do we choose relationships with people who hurt us? Why do we punish ourselves, tear ourselves down and sabotage our own success and happiness by a constant flow of negative, self-deprecating, self-destructive habits and behaviors? This comment by psychoanalyst Karen Horney, as provocative today as when she wrote it over six decades ago, gives an illuminating insight into those questions:

Self-torture is in part an inevitable by-product of self-hate. Whether the neurotic tries to whip himself into perfection impossible to attain, hurls accusations against himself, or disparages and frustrates himself, he is actually only tormenting himself.[135]

For many of us who were abused when we were young, negative internal responses and destructive behaviors sprouted and flourished in the dysfunctional environment in which we were raised. Since abused children have little or no power, in order to survive we learned early in life the feelings and behaviors that enabled us to cope with the treatment we encountered in our families.

As a result, some of these feelings and behaviors may sound very familiar to you. Self-blame and guilt; expecting-the-worst attitudes; the belief that nothing you can say or do will make much, if any difference; driving yourself to perform and produce; paying too much or too little attention to your physical appearance; perfectionism or passivity; withdrawal and denial; compulsive behaviors.

The problem is that even in adulthood, many of us continue to feel the same powerlessness we felt as children, although our current situations may be very different. However, destructive thoughts, attitudes, habits, and behaviors can be overcome. Here's how:

BE ON GUARD

Pay close attention to what you allow to enter and fill your heart, for "out of the fullness—the overflow, the super-abundance of the heart—the mouth speaks." (Matthew 12:34, Amplified.)

If you allow your heart to be filled with contaminating thoughts and feelings of bitterness, blame, self-pity, condemnation and fear, don't be surprised when your mouth overflows with words of rejection, hatred, mistrust and insecurity.

Closely monitor and guard what you think in your heart. The Scriptures reveal a vital, but often ignored, principle concerning the importance of our thoughts. Proverbs 23:7 declares that "As a man thinks in his heart, so is he."

Thoughts shape the soul. We can use words and actions to conceal, counterfeit, and misrepresent, but all the time our thoughts are determining who we are and what we will become. We are either being built up or destroyed from within.

For years my mind replayed my father's rejection and ridicule until I accepted it and repeated it to myself. Then I discovered that if I wanted to silence the nagging, negative voice within and replace it with a strengthening, encouraging winner's voice, my heart had to be filled with and focused on the healing and life-giving words of my heavenly Father:

> My son, give attention to my words; Incline your ear to my sayings. Do not let them depart from your eyes; Keep them in the midst of your heart; (Proverbs 4:20-21, NKJV.)

Now I have learned the importance of reading my Bible daily. I memorize verses focusing on my particular needs and meditate upon them. I cram my heart full of the Word of God so that when I think or speak, my thoughts and words will bring life and peace.

Proverbs 4:23-27 has also taught me to control what flows into and out of my heart by guarding what I say, what I see, where I go, and what I do:

> Keep *and* guard your heart with all vigilance *and* above all that you guard, for out of it flow the springs of life. Put away from you false *and* dishonest speech, and willful *and* contrary talk put far from you. Let your eyes look right on [with fixed purpose], and let your gaze be straight before you. Consider well the path of your feet,

and let all your ways be established *and* ordered aright. Turn not aside to the right hand or to the left; remove your foot from evil, (Proverbs 4:23-27, Amplified.)

Guard your heart!

BE FED

Have you ever been awakened at two or three o'clock in the morning by the cries of a hungry newborn baby? As the father or four children, I'll never forget the sounds of our tiny babies greedily gulping warm, nourishing milk. The first few noisy swallows sounded as if the milk was dropping ten feet into a hollow well!

God says that you and I are to be just as hungry for the nourishing milk of His Word in order that we may grow.

> Like newborn babies you should crave (thirst for, earnestly desire) the pure (unadulterated) spiritual milk, that by it you may be nurtured *and* grow unto [completed] salvation, (I Peter 2:2, Amplified.)

Reading the Bible should be more than an intellectual exercise, however. Learn to meditate on the verses you read. In your daily reading, watch for verses that tell you what you are to believe and what you are to do. Then, right there on the spot, turn those commands into specific prayers and intimate dialogue with God, asking Him to give you the power and desire to believe and do what He commands.

Our minds and spirits need to be nourished and fed, but certain problems should be starved. Remember the old saying: "What you feed grows; what you starve dies." Praying about the problems in your life is vital, but sometimes you must do more than pray if you desire to see some problems resolved. If a problem continues to grow, check to see if you are feeding it by what you are thinking, seeing, and saying. If you pray about it and starve it, it will eventually die. But in the meantime, don't forget to feed your mind and spirit with the Word of God.

BE CLEANSED

Did you know that you can get dirty on the inside just as easily as you can get dirty on the outside? But how can you take a spiritual bath every day? How can you cleanse yourself from everything that contaminates and defiles your body and spirit as God commands? (See II Corinthians 7:1.)

Ephesians 5:25-26 tells us that followers of Christ are cleansed by the washing of the water with the Word of God. Its truth not only nourishes, but purifies as well.

We are also cleansed by the blood of Jesus when we confess our sins and ask God's forgiveness:

> Like newborn babies you should crave (thirst for, earnestly desire) the pure (unadulterated) spiritual milk, that by it you may be nurtured *and* grow unto [completed] salvation, (I John 1:9, Amplified.)

If the springs of our heart are clogged and contaminated by sin, all that flows out—including our words and behavior—will be defiled.

BE CLOTHED

Healthy babies grow quickly. During the first couple of years or so in each of our children's lives, my wife sorted through the closet and dresser drawers in the nursery every two or three months.

She took out little undershirts, socks and outfits the babies had outgrown and carefully stored them for our next child or gave them away.

Again we can see the parallel in the spiritual realm. When we give our hearts to Christ and make Him Lord of our lives, our former nature with its defeating, destructive attitudes and actions must be outgrown, discarded and replaced by a new nature with its fresh mental and spiritual attitudes.

> But now put away *and* rid yourselves [completely] of all these things: anger, rage, bad feeling toward others, curses *and* slander, and foulmouthed abuse *and* shameful utterances from your lips! Do not lie to one another, for you have stripped off the old (unregenerate) self with its evil practices, And have clothed yourselves with the new [spiritual self], which is [ever in the process of being] renewed *and* remolded into [fuller and more perfect knowledge upon] knowledge after the image (the likeness) of Him Who created it, (Colossians 3:8-10, Amplified.)

Ephesians 4:22-24 says it like this:

> Strip yourselves of your former nature [put off and discard your old unrenewed self] which characterized your previous manner of life and becomes corrupt through lusts *and* desires that spring from delusion; And be constantly renewed in the spirit of your mind [having a fresh mental and spiritual attitude], And put on the new nature (the regenerate self) created in

God's image, [Godlike] in true righteousness and holiness (Amplified.)

We not only put on a new spiritual nature, but we are also to fully clothe ourselves in invisible spiritual armor so we can be ready at a moment's notice to fight and defeat Satan.

> Put on God's whole armor [the armor of a heavy-armed soldier which God supplies], that you may be able successfully to stand up against [all] the strategies *and* the deceits of the devil, (Ephesians 6:11, Amplified.)

BE FILLED

Have you ever left a pot of dirt outside through the winter after the annual flowers you planted were killed by the first heavy freeze? If so, did you notice what started sprouting as soon as the soil was warmed and moistened by the balmy weather and gentle rains of early spring? Little green weeds!

Our hearts are like the soil in that flower pot. Given the right conditions, something—regardless of whether it's good or bad—is going to grow there. Therefore...

> And do not be drunk with wine, in which is dissipation; but be filled with the Spirit, *speaking to one another* in psalms and hymns and spiritual songs, *singing and making melody in your heart to the Lord,* giving thanks always for all things to God the Father

in the name of our Lord Jesus Christ, (Ephesians 5:18-20, NKJV, emphasis mine.)

You're going to be filled with something, so make certain you're filled with the Spirit of God.

BE STRONG IN THE LORD

Shira Joy, our second child, whose name in Hebrew means "Song of Joy," was born prematurely and weighed only three-and a-half pounds at birth.

I noticed she was becoming very frustrated with her physical frailty and had difficulty keeping up after starting school, so I devised a plan to help her. Each night before she dropped off to sleep, I went into her room and talked with her. I told her what the Word of God said about her as His child. I quoted verses of Scripture, reminding her she was strong in the Lord.

Shira began to memorize and quote those verses to herself. Soon she was attempting physical challenges she had been afraid to try before. After a while, the whole family began to notice a remarkable difference in Shira's attitude as well as in her physical strength and endurance. The result? By the time she was nine years old, Shira could arm wrestle her mother and win.

Like little Shira, I know what it is to long for the strength and ability I see in others. I used to read Hebrews 11—the heroes of faith chapter—and sigh with envy.

I couldn't help comparing my doubts and feeble efforts with the unwavering faith and strength of those spiritual heavyweights. Then, in Hebrews 11:34, I noticed a phrase that turned my attitude around. The verse talks about how they "extinguished the power of raging fires and escaped the devourings of the sword." Then it says they, "out of the frailty and weakness won strength and became stalwart, even mighty and resistless in battle, routing alien hosts."

Remember that we talked about the butterfly fighting to free itself from the cocoon and how its struggles made it strong? Here is that principle again: The spiritual heroes of the Bible weren't always strong and stalwart. But out of weakness, they were made strong.

It's like doing spiritual aerobics. Each righteous response, every wise choice and right action makes us stronger. Every sincere prayer and time of meditation in the Word of God makes us more steadfast. With each success we gain confidence to confront other challenges.

The strength to make righteous responses and wise choices, to pray and study the Scriptures, comes from God, not from ourselves. So remember this:

> In conclusion, be strong in the Lord [be empowered through your union with Him]; draw your strength from Him [that strength which His boundless might provides], (Ephesians 6:10, Amplified.)

BE PATIENT

A friend of mine tilled the soil and prepared the rows for a small vegetable garden in her backyard. Just as she opened packages of green bean seed, her neighbor's two preschoolers wandered over and asked what she was doing. My friend told them she was planting beans and asked if they would like to help.

The next day she saw the children carefully examining the rows they had planted. "We're looking to see if the seeds are coming up yet," they replied.

My friend explained that it would take a while for the seeds to sprout and form little plants, but the following afternoon the youngsters were back, poking around in the dirt. They returned the next day and the next. Still nothing. Disappointed, the children didn't show their faces in the garden for a month.

When they did return, the children were shocked to see flourishing, green plants with their delicate tendrils winding around the poles and wire that my friend had erected so that the beans could climb.

Sometimes you and I are like those children: We know we need to change a habit or a behavior, so we put forth a big, all-out effort for a few days. But when we don't see immediate results, we give up.

It took months, sometimes years, to form our bad habits and behaviors, and it may take weeks, months, or years to replace them with edifying, constructive habit patterns. So refuse to give in to condemning thoughts. Reject the temptation to feel sorry for yourself. Accept responsibility for each failure, ask God's help, and move forward. Keep working at it until each new behavior, habit, or attitude is firmly established.

> But let endurance *and* steadfastness *and* patience have full play *and* do a thorough work, so that you may be [people] perfectly and fully developed [with no defects], lacking in nothing, (James 1:4, Amplified.)

BE PERSISTENT

How do you keep plodding when the going gets tough? Here are some suggestions:

1. Anticipate specific problems that may arise, and plan beforehand how you will deal with them.

For example, if the Christmas holidays or the annual family reunion are dreaded ordeals, what special plans or changes should you make to avoid or overcome the usual unpleasantness?

2. Set specific goals.

Did you know that of the people who make resolutions to change behavior, the most successful are those who have the most specific goals? In other words, don't say you want to lose weight. Instead, set a goal: "I will lose fifteen pounds by the time of my class reunion four months from now. Or, instead of saying, "I want to read the Bible and pray more," say, "I will rise ten minutes earlier each morning so I can read a chapter and talk to the Lord about the pressures and responsibilities I will face that day."

3. Don't try to do everything at once. Break big, threatening goals into a series of smaller, attainable goals.

Have a one-day-at-a-time attitude. Sometimes it's more realistic and effective to break a goal into a series of short steps instead of trying to accomplish everything in one giant leap. In the end, you will have an encouraging series of successes on which you can reflect and from which you can draw confidence.

4. When you fail in reaching a goal, refuse to cave-in and quit. Analyze what caused the failure and try again.

I once had a sound man named Tony working for me. He was a whiz at electronics and could coax temperamental microphones and public address systems into working their best. Tony told me at one point in his life he worked as a sound man for Ronald Reagan.

Tony said that when Mr. Reagan was governor of California, he was already planning his strategy and preparing to run for president. Part of that strategy was writing articles for newspapers, preparing brief commentaries for radio, making speeches and public appearances.

Tony told me that long before the presidential debates were to take place, Mr. Reagan was diligently researching his responses to questions that might be asked. Tony related that Mr. Reagan's first rehearsals were so bad and he made so many mistakes it sounded like "The Gong Show."

"You'd think, 'This man just couldn't be president of anything!'" said Tony. "But he just kept at it, rehearsing over and over again."

Soon, to Tony's surprise Mr. Reagan was performing comfortably, competently and confidently. Eventually even members of the media were referring to Ronald Reagan as "the great Communicator."

How did the future president gain his remarkable ability to communicate so effectively in the political arena? He planned for success.

Paul put it like this:

> And let us not lose heart *and* grow weary *and* faint in acting nobly *and* doing right, for in due time *and* at the appointed season we shall reap, if we do not loosen *and* relax our courage *and* faint, (Galatians 6:9, Amplified.)

WALKING DOWN A DIFFERENT STREET

Are you tired of walking down the same street? Then here's what to do:

1. Be on guard as to what you think in your heart and what you allow to enter it.

2. Be fed by nourishing yourself on God's Word.

3. Be cleansed daily from all that contaminates.

4. Be clothed with a new spiritual nature.

5. Be filled with God's Spirit.

6. Be strong in the Lord.

7. Be patient.

8. Be persistent.

Don't let self-deprecating, self-destructive attitudes, habits and behaviors keep you walking down the same old street. Put these eight principles into practice and get your life started in a new positive direction.

ESTABLISIHNG NEW HABITS AND BEHAVIORS

It was American humorist Josh Billings who said, "The postage stamp secures success through its ability to stick to one thing till it gets there." The following questions will help you develop your winning strategy and enable you to stick on one thing until desired attitudes, habits, and behaviors are firmly established.

1. Circle which of the following is your area of greatest need:

   a. Forgiving others
   b. Overcoming rejection
   c. Rebuilding shattered self-esteem
   d. Finding a God you can believe in
   e. Breaking a family curse
   f. Overcoming destructive thought patterns, habits and behaviors

2. List two specific, attainable goals you will begin working toward in order to address that area of need.

   a. Goal 1: _____

   _____

   b. Goal 2: _____

   _____

3. What are two possible problems that might arise as you work toward your goals? If those problems surface, how will you deal with them? Take a moment to think through and briefly outline a strategy to deal with each of those problems.

   a. _____

   _____

   b. _____

   _____

✤ 19 ✤

WELCOME TO A WINNER'S WORLD!

From prayer that asks that I may be
Sheltered from winds that beat on Thee,
From fearing when I should aspire,
From faltering when I should climb higher,...
From subtle love of softening things,
From easy choices, weakenings,
Not thus are spirits fortified,
Not this way went the Crucified,
From all that dims Thy Calvary,
O Lamb of God, deliver me.
"Give me the Love that leads the way
The Faith that nothing can dismay
The Hope no disappointments tire
The Passion that'll burn like fire
Let me not sink to be a clod
Make me Thy fuel, Flame of God."[136]

DEEP IN THE JORDAN DESERT near the ancient region of Moab stand the crumbling remains of a fort built and occupied by the Crusaders almost 1,000 years ago. The fort sits atop a mountain and consists of seven massive walls, each encircling the other. Therefore, in ancient times, even if an enemy could breach the outer wall, he was met by six other walls, each just as tall and strong as the first. The way the fort was constructed made it very unlikely that any enemy would ever be able to conquer it.

But an enemy army decided to attack the fort anyway. After laying siege for several days, they had not been able to break through even the first wall. Exhausted and discouraged, the enemy soldiers camped at a small oasis near the base of a mountain some distance from the fort.

One of the soldiers noticed a mongrel dog with unusual colors and markings that came each day to drink at the spring, then wander away. A short time later, the soldier was surprised to see that same dog walking along the top of the innermost wall of the fort. The next day, the dog again came to the oasis to drink. And just as before, minutes after the dog left, it could be seen walking on the massive inner wall.

The enemy soldier knew there had to be a way for the dog to get in and out of the fortress. As he watched, he formed a plan.

The following day when the dog came to drink, the soldier watched and followed it. At the foot of the mountain, the dog picked its way through brush and rocks and entered the mouth of a cave obscured by huge boulders. The soldier followed the dog into the cave and through a narrow tunnel leading into the very heart of the fort.

Covered by dust and trembling with excitement, the soldier rushed back to inform his commander of the amazing discovery. In less than an hour the enemy army had slithered through the tunnel and burst into the fort, surprising and totally overwhelming the unsuspecting Crusaders.

Once the fort containing and food and other supplies needed by the Crusader armies in the area was conquered, the battle was over.

Since the first time I heard it, that story has fascinated me because in it I can see a picture of the warfare that goes on in the spiritual realm. Our enemy sets up camp outside the castle of our hearts. After building strongholds—heavy obstacles and barriers—in front of his forces to protect them, he begins attacking and harassing us. He constantly seeks to cut the supply lines through which we receive spiritual food, water, ammunition, and reinforcements. And he is always searching for the weak places and vulnerable points in the walls through which he may gain entrance. Imagine his delight when he finds an unguarded tunnel dug by our own careless habits, undisciplined actions and sinful thoughts, giving him access to the very core of our being.

DEFENDING THE CASTLE OF YOUR HEART

How do you turn the battle around and defeat the clever enemy assaulting your mind? First of all, you starve him out. You cut off his supply lines and reinforcements. You refuse to toss him a scrap of food. You stop up the springs that water the comfortable little oasis at which he loves to camp.

Next, you assault the strongholds of lies, fear, and hopelessness that he has constructed in your path. You tear them down, exposing his forces and resources to attack. Every time one of his subtle lies, evil imaginations, discouraging doubts or deceiving thoughts (cleverly disguised as a sympathetic friend) attempts to scale the walls of your mind, you recognize it and instantly cast it down.

Paul described the weapons and tactics you and I must use if we want to defeat this subtle enemy:

> For though we walk (live) in the flesh, we are not
> carrying on our warfare according to the flesh *and*
> using mere human weapons. For the weapons of our

warfare are not physical [weapons of flesh and blood], but they are mighty before God for the overthrow *and* destruction of strongholds, [Inasmuch as we] refute arguments *and* theories *and* reasonings and every proud *and* lofty thing that sets itself up against the [true] knowledge of God; and we lead every thought *and* purpose away captive into the obedience of Christ (the Messiah, the Anointed One), (II Corinthians 10:3-5, Amplified.)

Satan has declared an all-out war on you. If you let him, he will use your personal problems, your pain and your past as weapons to damage and, if possible, destroy the person you were meant to be.

RENEWING YOUR MIND

How can we strengthen and fortify ourselves against attacks by the enemy?

As followers of Christ, you and I are not to live like those who don't know God. We are not to be conformed to the world's customs or allow ourselves to be squeezed into its mold. Instead, we are to submit ourselves to God and let Him remake us so that our whole mental attitude is transformed.

Do not be conformed to this world (this age), [fashioned after and adapted to its external, superficial customs], but be transformed (changed) by the [entire] renewal of your mind [by its new ideals and its new attitude], so that you may prove [for yourselves] what is the good and acceptable and perfect will of God, *even* the thing which is good and acceptable and perfect [in His sight for you], (Romans 12:2, Amplified.)

When you submit to the principles and power of God, you will undergo a supernatural change which finds expression in your nature and character, as well as your thought patterns and behavior.

> For those victims of abuse who have had difficulty loving and relating to God because they've had such a badly distorted image of Him, Colossians 3:10 contains an important key regarding this subject of renewal. As a believer in Christ, your new spiritual self is "being renewed *to a true knowledge* according to the image of the One who created him" (NAS, italics mine.)

Our minds can be renewed and remodeled into a fuller, more accurate knowledge of God that is after His true image and likeness. How? By pursuing a deep, intimate relationship with Jesus. By consistently scheduling time each day to commune with the Lord in prayer, getting to know Him intimately and opening the depths of your being to Him. By reading and meditating on His Word on a regular basis, dialoging with Jesus and committing to believe its truths and obey its commands.

I'll let you in on one of the little secrets I use to help renew and remold my mind: I copy Scriptures and tape them in places where I know I'll see them every day—on the mirror, in the car, on the refrigerator, on my computer screen. I change the verses from time to time, depending on the particular area of my life that I'm concentrating on strengthening or rebuilding.

When a negative thought comes against me and assaults my feelings, the powerful spiritual truths I've stored up in my mind undergird me with strength, helping me cast the thought down and respond constructively. This is how it works:

Thought: What do I have to live for? Life is miserable.

Feeling: Sad

Scripture: Ephesians 2:10—I am God's workmanship; He has a special plan for my life.

Action: I will obey God and put Him first. He will give me purpose and fulfillment.

Thought: I'm a piece of junk. My life is a wreck, and it is my fault. I will never amount to anything.

Feeling: Self-hatred

Scripture: Psalm 139:13-18—You are my Creator; I am fearfully and wonderfully made. Your thoughts of me are more in number than the grains of sand on earth's seashores.

Action: Instead of griping and doubting, I will read a Psalm each day and praise God. I will focus on Him whenever I feel discouraged.

Thought: People think poorly of me and don't particularly like me, so why bother to make friends.

Feeling: Isolated and lonely

Scripture: Proverbs 18:24—If I want to have friends, I must be friendly. The Lord is my closest friend.

Action: I will develop the qualities in myself that I would like my friends to have. I will reach out to and serve others and refuse to be self-centered.

TRANSFORMATION VERSUS RENOVATION

When I talk of the transformation of your character, inner nature and personality, I'm not referring to renovation. I'm talking about transformation in the very center of your being through the life and power of God. I'm talking about becoming progressively more intimately acquainted with Jesus Christ. I'm talking about diligently inquiring of Him and acquiring Him as your most vital necessity. Having the roots of your being firmly and deeply planted in the Lord. Being continually built up in Him, undergirded, strengthened and transformed by Christ's mighty power in your inner man.

MORE THAN WILLPOWER

To pull this off, in the long run you will need much more than willpower and a positive mental attitude. Such a radical transformation will never be accomplished through self-improvement techniques and willpower alone. Perhaps an illustration will clarify this:

> The latch on the portable car seat had just broken, so my friend used the seat belt to strap her two-year-old son securely into the seat beside her as she drove along a narrow, winding road. While carefully navigating an especially sharp curve, she flung out her right arm to steady him and cried, "Hang on tight, honey." Quick as a flash, the little fellow grabbed one of his shoe laces in each chubby fist and said, "I'm holdin' on, Mommy."

I'm afraid that's exactly what most of us have tried to do in our quest for healing and wholeness. We've held on to our shoelaces of self-help and willpower instead of clinging with all our might to God, believing what He tells us to believe and doing exactly what

His Word instructs us to do. Then we've wondered why every sharp curve in the road has thrown us off balance.

This will keep you secure and hold you steady: An intimate relationship with Jesus and an ever-deepening friendship with Him; faith in God's loving ways and wise purposes for your life; learning to lean your entire personality on Him in absolute trust and confidence in His power, wisdom and goodness; and, renewing your mind after the true knowledge of Him.

You and I are engaged in a spiritual struggle. As we explore our pain and restlessness, more and more we will discover that at the root of it all is a yearning for a personal, intimate relationship with God. Only in Him will we find the depth of love, forgiveness, acceptance and approval that we need and crave.

That is why you cannot find true release from your past or realize lasting personal growth and fulfillment by following formulas and rules. You need firm faith and a real relationship with the Lord Jesus Christ.

THEY THAT SOW IN TEARS...

Do you know what picked me up out of total despair and started me on the path to healing and wholeness when I was eleven years old? It was hearing the wonderful words of a loving Christ who walked into my darkened bedroom, looked into my tear-stained face, and said, "Son, I love you and I have a wonderful plan for your life."

That one brief sentence told me so very, very much. I was accepted. I was loved. I was not an accident or a blunder—the result of an adulterous affair. The awful things that had happened to me had not ruined me beyond repair. God had a plan—a wonderful plan—for my life.

God's plan for your life is different from mine, but it is no less wonderful. You can rest assured that His perfect plan for your future includes neither barrenness nor bitterness.

As a victim of abuse you have every right to weep. There is a time for tears; but there also comes a time when you make the decision to reclaim lost ground. It is a time to blink back the tears and attack the flourishing outgrowth of symptoms, pain and thorny problems produced by the abuse—a time to expose the root system and deal with its poisonous fruit. It is time to allow the Holy Spirit to bring His plow and break up the fallow ground of your life so that you do not sow the precious seed of your future among the choking weeks and painful thorns from your past.

> They who sow in tears shall reap in joy *and* singing. He who goes forth bearing seed and weeping [at needing his precious supply of grain for sowing] shall doubtless come again with rejoicing, bringing his sheaves with him, (Psalm 126:5-6, NKJV.)

HOW WILL YOU DEAL WITH YOUR PAST?

God longs to do a new thing in your life. He wants to help you deal with your past so you can conquer the present and confront the future.

As a victim of abuse, you can choose any of several different ways to deal with your past:

- » You can replay the past and live to get even.
- » You can repeat the past, blame everyone else and live with a grudge.
- » You can regret the past, blame God and live with grief.

> » You can repress the past, blame yourself and live with guilt.

> » Or, you can release the past, believe in the God who makes all things new and live in grace.

God can help you reclaim the untilled, unproductive soil of your soul and make life fruitful. He can transform your tears of pain and regret into tears of joy.

Reach out now and take His hand. He wants to welcome you to a winner's world.

ENDNOTES

1. Jeff Van Vonderen, *Good News for the Chemically Dependent* (Nashville: Thomas Nelson Publishers, 1984), pp. 78-80.

2. US Department of Health and Human Services (HHS), *Child Abuse and Neglect: Critical First Steps in Response to a National Emergency*, (WDC 1990.)

3. US Department of Health and Human Services, *Child Maltreatment 1992: Reports from the States to the National Center on Child Abuse and Neglect* (Washington, DC, 1994), p. 9.

4. Peter E. Quinn, *Cry Out* (Nashville: Abingdon Press, 1984.)

5. Susan Forward and Joan Torres, *Men Who Hate Women and the Women Who Love Them* (New York: Bantam Books, 1986) pp. 144-145.

6. Yvonne Vissing, Murray Straus, Richard Gelles and John Harrop, "Verbal Aggression by Parents and Psycho-Social Problems of Children, Child Abuse and Neglect," Vol. 15, 1991 (Kidlington, UK: Elsevier Science Ltd.) Reprinted and used with permission.

7. Ibid, p. 233

8. "America's Children: How Are They Doing?" American Humane Association; http://www. americanhumane.org/children/stop-child-abuse/ fact-sheets/americas-children.html; accessed March 2014.

9. Burton Stokes and Lynn Lucas, No Longer a Victim (Shippenburg, PA: Destiny Image Publishers, 1988), pp. 136-137.

10. Ibid., p. 138

11. Ibid., p. 136

12. Ibid., pp. 137-144

13. Child Welfare.gov, https://www. childwelfare.gov/pubs/factsheets/fatality. pdf#page=2&view=How Many Children Die Each Year From Child Abuse and Neglect? Accessed March 2014.

14. Bridgette Y. Rose, "Abuse Provokes Questions," *The Dallas Times Herald*, November 1991, pp. A_13, A-15.

15. HHS Reports from the States (WDC 1994), p. 18.

16. Child Welfare.gov, https://www. childwelfare.gov/pubs/factsheets/fatality. pdf#page=2&view=How Many Children Die Each Year From Child Abuse and Neglect? Accessed March 2014.

17. Corrie ten Boom (with John and Elizabeth Sherrill), *The Hiding Place* (Chappaqua, New York: Chosen Books, 1971), pp. 30-31.

18. Martha Janssen, Silent Scream (Fortress Press, 1983). Reprinted with permission of Augsburg Press.

19. National Children's Alliance, http:// www.nationalchildrensalliance.org/ NCANationalStatistics; accessed March 2014.

20. Jane F. Gilgun, "Resilience and the Intergenerational Transmission of Child Abuse" in *Family Sexual Abuse*, Michael Quinn Patton (ed.) (Newbury Park, CA: Sage Publications, 1991.)

21. David Finkelhor, Child Sexual Abuse: New Theory and Research (The Free Press, MacMillan Publishing Company, a member of Paramount Publishing), pp. 192-193. Reprinted with permission.

22. Ibid., p. 193

23. Ibid., p. 194

24. Ibid., p. 194-195

25. Stokes and Lucas, PP. 106-115

26. Ibid., p. 115

27. Ibid., pp 116-117

28. Dr. Dan B. Allender, *The Wounded Heart: Hope for Victims of Childhood Sexual Abuse* (Colorado Springs: NAVPRESS, 1992), p. 128.

29. Stokes and Lucas, p. 119.

30. Allender, pp. 91-98.

31. Child Abuse and Neglect Statistics, http://www. firststar.org/library/national-statistics.aspx; accessed March 2014.

32. UCLA, http://classes.dma.ucla.edu/ Winter05/154B/anti_violence.pdf; accessed March 2014.

33. Stokes and Lucas, pp. 125-131.

34. Elia Wise, *For Children Who Were Broken* (New York: Berkley Books, 1989.)

35. Rita-Lou Clarke, *Pastoral Care of Battered Women* (Philadelphia: The Westminster Press, 1986), p. 15.

36. Angela Browne, *When Battered Women Kill* (New York: The Free Press, 1987), p. 4.

37. Ibid., (Browne takes this statistic from a Bureau of Justice Statistics publication, "intimate Victims: A Study of Violence Among friends and Relatives: 1980, WDC.)

38. Drs. Murray Straus and Richard Gelles, *Physical Violence in American Families: Risk Factors and Adaptation to Violence in 8.145 Families* (New Brunswick, NJ: Transaction Publishers, 1990.)

39. Clarke, pp. 17-18.

40. Domestic Violence and Abuse Statistics, http:// www.statisticbrain.com/domestic-violence-abuse-stats/; accessed March 2014.

41. Murray Straus, "Conceptualization and measurement of Battering: Implications for Public Policy (1991), published in *Woman Battering: policy Responses*, Michael Steinman (ed.) (Cincinnati: Anderson Publishing.)

42. Violent Crime Between Intimate Partners by Sex of Victim, 2008, http://www.census.gov/ compendia/statab/2012/tables/12s0318.pdf; accessed March 014.

43. Browne, p. 43.

44. J. Alsdurf, "Wife Abuse and the Church: The Response of Pastors", http://www.researchgate. net/publication/232605972_Wife_abuse_and_ the_church_The_response_of_pastors; accessed march 2014.

45. R.E. Dobash and R.P. Dobash, *Violence Against Wives: A Case Against the Patriarchy* (New York: The Free Press, 1979.)

46. S.E. Eisenberg and P.O. Michlow, *The Assaulted Wife: "Catch 22 Revisited"* (Ann Arbor, MI: University of Michigan Law School. Unpublished manuscript, 1974.)

47. Browne, p. 47.

48. Ibid, pp. 42-45

49. Lenore E. Walker, *Terrifying Love: Why Battered Women Kill and How Society Responds* (New York: Harper and Row, 1989.)

50. Lenore E. Walker, *The Battered Woman* (New York: Harper and Rowe, 1979), pp. 73-75.

51. Browne, pp. 90-91.

52. Walker, *Terrifying Love*, pp. 51-52.

53. Connie Dorn, "The Missionary Position: The Role of Rescue Fantasies in Maintaining Abusive Relationships" (Paper presented at a September 1980 meeting of the American Psychological Association, Montreal, Canada.)

54. John and Elizabeth Sherrill, *Glimpses of Glory*, 1991 by Guideposts Associates, Inc. (Used by permission of Tyndale House Publishers, Inc. All rights reserved.

55. Robin Norwood, *Women Who Love Too Much* (The Putnam Publishing Group/Jeremy P. Tarcher, Inc., 1985), Reprinted with permission.

56. Ibid., *Introduction*

57. Ibid., p. 14

58. Ibid., p. 102

59. Ibid., p. 103

60. Ibid., p. 107

61. Ibid., p. 15

62. Ibid., p. 136

63. Ibid., p. 125

64. Forward and Torres, p. 38

65. Ibid., p. 39

66. Browne, p. 11.

67. Norwood, P. 247.

68. Ibid., p. 21

69. Ibid., p. 247

70. Ibid.

71. Ibid.

72. Gerald T. Hotaling and David B. Sugraman, "A Risk Marker Analysis of Assaulted Wives," (*Journal of Family Violence*, Vol. 5, No. 1, 1990, p. 2

73. Ibid., p. 9

74. Ibid., pp. 8-9

75. Ibid., pp. 10-11

76. Ibid., pp. 10-11

77. Ibid., p. 11

78. Ibid., p. 12

79. Walker, *The Battered Wife*, p. 93.

80. Ibid., pp. 114-115

81. Ibid., p. 115

82. Ibid., p. 117

83. Ibid., pp. 117-119

84. Ibid., p. 129

85. Ibid., p. 130

86. Ibid., p. 131

87. Ibid., p. 132

88. Ibid., p. 139

89. Ibid.

90. Ibid., p. 148

91. Ibid., pp. 170-171

92. Forward and Torres, p. 42.

93. Walker, *Terrifying Love*, p. 136

94. Ibid.

95. Ibid., pp. 137, 146, 150

96. Ibid., p. 152

97. Ibid., p. 164

98. Ibid., p. 146

99. Ibid., p. 254

100. Ellen Bass and Laura Davis, *The Courage to Heal: A Guide for Women Survivors of Child Sexual Abuse* (New York: Harper and Row, 1988), p. 150.

101. Ibid., p. 149

102. Ibid.

103. Ibid., p. 150

104. Ibid., p. 151

105. Ibid., p. 149

106. Amy Carmicheal, "If".

107. Bass and Davis, p. 153.

108. William Barclay, *The Daily Study Bible* (Edinburgh: St. Andrew, 1962), pp. 262-268.

109. Lisa Wells Isenhower, "The Jagged Memory," *Guideposts* (Rights and permissions: New York, January 1992), pp. 20-22.

110. Phillips Brooks was an American clergyman and author, who briefly served as Bishop of Massachusetts in the Episcopal Church during the early 1890s. In the Episcopal liturgical calendar he is remembered on January 23. He is known for being the lyricist of "O Little Town of Bethlehem".

111. Zick Ruben and Elton B. McNeil, *The Psychology of Being Human*, 3rd Edition (New York: Harper and Row, 1981), p. 317.

112. Ibid.

113. Morris Rosenberg, *Society and the Adolescent Self-Image* © 1965 (Princeton University Press. Copyright renewed 1993 by PUP. Used with permission.)

114. Rubin and McNeil, p. 317.

115. Ibid.

116. Ibid.

117. Ibid.

118. Samuel Osherson, *Finding Our Fathers: The Unfinished Business of Manhood* (New York: The Free Press, 1986), p. 3.

119. Ibid.

120. Philip Yancey, *Disappointment with God* (Zondervan Publishing House, 1988), p. 183.

121. Bass and Davis, p. 156.

122. Yancey, p. 192

123. Derek Prince, *Blessing or Curse? You Can Choose* (New York: Chosen Books, 1990,) p. 27.

124. Merrill F. Unger, *Unger's Bible Dictionary* (Chicago: Moody Press, 1966), p. 231.

125. Prince, *Blessing or Curse?*, pp. 15-19.

126. Ibid., pp. 45-58.

127. Corrie ten Boom, *Defeated Enemies* (Christian Literature Crusade, 2002), pp. 8-9.

128. Ibid., pp. 11-12.

129. Ibid., pp. 16-17.

130. Prince, *From Curse to Blessing*, pp. 42-43

131. Floyd McClung, *The Father Heart of God* (Eugene, OR: Harvest House, 1985), p. 62.

132. Adapted from: Prince, *From Curse to Blessing*, pp. 50-51.

133. John Garlock, *Discouragement: The Cause and the Cure* (Dallas: Christ for the Nations, March 1992), P. 14.

134. Bass and Davis, p. 183 ("Autobiography in Five Short Chapters" by Portia Nelson.)

135. Karen Horney, *Neurosis and Human Growth* (W.W. Norton and Co., 1950.)

136. Excerpted from "Soldier's Prayer" by Amy Carmichael, a missionary to India, http://mylordsroom.bravepages.com/aprayer.html; accessed March 2014.

MICHAEL DAVID EVANS, the #1 *New York Times* bestselling

author, is an award-winning journalist/Middle East analyst. Dr. Evans has appeared on hundreds of network television and radio shows including *Good Morning America, Crossfire* and *Nightline,* and *The Rush Limbaugh Show,* and on Fox Network, *CNN World News,* NBC, ABC, and CBS. His articles have been published in the *Wall Street Journal, USA Today, Washington Times, Jerusalem Post* and newspapers worldwide. More than twenty-five million copies of his books are in print, and he is the award-winning producer of nine documentaries based on his books.

Dr. Evans is considered one of the world's leading experts on Israel and the Middle East, and is one of the most sought-after speakers on that subject. He is the chairman of the board of the Ten Boom Holocaust Museum in Haarlem, Holland, and is the founder of Israel's first Christian museum—Friends of Zion: Heroes and History—in Jerusalem.

Dr. Evans has authored a number of books including: *History of Christian Zionism, Showdown with Nuclear Iran, Atomic Iran, The Next Move Beyond Iraq, The Final Move Beyond Iraq,* and *Countdown.* His body of work also includes the novels *Seven Days, GameChanger, The Samson Option, The Four Horsemen, The Locket, Born Again: 1967, and his most recent, The Columbus Code.*

Michael David Evans is available to speak or for interviews.
Contact: EVENTS@drmichaeldevans.com.

BOOKS BY: MIKE EVANS

Israel: America's Key to Survival

Save Jerusalem

The Return

Jerusalem D.C.

Purity and Peace of Mind

Who Cries for the Hurting?

Living Fear Free

I Shall Not Want

Let My People Go

Jerusalem Betrayed

Seven Years of Shaking: A Vision

The Nuclear Bomb of Islam

Jerusalem Prophecies

Pray For Peace of Jerusalem

America's War: The Beginning of the End

The Jerusalem Scroll

The Prayer of David

The Unanswered Prayers of Jesus

God Wrestling

The American Prophecies

Beyond Iraq: The Next Move

The Final Move beyond Iraq

Showdown with Nuclear Iran

Jimmy Carter: The Liberal Left and World Chaos

Atomic Iran

Cursed

Betrayed

The Light

Corrie's Reflections & Meditations

GAMECHANGER SERIES:

GameChanger

Samson Option

The Four Horsemen

THE PROTOCOLS SERIES:

The Protocols

The Candidate

The Revolution

The Final Generation

Seven Days

The Locket

Living in the F.O.G.

Persia: The Final Jihad

Jerusalem

The History of Christian Zionism

Countdown

Ten Boom: Betsie, Promise of God

Commanded Blessing

Born Again: 1948

Born Again: 1967

Presidents in Prophecy

Stand with Israel

Prayer, Power and Purpose

Turning Your Pain Into Gain

The Columbus Code

Christopher Columbus, Secret Jew

TO PURCHASE, CONTACT: orders@timeworthybooks.com

P. O. BOX 30000, PHOENIX, AZ 85046